A YEAR ON THE FROG

(The Misadventures of Two New Narrowboaters)

This book is dedicated to my wonderful wife, Pip, who shared this amazing adventure with me. Thank you for your humour, resilience, forbearance and love. I can't think of anyone else who would have survived a Year on The Frog with me!

'You don't stop laughing when you grow old, you grow old when you stop laughing.'

GEORGE BERNARD SHAW

INTRODUCTION

'You numpty!'

Derek's comments had stopped stinging a long time ago. He had used this particular adjective many times since we had met.

Derek, and his wife, Emma, were based at Ham Manor Marina in Newbury, a temporary home of our narrowboat 'Frog in a Bucket' (The Frog). His latest assessment of my complete inadequacy as a boat owner was made in late 2019 - a few months after we had purchased our lovely Frog and about a year before we began the odyssey that is the main subject of this book. But I am getting ahead of myself. The full tale begins in early 2019 when Pip, my lovely wife and I were planning our future after my retirement.

When jotting down these ramblings, I thought I should be clear what I was actually trying to achieve. Having kept a diary, written a number of Blogs and recorded over forty YouTube Vlogs (both these social media addresses can be found at the end of the book), we had a wealth of recorded material covering the odyssey. The Vlogs already serve as a wonderful reminder of our bucolic year afloat and keep the trip alive for us. What they don't reveal, however, are the extra details I recorded in my diary. Furthermore, as they did not start until we undertook a practise cruise on the Kennet and Avon, in July 2020, they miss out lots of important background: the trials of buying a boat, the traumas of our early cruising experience, the preparation for our odyssey and our wonderful interactions with Derek in Ham Manor Marina.

As well as creating a single record that paints the whole picture for Pip and our family, I also felt that it was a great opportunity to help and inform new boaters. So, early on, I share a lot of basic details about the boat buying process, boating itself and living aboard. This background may feel a bit dry but, even if you are not planning a similar enterprise, I think this insight will help you later, as the incidents I record in the book may make more sense. But it's not compulsory - so feel free to skip ahead if you prefer.

The book is mostly a travelogue and I am meticulous in recording the names and numbers of bridges and locks. I also make sure I have recorded where we moored each night. Again, this is partly for navigational (anal) accuracy, but hopefully, it will also help any boater, experienced or not, who is planning to cruise a waterway for the first time.

Finally, this is a book for experienced boaters who will not only know the waterways I am describing but may also recognise, and chuckle over, the incidents and mishaps that punctuated our odyssey.

Along the way I have tried to share a little of the history behind the waterways we cruised and the places we visited. My sources were varied and, I hope, accurate - but I could not verify them all. So I apologise if some of this background has been created. I do not intend to mislead. My detailed explanation of the boat buying process is accurate in that it reflects the process we went through. I recognise that other people may have had different experiences and may consider different factors to be more important than those detailed below.

I hope you enjoy our Year on The Frog. On our adventure we had fun, made mistakes, made great friends, learned a lot about ourselves and grew as people. All of this happened against the dark background of the worst pandemic in two generations.

CHAPTER 1: HOW ABOUT A NARROWBOAT?

After a 35 year career in a large corporate organisation I was finally hanging up my boots and retiring. Pip had stopped working a few years earlier and was desperate for me to join her. My job was demanding and kept me away from home on long days and involved lots of driving as I scuttled across the South West of England from our home in Cornwall.

When retirement was imminent we started to think about what the future may hold. My stepson, and his family (including three grandchildren) were planning a move to the Bristol area and my three children already lived in the city. Cornwall is lovely but it is so far from anything and anyone. So - it was agreed: we would sell up and move to be closer to them all.

We were seasoned house movers. Pip often points out that she has never lived in a house for more than 7 years in her life. She left the UK in 1981 and spent 20 years in Canada. She was married to a navy clearance diver and, as such, 'ping-ponged' between British Columbia and Nova Scotia. She even moved back to the UK for a few years in the early 1990s. My career had seen me move every three to four years until I moved back to the South West and we began our seven year stint on the edge of Bodmin moor. Our many house moving experiences served to highlight the ridiculous UK house buying process and I did not fancy yet another challenging move. With this in mind I approached Pip and this is roughly how the conversation went:

Me: 'Why don't we sell up here and move into rented accommodation and then buy something near Bristol as cash buyers?'

Pip: 'No - I don't want to move twice!'

Me: 'OK'

A short exchange, as you can see. And there it rested - or so I thought.

I can't remember exactly when the follow up counter proposal was made but it went a bit like this:

Pip: 'You know you wanted to sell the house and move into rented accommodation before buying near Bristol?'

Me: (naively and probably off guard playing on my tablet) 'Yes'.

Pip: 'Well I've been thinking. (Warning bells ringing in the distance). I still don't want to move into rented accommodation but what about moving onto a NARROWBOAT?'

It's appropriate to give a bit of background here. Pip loves narrowboating. She had several previous adventures with her first husband and other family members on her short posting in England and fell in love with the pace of life on 'the cut' (a colloquial term for the canal network). My only previous experience was a family holiday in 2004 - shortly after meeting Pip - when we took my three then young teenage children and Pip's second child around the Warwickshire Ring (a well known holiday cruising route and not a medical condition affecting South Midlanders). On this voyage I had realised how difficult it was to handle a narrowboat and I entertained everyone by falling in whilst walking on the gunwale. The gunwale (pronounced 'gunnall') is a four to five inch ridge halfway down the flank of a narrowboat, where the top part of a narrowboat's body meets the hull. It serves as a VERY NARROW walkway running the full length of the boat. So, with this background, it was not surprising that my slightly less positive boating experience meant that the prospect of not only buying but LIVING ON a narrowboat was not high on my retirement bucket list (in reality, it was not on the list at all).

Pip was a financial adviser and relationship manager in her working life. Over the next few weeks she used all of her innate skills to positively position her proposition. Firstly she introduced the concept of a 'gap year'. This was clever. Gap years are what prospective students take before they start studying. Gap years are a fun time before the burden of academia kicks in and are what adventurous, young people do! See what she did there? Secondly, as we are both bell-ringers, Pip suggested that, if we undertook this odyssey, we would be able to visit lots of churches and join in with the local ringing team to try out their bells. Next she also reminded me of the many fantastic waterside pubs that the canal network is famous for - all just waiting for our custom!

So her campaign was off to a great start. The next thing she had to do was to remove the fear element, as well as appeal to my slightly OCD 'need for detail'. Pip summarised the next step in her 'win Rob over' process in this extract from her first *'Blog From The Frog'*:

'What if, instead of living in a rented house, we lived on a narrowboat? Crazy, but it could just work. It would mean packing up our 4 bedroom house and putting it all into storage. It would mean going from living in a large house to living in the equivalent of a floating caravan. But it would also mean a fantastic, life changing adventure that could give us many memories to keep us warm for years to come. The more I thought about it the more it seemed like the perfect solution. Rob, surprisingly, didn't dismiss it right away and even seemed to warm to the idea. We did much research, subscribed to a canal boat magazine, read loads of online articles, and watched many hours of YouTube vlogs by people living our dream.'

We did indeed do our research and, as Pip says, over time I did 'warm to the idea'. In essence, the more information I took on board, the less daunting the decision became. Finally we agreed: we would do it. All we needed to do now was find a boat!

CHAPTER 2: FINDING 'THE FROG'

We soon realised that choosing a narrowboat was no easy task. Where do you start? We didn't even know what questions to ask.

Here I should give credit to a really helpful Narrowboat Vlogger whose YouTube output was appropriately called '*Cruising the Cut*'. David Johns, who compiles the vlog, already lived aboard his narrowboat and, as such, had huge credibility; he really was 'walking the walk' or should I say 'cruising the cruise'. He is also a great communicator and he became our first information source. He was not only asking the questions but was also answering them for us.

As an aside, David is a very generous man. We met him twice - fleetingly at the Crick Boat show in 2019 when we were still boat hunting (more about this later) and again in the summer of 2021 on the infamous Rochdale Canal when he was working on his latest project identifying the best pubs on our waterways (a tough assignment but David was brave enough to take it on). At this second meeting we had already been cruising for some months and had published over twenty five of our own Vlogs. David recognised The Frog and told us he had seen several of our Vlogs and liked our 'bucolic style'. After a brief chat, he filmed us leaving Callis Lock and included not only these pictures in his next Vlog but also a link to our own. As I write he has over two hundred thousand subscribers to his YouTube channel and I remember sitting one evening, in the summer of 2021, and watching our own subscribers soar towards the giddy heights of a thousand on the back of his generous posting. Thank you David.

So, what did we learn from Cruising The Cut? Well we learned that there are many variables that you need to consider when you buy a boat. Some of these are obvious, some less so but, for those planning to live-aboard, still very important. This is potentially where my tale turns into an 'infolog', looking like it is aimed at would-be boat buyers. You may feel I am going into unnecessary detail but I ask that you please humour me. Full appreciation of the odyssey, and the challenges and adventures therein, will be helped by having an understanding of the many references to toilets, boat length, beam, draught etc. So please bear with me and 'plough through' the following few pages. I will of course try to make them as gripping as possible!

Length: Unlike in life, bigger is not always better! A decision on the size of your boat is driven by two contradictory considerations: the understandable desire for lots of living space countered by the equally understandable desire to be able to cruise as much of the network as you can as easily as possible.

What do I mean? The canal network is peppered with locks. Locks were the canal engineer's most common solution to the problem caused by changing heights in the landscape surrounding a waterway. For the canals to be navigable, white water weirs, such as those you find on rivers, are not an option. A lock is, in essence, a chamber that can be closed at either end with the use of gates. When a boat is ascending, the empty chamber can be filled with water by opening paddles (covering sluices) that allow water to run in (or emptied by allowing water to run out if descending). In most cases the paddles are moved using a windlass - a hand held metal tool that all narrowboaters will carry. Locks are very clever examples of great engineering and whilst they are all similar in design, they do have some important variables. The relevant one here is length. You may ask why different canals have different length locks. There are a number of reasons - some were engineering restraints and some others the result of the commercial nascence of the canal system. Different canals were owned by different companies and having different lock lengths was a way of controlling traffic and generating additional income. The most obvious example of this is the Calder and Hebble (C&H) Navigation. This stretch of waterway begins at Sowerby Bridge in Yorkshire and runs twenty one miles east to Wakefield. It is now linked to the Rochdale Canal but until the restoration of the Sowerby end of the Rochdale in 1996, it was a 'cul-de-sac' with its terminus at Sowerby. The locks on the C&H are less than sixty feet long, as they were designed to accommodate particular vessels called Yorkshire Keels. This meant any longer boats, travelling east towards Leeds and Wakefield on the Rochdale Canal (from Manchester), had to stop at Sowerby, unload their goods, possibly into a Sowerby warehouse, and then reload them onto shorter vessels to continue the journey. This ensured an income stream for the Sowerby warehouse owners, the Yorkshire Keel owners of the C&H and the company who owned the C&H Navigation.

Enough of the history lesson. The net result of this variation in lock length is that there is an optimum narrowboat length - about fifty seven feet - that allows you to navigate the vast majority of the system.

By the way, you notice we are not discussing the width or, more accurately, the beam of our boat. Narrowboats, by definition, are all narrow and are typically just under seven feet in width. It is possible to buy what is known as a wide beam. However, whilst this would have given us significantly more living space, it would have seriously restricted our cruising ability stopping us from travelling on any waterway that does not have double locks - and that is a long list.

So we now know how long we want the boat to be. But even that is not the full consideration when it comes to living space. The next question was what stern did we want?

For simplicity I will say narrowboats have a choice of three sterns: traditional (or trad), semi-traditional (or, you guessed it, semi-trad) or cruiser. Trad sterns are typical of the old working boats. There is only really enough room for the helmsman and the tiller and that's it. The main benefit of a trad stern is obvious - more of the boat is dedicated to 'indoor' space. The downside of course is that the helmsman is alone and isolated from the rest of the crew. So, in short, trads are better for the additional indoor space they allow but are quite anti-social.

At the other extreme, on a cruiser stern, the space at the aft of the boat is much bigger, with enough room for several people and the helmsman. There are usually bench seats that still allow the tiller to be safely manoeuvred. With these 'party boats' the obvious compromise is on indoor space - especially if you have opted for a boat that is only fifty seven feet long.

Semi-trad sterns sit in between. There is less external room than a cruiser but more than a trad. This is a good compromise, where less space is lost inside the vessel but the helmsman can be joined by a couple of people helping to wile away the long hours at the tiller and making switches in control from one person to another a lot easier. As we would spend most of our time on our own, for Pip and I the semi-trad felt like the right option.

Ok so we are now looking for a fifty seven foot narrowboat with a semi-trad stern. Feels like progress.

We then needed to decide on the preferred interior layout. Despite the obvious space restrictions, there are many variables within a narrowboat layout. I am not going to describe them all here, as when it comes to things like the dining area, it is almost certainly best to view a narrowboat in person and picture yourself eating and moving through that space before making a decision to buy. Rather, I will simply deal with the more 'macro' consideration of choosing either a traditional layout (living area at the front of the vessel and bedroom(s) at the rear) or opting for what is commonly known as a 'reverse layout'. In this latter design option, a living area (typically the galley or kitchen) sits directly in front of the helmsman at the stern and the bedrooms are positioned in the bow (front of the boat).

This was an interesting process of discovery for us. We instinctively wanted a reverse layout. We pictured one of us at the helm whilst the other pottered about in the galley just a few feet away, making cups of tea whilst listening to Pop Master (note for the under forties: Pop Master was a Pop Quiz, hosted by Ken Bruce, on BBC Radio 2 every weekday at ten thirty am). I guess we persisted with this wish until we started viewing boats in person and finally saw The Frog (which has a traditional layout). After our searching we concluded that with a bigger and more accessible well-deck (the space at the bow of your boat where you can get on and off and often have a sociable seating area) a traditional layout felt right for us. When we were sitting in our 'lounge' in the evenings, we thought it would feel comfortable to be looking forward through the double doors at what lay ahead of us. It also meant that when we had visitors the combined external and internal social space was much bigger at the bow than it would be at the rear with our semi-trad stern. So, it wasn't just because we fell in love with The Frog that we changed our minds. In the end we both agreed a traditional layout was right for us. Good friends of ours (friends made whilst cruising) had a cruiser stern and a reverse layout (they designed their boat and had it built) and this worked for them. They had two big dogs and spent their evenings at the stern with direct access to the galley/beer fridge. For us, the bow well-deck and our lounge/diner gave us more space and seemed more 'natural'. Oh - and of course we did fall madly in love with The Frog. So that was that!

What about the number of bedrooms? With a fifty seven foot boat this was really a no-brainer. It made no sense to have a second bedroom that would reduce our living space, when most of the time we would be alone. Instead, we simply needed to ensure we had separate beds available in the living area as and when needed. This is quite normal on a narrowboat. If you are a caravaner, you will also recognise this practical solution to increasing temporary bed space for guests. In our case, The Frog had a leather banquette with removable cushions. The whole thing pulled out from the wall creating a large flat wooden surface upon which the cushions could be arranged to make a double bed. Having slept on it many times I can vouch for how comfortable it was (albeit a bit noisy when you turned on the squeaky leather cushions). We also bought a bespoke bed settee - which was great for relaxing on and gave us an option for even more sleeping space.

Bathrooms presented another conundrum. There are typically two bathroom layouts. The first is known as a 'walk-through' bathroom. Quite simply, the bathroom is built across the entire beam of the boat and is accessed from either end - typically from the galley/living area and, at the other end, the bedroom. The second I will describe as a 'train carriage' or 'corridor' bathroom. This is where the bathroom is set on one side of the boat and is accessed via a door off a narrow corridor on the other side of the boat.

If a boat is shared with others, regularly, then a corridor bathroom may be better. It gives greater privacy (although privacy is a relative term in such a small space) and allows you to have bedroom doors open, if you want to, when guests are on board. In the walk-through option the doors are normally closed when guests are on board to avoid the obvious embarrassment of walking in on a midnight pee-er as you head to the galley for a drink of water.

We wanted a walk-through bathroom. No, not just because The Frog had one. This was one stipulation we were definitely looking for and The Frog, coincidentally, offered it. I have said a few times that we would spend most of our time on the boat alone - so privacy was not a big issue for us. We would much rather have a larger bathroom - which typically the walk-through option offered - being, as it is, the full width of the boat. Remarkably, The Frog had enough room in its bathroom for a three quarter size bath - a luxury that water shortages meant we never actually made use of.

Toilets were not a 'shall we shan't we' consideration; a toilet was an obvious essential, however here we have one of the most potentially divisive decisions that a new boater has to make. There are several toilet options. These are the most common: Pump out (either 'drop through' or macerator), cassette and compost.

Pump Out does what it says on the tin: your boat has a big 'poo tank' (technical term) into which the waste flows and is stored pending an opportunity (or NEED) to pump it out (much more about this when we are on our travels). The different pump out options are, again, fairly descriptive: in a 'drop-through' system the waste does just that, it drops directly into the tank. Holiday narrowboats almost always have this option as it is the simplest and the least likely to break/be broken. If you choose a macerator, you will have a pump and a macerator under the toilet bowl that breaks up any solids before passing them into the tank. The main benefit of the latter is that the tank can be more remote from the bathroom, be almost completely sealed and, therefore, less likely to create a nasty smell when it is half full. It may also mean that less 'Blue' has to be added to the tank. Blue (or Pink if you prefer) is a chemical solution that is poured into your poo tank - usually when you pump out. It mixes with the water in the tank and helps to break down solid material (aiding pump outs) and reduces odours. The macerator system is better, in our opinion, but it is subject to malfunction as we found out, to our cost, a few months after owning The Frog. Oh - and The Frog had a macerator!

The most common alternative to pump out toilets is the cassette. With this system you own a plastic container that sits under your toilet. Most boaters have at least two - one for use and one for spare. The waste material is stored temporarily in the cassette which can be moved and carried away from the boat for disposal in an Elsan (a special facility offered on waterways for the very purpose of emptying a cassette). An Elsan is not much more than a sink/funnel with a tap above it into which a cassette can be emptied and 'flushed".

Compost or separator toilets capture all solid material in a tank and so begins a process of natural dehydration and decomposition that may take over three months to complete. They are increasingly popular as they are 'greener' options than the more common pump out and cassettes (they do not use any chemicals and use a lot less water). However, because of the time it takes for material to decompose you need to have sufficient space on your boat to store 'work in progress' as disposal of partially processed 'material' in any canalside bins was prohibited. When we bought The Frog these toilets were a very new concept and, for the same reason we did not like the thought of handling a cassette, we were very glad to find that The Frog had a pump out system.

Whatever option you choose, if you live aboard you will still be forever conscious of the consequence of pooing on your boat. Not only are there the obvious privacy issues (not such a problem for a married couple) but you will be very aware that every 'deposit' will take you one step closer to needing to pump out or empty the cassette. Consequently, whilst on our odyssey, we dedicated a lot of energy and planning to finding anywhere else we could to go to the loo. The lack of pubs open in lock down did not help but we are greatly indebted to the many supermarkets and other facilities we managed to find along the way!

Controlling a narrowboat can be a challenge - especially turning a sharp corner, turning around (or winding as it is known) or even just getting out of a tight spot. On a narrowboat all of these moves have to be completed using just forward and reverse gear and the tiller. You cannot steer a narrowboat in reverse (explained later) and this makes turning dependent on forward momentum and your tiller skills - unless you have a bow-thruster. A bow-thruster is a two way mini propeller that is set in an underwater channel cut through the bow of your narrowboat. It is controlled using a couple of switches at the stern near the tiller and allows the helmsman to move the bow left or right even if there is no forward momentum or if the boat is reversing. Many purists scoff at the idea of having a bow-thruster. The colloquial and misogynist term used by such boaters to describe a bow thruster is 'lady button'. The obvious inference being that if you need one you are not only not a real man but that you handle a boat 'like a lady' - as if this were somehow a disability! I can tell you from my long months on the Frog that this term is not only insulting and anachronistic but also highly inaccurate. Some of the best boat handlers I encountered were female. I remember an embarrassing afternoon in Crick marina when the high winds were stopping me bringing the Frog around. Who came to my rescue? One of the marina team who was also a boat mover by trade. I have never seen a narrowboat in more competent hands and she was a thirty-something lady.

Did we want a bow-thruster - well the propaganda of the purists had done its work and we decided against it. Were I to make the decision again, I think it would be a different one. Not only were there many occasions when we would really have benefited from a thruster but we have also spent time aboard a narrowboat which had one and seen it in action. Much more of this later as we near the end of our Odyssey.

I have not mentioned, yet, how much we should pay. We naively had a figure in mind when we started our boat search. David Johns was helpful again. He produced a very informative vlog putting monetary figures against categories of boat and illustrating his analysis with some external shots of actual narrowboats. Based on this vlog we came to the conclusion that we would spend £45,000-£50,000. If we invested this amount then we would be buying a sound, ready to go boat with probably some minor work (decor for example) needed before we were ready to set off on our odyssey.

So we now knew: how long, how wide, what layout, what bathroom, what toilet, what stern and what cost we were planning for as we started our boat search. All we needed to do now was get out there and find a boat!

One final point I should make. An option available to all new boaters is to buy a brand new boat. We quickly dismissed this idea. Most new boats are built 'to order'. This is great as most new boat builders will give you the opportunity to input on features, layout etc so you can tailor the vessel to suit your specific needs. It follows, however, that a new build will take time - often quite a long time - and for us the clock was ticking. The other downside is that much like a new car, in a normal market, a brand new boat will depreciate significantly. There are also different VAT rules for a new boat and as we knew we would sell our boat at the end of the Odyssey, these were very important considerations. Finally, to buy a new boat you would probably need a budget in excess of £100,000. So, in the end, it was a simple decision: we were looking for a pre-loved boat.

You will not be surprised to hear, in these high tech times, that our search started online, not least because we lived more than a two hour drive from the nearest canal. We started bookmarking certain online sites and found what we thought were boats worth looking at. By coincidence The Crick Boat Show, the largest boat show in the UK, was taking place in May 2019 and this seemed like a good opportunity to see some boats and talk to people whose brains we could pick for advice. Crick itself is a small village in Northamptonshire and is physically central to the canal network being positioned just up the Leicester Line of the Grand Union. We did not know it then, but It would be where we would spend three months of the winter of 2020/21, including Christmas and New Year. Oh, and my sister, Helen and her husband Graham, also live in the village.

Crick is a boat owner's dream day out. Sellers of everything you can imagine from high tech onboard wifi to solid fuel, are there - along with most of the country's big boat brokers. Or at least enough to make it a great location to go boat hunting. As luck would have it, one of the boats that was within our budget and that we liked the look of, was going to be on display at the show. So we set off, hopeful that we would make the five hour drive worthwhile, as well as enjoying a lovely weekend with Helen and her family.

We spent a whole day at the show and had a great time looking at all the many great stalls, almost buying a wifi set up before we even had a boat to put it in. We explored the inside of many new boats that we knew we could not afford or want (see above) gleaning the latest design ideas and ruling things off and onto our wish list. We managed to view the boat we had spotted online as well as five others we found whilst there. This turned out to be the only disappointing part of the day: viewing of the boats in our set price bracket. They were 'fine'. I use that word deliberately. They absolutely met the classification that the Cruising The Cut Vlog suggested they would at the price they were offered but they were just not right. We didn't need to over-analyse things; Pip and I agreed - if we were going to spend a year or more of our lives in a floating home it would have to offer more comfort than those we saw.

We needed to spend a bit more to get the finish we were looking for. So that night, after a lovely pub meal with my sister and her husband, we went back to the drawing board. Well back to Google anyway. We wanted to find some other options whilst we were in the Midlands as, put simply, that is where the boats are. We made a few calls and lined up three more boat viewings on our way home from Crick to Cornwall, one in Whilton Marina (just down the Grand Union main line) and two in Gayton Marina (situated where the Northampton Arm meets the Grand Union near Blisworth).

The Whilton Marina boat had sold that morning. So we moved onto Gayton where the first viewing was a let down. It was a boat called Rachael (Pip's daughter's name) and, like the other vessels we had viewed, she looked lovely with the clever photography used in her publicity shots. The reality was much less flattering and our heads dropped again.

The next boat we would view had just come onto the market. We were the first to see it and three other people were lined up to see it that afternoon. She was a beautiful, marine blue colour and had magnificent, large, silver portholes that sparkled in the late morning sunshine. Upon entering the semi-trad stern (tick), we came down the steps into the bedroom which had a double bed with a memory foam mattress and built-in wardrobes. Next there was a walkthrough bathroom (tick) which had a pump out, macerator toilet (tick). It also had an almost full size bath with a shower over it, lovely for lounging in after a hard day of doing locks (that never happened). Going into the main part of the boat, Pip and I both drew involuntary breaths: she was beautiful. The galley and lounge were fitted with oak cupboards. The work surfaces in the galley were solid granite. She had a built-in washing machine, loads of cupboard space and even an integrated dishwasher! Green leather cushions surrounded the dinette and beautiful oak parquet-style flooring led into a lounge where we saw the icing on the cake; a wood burner.

We were of course on 'The Frog' (full name 'Frog in a Bucket') and we were, of course, in love!

We looked at each other and words were not necessary. I could see it in Pip's eyes and I knew she could see it all over my rubbish poker face. We grinned and then grinned some more. We ran our hands over the granite and sat on the leather seats. We walked outside and looked at the gleaming, near perfect paintwork and marvelled again at what we knew, even with our limited experience of boat hunting, were an amazing feature - those enormous portholes. We looked at the shining chrome and then our eyes rose to the unusual white roof cut into sections by perfectly painted blue lines crossing her beam. Only then did we notice the three chrome skylights that finished off the roof beautifully as well as explaining why the interior was so light and welcoming (unlike most of our previous viewings). The interior walls were also painted in a light cream colour and this was very different to most of the other vessels we had viewed. These were typically wood-lined and much darker as this surface absorbed, rather than reflected, much-craved light. We went to the stern. Pip posed at the tiller - a position we were both destined to spend many many hours in - whilst I took a photograph. THE FROG WAS BEAUTIFUL and we wanted her!

So, down to earth. We walk back to the office and try to put our negotiation faces on. The conversation went a bit like this:

Broker: 'So what do you think?'

Me: 'Yes, she's a nice boat. Tell me a little about the vendor's situation' (more relevant to house buying I think but we were new to this game).

Broker: 'The vendor is actually the widow of the previous owner who died suddenly quite recently. She does not use the boat and wants to get rid of it. You are the first viewers and there are three more later today. We think it will be easy to sell'.

I look at Pip. Again without needing to say anything I turned back to the broker: 'We like it and want to ensure you do not sell it to anyone else. I am happy to offer the full asking price on the condition it is immediately marked 'under offer' and no more viewings are allowed'.

Broker: 'Ok - let's do the paperwork'

What a negotiation! Had we been contestants on The Apprentice I am certain Lord Sugar would have berated me for my immediate 'cave-in' and the sorry exchange would have been replayed many times over in the after show following my deserved 'firing'!

In reality, the vendor was away on holiday and would have the final say on whether the asking price was acceptable - but to all intents and purposes we had taken the first massive step to becoming the proud and very happy owners of the Frog! We drove back to Cornwall with a mixed feeling of excitement (an air punching 'YES') and nervous anticipation (have we really just bought a boat for £69,000?)

Pip, as always, had her feet firmly rooted on the ground. We knew the Frog needed to be 'blacked' and that we should really have a survey completed. Blacking is a process that every narrowboat should undergo regularly. It's quite an expensive thing to do as the boat has to be removed from the water. In Gayton this would be by crane - one of the most expensive methods - and it would set us back about £300 just for the lift. The blacking would then have to be added to the bill - both the material used and the labour. In total we would pay over £700 for the whole job. Blacking protects your hull and lengthens its life. It is typically done every two to three years but some boaters choose to leave it longer whilst others, who can afford to, may have it done every twelve to eighteen months. There are two types of blacking: Bitumen and Two Pack Epoxy. The latter will last up to five years whilst the former needs to be topped up typically after two years. The cost of each reflects this resilience.

A survey, much like a house survey, is strongly recommended when you buy a boat. The surveyor needs access to the hull exterior so it made sense to order it at the same time as the blacking - hence the need to act quickly to secure a surveyor. We booked one and waited to hear final confirmation from the vendor that our offer was accepted. The news did not take long to come and a few days later we were popping open a bottle of wine to celebrate. We would soon own The Frog and we now just had to deal with the separation anxiety that having a new member of the family would bring. We couldn't wait to get back up to see her.

For those who are interested I will add a bit more detail about The Frog. She was constructed in 2008 at Cauldon Boats near Stoke on Trent and has a Piper shell. This latter name will mean something to boat owners. Piper design great boats (other boat designers are available) and we received many comments on our travels about how sleek she looked. She certainly 'travelled' well and the hull design would have been a factor in this. I would go as far as to say if Katherine Hepburn had owned her she undoubtedly would have described her as 'Yar' (credit: *The Philadelphia Story* (1940)). She had a forty three horse power Beta Marine engine - which was more than up to the job. I will say no more about the electrics as this is mentioned later (one to look forward to!). If at this stage you would like to have a tour of The Frog you can go to our second Vlog and take a look (not compulsory and I know many of you will prefer to let your imagination do the heavy lifting).

CHAPTER 3: JUST A FEW MORE HOPS!

May turned to June and we were thinking about where we would moor our new acquisition until we started our Odyssey. A safe mooring location is a necessity. Canals have an 'on' and 'off' side. The 'on', or towpath side, is typically controlled by the Canal and Rivers Trust (CRT) - the charity that replaced British Waterways in managing most of the waterways in the UK. When cruising, the on side is where you can and should moor (with very rare exceptions). How long you can moor will vary. Where there are no instructions to the contrary, mooring is normally limited to fourteen days. In more popular locations, for example in the centre of towns or at beauty spots, mooring will be restricted still further to as little as twenty four or forty eight hours. The 'on' side, because it is the towpath side, is also accessible to the public and, depending on location, this carries obvious risks. A boat left unattended may soon become the target of vandals or thieves. We saw evidence of this ourselves near the Watford Flight on the Grand Union Leicester Line and if you follow social media, unfortunately, you will hear of other examples. My intention is not to scare. For balance, most of the network is relatively safe but some areas are notoriously high risk and even normally benign sites can see opportunists, or idiots, causing problems. I will explore more on this subject as we set out on our Odyssey. It is obvious from the above, however, that leaving our lovely Frog on the side of the canal was never an option.

The 'off' side is typically where privately owned land meets the waterside and is normally out of bounds for boaters. A lot of marinas are accessed via the 'off' side and some landowners also create private moorings which they charge for. Facilities will vary but usually include water and power. Marinas are normally more expensive but tend to offer more facilities - like laundry, chandlery, pump outs etc. They are also usually more secure. We concluded we wanted to moor in a marina. The question was: which one?

We had two considerations: cost and accessibility. I won't bore you with the full details here but in short, cost will depend on a combination of the proximity to places people want to be, the facilities offered and the resultant demand for berths. We chose

Ham Manor Marina on the Kennet and Avon (K&A) Canal in Newbury. Our logic was sound: the closer you got to London or Bath the higher the price - Newbury was well placed in between the two. Ham Manor had some facilities but not too many - both factors made the mooring fees reasonable. It was also situated not far from the M4, making it a mere three hours from home. Finally, we had cruised the K&A in March of that year on a hire boat and liked the canal and thought it would make a good practice waterway to cut our teeth on before the odyssey. We also fondly remember the very first phone call we made to Emma, wife of the infamous Derek mentioned above, who managed most of the administration at the marina. She was so warm and welcoming.

Our berth booked, Pip and I called into the marina on a return trip from somewhere I have forgotten. The visit merely confirmed that we had made the right decision. Emma continued to be warm and accommodating and the marina was really picturesque and we had yet to meet Derek!

Back at Gayton, the survey had been completed and the hull had been blacked. The survey report was sent to us very quickly and a few 'minor' problems involving the inverter and the electrical system were highlighted but nothing major (or so we naively thought). The only significant job that needed immediate attention was to move the wood burner. It transpired that the stove had never actually been fixed to the boat properly and it was also too close to the hull to be safe. The previous owner was contacted and agreed to pay the cost to bring this up to safety standards, as well as fixing a few other minor problems (not the electrics) mentioned in the report.

One upside was that the surveyor had valued The Frog at four thousand pounds more than we paid. We were not so naive that we did not realise that this valuation was only one man's opinion but it still made us even more happy with our purchase decision. As a final step, the surveyor issued us a safety certificate (needed for insurance and to secure a CRT licence) and we paid across the final balance of the purchase price. The Frog was now fully ours!!

We quickly arranged insurance (surprised that it was only about two hundred and fifty pounds a year) and paid for our first CRT licence. To have a vessel on CRT water you must hold a valid licence. It covers the maintenance of the waterways, towpaths and the other facilities the CRT offers. As such, it's a bit like a combination of Council Tax and Road Traffic Tax. It cost us about nine hundred pounds (when we left the Frog, over two years later, the annual cost was around twelve hundred pounds and I know it has risen even more since).

CHAPTER 4: WELCOME TO THE FROG - WHAT'S THAT SMELL?

The driving distance from Gayton to Newbury is sixty four miles and Mr Google tells me the journey will take about seventy five minutes. By water, the same trip is one hundred and twenty nine miles and will take about sixty two hours of cruising time! Put another way, assuming you cruise for seven hours per day (which is very demanding) it will take you nearly nine days to complete the trip. The route involved cruising the Grand Union Canal, tackling the Braunston Tunnel, moving onto the Oxford Canal, the River Thames and finally the River Kennet and the K&A itself. It also involved negotiating eighty six locks - some of which are challenging river locks. A tall order for any inexperienced boater.

Unfortunately, I was still working at this point and I could not take the time off to move The Frog ourselves. Some research told us that there are professional boat movers who can be hired for this very purpose. A google search enquiry saw us quoted the princely sum of twelve hundred pounds for the service.

So - what to do? The answer came fortuitously from our sister-in-law, Sue. She was following our exploits and knew we needed to move the boat. She had a coffee with a friend one day. Jackie, (the friend) was the wife of an experienced yachtsman who had mentioned he fancied a narrowboat holiday. Sue's grey cells lit up: 'Funny you should say that Jackie, I have relatives who have just bought a narrowboat and need to move it from Northampton to Newbury. If you did it, they would get a free move and you would get a free holiday. What do you think?'

I now know that Neil, Jackie's husband, is a very cautious and considered individual and the next step was a facetime call between the four of us to say hello and talk through the process. Whilst Neil had never handled a narrowboat before I knew that sailing a yacht was far harder but we still agreed that they would come up to Gayton and take the helm for a trial run to see how they felt about the enterprise.

July 11th is Pip's birthday and we had already decided we would spend that night as our first night on board. We agreed to meet up with Neil and Jackie the next morning and complete the seven locks in the Stoke Bruerne flight with me at the helm. Then we would wind (pronounced as in a weather report and not the, arguably more obvious, what you would do with a bobbin). Put more plainly: we would turn the boat around. This is done in special locations called winding holes (the canals being far too narrow to turn a narrowboat around anywhere you like.) A winding hole is normally nothing more than a rough diamond shape cut out of one bank of the canal. This indentation allows the boater to put the bow of the narrowboat into the angle and swing the stern around using a combination of forward and reverse gears (and a bow thruster if you have one). In the most forgiving winding holes you can even place your bow actually into the bank and, using mostly forward gear and the rudder, swing the stern around. Sometimes the 'corner' of the hole was full of weeds/silt or was made of concrete or armco (more about armco later) which was unforgiving and this is when you needed to keep the bow in the canal and use both gears to complete your move - avoiding the bank altogether. Again, I know this is a long aside but winding is an important part of boating and one of the biggest challenges for a novice. It is important when we talk about winding on the odyssey that you can picture what we mean - hence the detailed explanation.

After we had turned the boat around, Neil would take the helm and bring her back up the seven locks. Between us and this trial run lay our first night on The Frog and the Blisworth tunnel. The latter was an obvious challenge, which I will go into much more detail about later. The former, on the face of it, should not have been a challenge.

We arrived at the marina late in the afternoon having been delayed in traffic on what was already a very long journey. We just about had enough time to collect the keys and unload the car before the marina office closed up and everyone went home. Earlier I explained that the former owner had sadly passed away and the boat had not been used for some months as the mourning family made decisions about what to do with her. As a result, what had been in the poo tank had been there for some time. I mentioned earlier that the potential smell hazard from the tank was suppressed by using 'Blue'- a chemical additive. It was also abated by regular emptying of the tank and 'flushing through' when pumping out. On the day of our arrival however: the Blue had long since lost its power and the boat had not been pumped out for some time - unbeknownst to us. We had not noticed anything awry when we viewed The Frog as the contents of the tank had lain undisturbed and were, consequently, completely inoffensive. This changed very quickly however when I needed to spend a penny. Excited about using the electronic button pad above our loo, I finished my visit and innocently pressed 'Flush'.

The result was instantaneous. The odour that rose from the now disturbed poo tank was overwhelming. Pip was in the bedroom - the worst possible position (the poo tank is under the bed). I was obviously in the adjoining bathroom. We both voiced suitably shocked expletives and sprinted for the steps at the stern to get out of the door as quickly as possible. We emerged gasping for air and wondered what on earth had just happened. I can set the scene for this now in detail but only with the benefit of hindsight. At the time, you can imagine what we were thinking: is this what is going to happen every time we use the loo? Have we actually just bought a 'poo in a bucket'? Once our lungs were filled with oxygen and we were able to think more clearly we started to rationalise: we thought through the history of the boat, we had not heard of Blue at this point but we did know the boat had lain dormant for some time. We concluded (and hoped) that this would be a temporary problem, cured as soon as we could pump out. The problem was, this could not happen until the next morning. Everyone had gone home.

Luckily for us the marina had its own loos so we decided we had no choice but to take a walk to the facilities whenever there was a call of nature that night in order to avoid nearly suffocating ourselves again. We made several unsuccessful attempts to go back on board before the atmosphere was fit for human habitation and even then we feared that sleeping above the offensive material was not going to be pleasant.

As it turned out, the lingering odour of the poo tank would be the least of our sleep inhibitors that night. Remember the boat inspection report and the few 'minor' problems involving the inverter?

Before I go further I need to explain what an inverter is and how narrowboats generate and use electricity. An Inverter is an essential piece of equipment on a narrowboat. It converts Direct Current (what the engine alternators, solar panels and wind turbines (if you have them) generate) into Alternating Current (what your boat and all its devices use for power). It also allows you to run devices that need 240 volts of power from batteries. Narrowboats typically have two electrical systems: A 12 volt and a 240 volt. On the Frog we had a 12 volt fridge and some of the lights ran from the 12 volt system but everything else was 240 volt. It will be apparent, therefore, that narrowboat's electricity can come from different sources which, for simplicity, I will summarise as either shoreline or generated.

Shoreline: the boat has an external electricity input socket that allows you to attach to the national grid and receive 240 volts of power directly into your boat. If you stayed in a marina attached to a shoreline the whole time you would not need an inverter.

Generated: I use this general term deliberately as electricity can be generated in a number of ways on a narrowboat. The most common way to generate power is via the engine (alternators act effectively as mini turbines that use the boat's engine to generate power). This is the same as any internal combustion-engined car, however, The Frog had three of these. When cruising it used the power generated by the engine to top up the six marine grade batteries we had on board. Many boats also have a solar supply via panels and some even had a wind turbine. Others may carry a separate petrol or diesel generator.

At the time of our first night aboard we did not have solar panels (we added them in Newbury) and the boat had been attached to the shoreline for a very long time. As it turned out this had degraded the batteries (which I think were original to the boat and were therefore about ten years old). It had also 'buggered' (technical term) the inverter - which ironically was not needed when attached to a shoreline. Not, that is, as long as the power was flowing. The shoreline in Gayton required a prepaid card to be bought at the office and inserted into the meter on the pontoon. This allowed electricity to flow until the value of the credit on the card ran out. Of course it had to be that night that our card ran out - at two AM to be precise! When the shoreline stopped working, the batteries were called upon to take over and the inverter kicked into life. In our case, a better description would be the inverter was prodded begrudgingly into a semi comatose state, not at all resembling life and then reacted very badly to being disturbed. It sounded a very shrill alarm, which, we now know, meant that the batteries were not holding their power.

Pip wears ear plugs (my snoring being a little too enthusiastic at times) - but I don't. I woke up with a start and banged my head on the hard barrier between the bed and the stern stairs. The inverter was literally three feet from my ears and the alarm was so loud it could probably be heard in the marina office - so I really wanted to turn it off as soon as possible. Pip stirred, eventually, conscious of me using a torch and peering into the control box, wearing nothing but underpants and swearing at my inability to quell the dreadful noise.

In the end I had to concede defeat and, inwardly apologising to all other nearby boaters also trying to sleep, I borrowed one of Pip's ear plugs and put the pillow over my head. It was, needless to say, a horrible first night experience, which was made worse when, the next morning, an engineer from the marina put his hand into the control panel and flicked a small switch on the top of the inverter, turning the alarm off easily! A memorable first night.

CHAPTER 5: 'THEY MAKE FOOLS OF US ALL'

We made a mental note that we would need to have a serious overhaul of all the electrics on board but in the meantime we still needed to meet our boat movers: Neil and Jackie. As I have already explained, my narrowboating experience was limited and I started the engine and disconnected the shoreline with mixed feelings. I loved The Frog and was so excited at the prospect of the Odyssey to come. However, the cold reality of manoeuvring this beautiful fifty seven foot boat out of the marina and onto the pump out station without making a fool of myself and without damaging her (we were still precious at this point and had not heard Derek's description of boating as 'a contact sport') - gripped at my bowels! Not only that, our disturbed night meant we were both bleary-eyed and slightly dishevelled as we left the berth and headed for the narrow exit.

Remarkably all went to plan. We came out of the marina and headed north up the Northampton Arm a few hundred feet to moor again at the pump out station. I took a little while to pull in and the marina staff helped by grabbing our bow and stern lines (ropes). My confidence grew however when we started chatting with the team. Firstly, they said how much they loved The Frog and how delighted they were to see her being taken out for a cruise. They all agreed this was a boat made for cruising! I commented on my inexperience and my inadequate mooring at the pumping station. A sympathetic employee said the words that will live with me forever - not least because now, after our thirteen month odyssey, I know them to be oh so true: 'I've been boating for thirty years and I know they make fools of us all'!

A chance to talk about pump outs. In an earlier chapter I explained what a macerator toilet was and that, with a poo tank option, you regularly (in our case about every ten days or so) had to pump out the tank. But what does this actually look like?

Whilst I was still working and telling my team about our odyssey plans, the bit that always fascinated them and made their noses twitch was the act of pumping out. It sounds distasteful and I guess if you really think about what you are doing and the material you are 'handling' (not literally - unless you are very careless) I guess it is.

Most marinas have a pump out station and most offer the service to all boaters - whether they are moored in the marina or just cruising by. In a lot of cases, an employee of the marina will do the pump out for you and it typically costs around £20 (at the time of our odyssey). A few places were a bit more expensive: I remember one marina on the Thames that charged £25. You may think this is good value - avoiding the need to get down and dirty yourself. The problem is you did not know until you arrived whether the marina pump out was self service or attended and beggars (with full poo tanks) can't be choosers.

The CRT also offered a number of self-operated pump outs, positioned at some water points. These were a god-send but were few and far between. They were card operated and gave you about eight minutes of suction per card. When we were cruising, the cards could be purchased for around £16 each. We did not need to buy any when we were out as I prudently, Pip would say over-zealously, purchased twenty cards before we set off for only £12 each. To put this into context, over the thirteen months of our odyssey we used fourteen cards and sold the remaining to friends, staying out on the cut, for our original purchase price. These numbers reflect just how rare the CRT self-service sites are (and, partly, how often they were actually operational).

So what is a pump out? Both the marina machines and the CRT machines operate in similar ways. A long hose about two to three inches in diameter has a nozzle on one end with a large lever that can be twisted to open and close it. The other end is attached to a VERY STRONG pump that creates a powerful suction. Every boat poo tank has an external outlet, usually accessed using a hexagonal-shaped key (an essential piece of equipment for every narrowboater) which was used to unscrew a metal cap. The nozzle is inserted into the outlet and the pump is turned on. Most pump out hoses have what is best described as an 'observation' window just below the nozzle. This allows the 'pumper' to take note of exactly what is being sucked out of the tank. You may ask yourself why anyone would want to look at this flow but later in the process, when the tank is being washed out, the sight of clear water rushing up the hose means your job is done (no pun intended).

So your nozzle is inserted and the machine turned on. The pumper, ensuring the nozzle is firmly in place, tentatively twists the handle and presses down hard to ensure the best possible seal (a poo tank is quite large and, whilst the pump is strong, a vacuum needs to be created to draw the contents in the right direction). The initial surge is always a very liquid, very brown combination of waste material. This will last for about three to four minutes and then the pump will start to buck slightly and the flow will become less rapid. Now you are starting to move the heavier solids that sit at the bottom of the tank. You let this continue for maybe a minute and then pause the pump and turn the handle back into the closed position. Remove the nozzle, being very careful to avoid covering your boat/the pump out station/your shoes with the inevitable small backwash that happens at this point. Next you insert a hose (NOT your water tank hose, for fairly obvious reasons) and let a generous amount of water into the tank to, hopefully, disturb the remaining solids. Then insert the pump hose again and turn the pump back on. You then repeat this as often as the timer will allow. In the periods when the pump is off, go aboard and flush the loo a few times. This also helps to 'move things on'. We learned it is best not to flush when the pump is on as this breaks the vacuum and creates a very strange sound in the toilet when you do so. Finally, after pumping out, replace your cap, being careful not to drop it in the canal. I did this in the New Islington Marina in Manchester and realised the value of carrying a spare. Most marinas will pour Blue into the outlet when they finish the pump out. There is no harm in this but in our experience it is much better to pour the Blue into the toilet pan and flush it through the entire sewerage system and into the tank.

There you have it. Pumping out de-mystified. I have to say it is not as bad as it sounds. Personally I have seen much worse sights and experienced much stronger odours when passing an Elsan (where toilet cassettes are emptied). Pumping out is rarely dirty and whilst there is a faint smell, it is bearable.

My worst pump out experience? Well I can think of two, the first of which had nothing to do with the pump out itself. We had moored near the junction of the Oxford and Grand Union canals and set off in the morning to pump out at Ventnor marina. I always phoned ahead and got the answers to a few basic questions: do they offer pump out? (sometimes the Nicholson Guide is out of date - more on

Nicholson later). Is it actually working? Is it canal side and if so what bank? If in the marina, where EXACTLY is it? Later I added: and how do I approach it? This last question was added following my 'Ventnor experience'.

The helpful lady on the phone at Ventnor answered the first four questions and we set off. It was a Saturday morning and the rain had just started. Worse still, the wind had got up and by the time we reached Ventnor it was really whipping across the canal. Ventnor marina is a large open expanse (two expanses to be precise) and, consequently, manoeuvring the Frog was very tricky in the wind. I had been told that the pump out was situated next to the flagpole. As I entered the marina the flagpole was very obvious, despite the rain, so I set the nose of the Frog directly for it. It was situated on the left hand side of the marina as you enter and turn to the right. So I made a diagonal course across and towards it. What I had not been told was that whilst the flagpole was at the end of a pontoon, the pump out was set down a very narrow berth alongside that pontoon, necessitating a very tricky turn to take the boat in at right angles to the course I was travelling on. Not only that, I did not realise this until I reached the flagpole - far too late to turn!

At this point the wind got up even more and despite my efforts to pull out from the end of the pontoon I was forced sideways into both it and the opening of a dry dock/work area next to the pontoon. The pump out operator stood with his arms folded and a smile on his face. He had probably cursed the phone call that meant he had to drive down to the pontoon and perform a pump out, so the spectacle of me struggling, in vain, to avoid a collision was some entertaining compensation at least. He certainly looked like he was enjoying himself!

I finally got clear of the pontoon and took The Frog out into the middle of the marina and conducted a challenging 450 degree turn to bring her back towards the pontoon at the right angle. I still managed to hit the end of the pontoon with the bow before 'bouncing' down the narrow gap into place for the pump out. This will not be the last time I struggle to turn in a marina - as you will discover as the odyssey unfolds. The words of the Gayton employee came back to me as I stood, dejected, on the pump out pontoon - they really do 'make fools of us all!'

The second pump out that sticks in my mind was during our 'practise' run down the K&A. We had left Hungerford and headed west towards Great Bedwyn. I had secretly arranged for Pip's sister's family to meet us for lunch at Froxfield as it was Pip's birthday. The reunion was a great success and we cruised with the new enlarged crew onto Great Bedwyn where we moored for the night. Trish, Pip's sister, commented on the smell of the canal - 'in this area". We agreed and said it had been like that for a couple of days. We then went for a walk along the towpath and into the village. It was only as we were returning and nearing The Frog that we realised the smell was getting stronger. This was puzzling. The next morning we moved down to Great Bedwyn Wharf to top up the water. At the water point the bank was much lower and I could see the poo tank overflow outlet clearly on the hull of The Frog. This 'vent' is designed for just that: to allow any nasty gases, that may accrue in the tank, to escape. However, I noticed, with dismay, that as well as gas, we also had a slow trickle of 'liquid' running down our hull and into the canal. In short our poo tank was so full the contents had reached the very top of the pump out outlet and were being forced out through the vent.

We felt terrible! We knew we were polluting the canal and there was nothing we could do until we could pump out. To be fair to us, whilst the poo tank had a gauge, telling us how full it was, at that point we did not realise that it was a 'floating gauge' - which worked fine until the poo tank neared capacity. Then it simply fell over and the meter dropped back to zero. I phoned Derek at Ham Marina for advice. It was a Sunday afternoon and on reflection I am not sure what I was expecting him to say. He told me everything that I had worked out for myself and suggested I get a pump out smartish! A quick look at our Nicholson Guide and we realised the next facility was at Pewsey eight and a half miles, twelve locks and a short tunnel away. We had to moor at Crofton that night to allow our guests to leave and it was only the next day that we reached Pewsey after a very long cruise.

So it was with a very full poo tank that we pulled up to Pewsey Wharf. When we arrived another boat was moored there with its hose running into the water tank on board. We waited, and waited, and waited (we know how long water tanks can take to fill) and eventually a head appeared at the well deck: 'Oh sorry, are you waiting? We finished topping up sometime ago and were just grabbing a spot of lunch'. 'No worries' I said, through gritted teeth, thinking and feeling the complete opposite. They untied and pulled off.

This is where it got interesting. The pump out box was sited right at one end of the wharf where the bank bent in close to a bridge entrance. I moored The Frog and tried to pull the hose to the pooh tank outlet. It would not reach. My only option was to move us down about 20 feet and moor at an angle across the corner of the mooring - meaning I could not pump out from the bank. Instead I had to walk down the gunwale carrying the pump out and water hoses. Bear in mind, at this point I had fallen off the gunwale on three previous occasions (how can I bear this in mind, you ask yourself, when you haven't told me about this yet - I promise I will later). Needless to say, I moved slowly and awkwardly, carrying, as I had to, the heavy pump out hose and the lighter, but fiddly, water hose, whilst trying desperately not to drop the pump out keys into the canal. I made it to the outlet and grabbed hold of the gangplank housing on the roof of The Frog very tightly. I bent my knees sideways (sounds painful - but you know what I mean) to avoid pushing myself off the side of the boat and began to undo the poo tank cap. Not surprisingly the 'liquid' was right up to the top and actually spilled over the rim when the cap was removed. More was displaced as I inserted the nozzle. Remember, all of this had to be done one-handed as I hang on for dear life with my other hand. Pip turned on the pump, I managed somehow to turn the handle allowing the waste to flow and breathed (not too deeply) a sigh of relief. At last we were no longer killing fish or annoying other boaters by sharing our effluence with the UK's waterways!

Above, I have described in detail what a pump out consists of, so you should now have a picture of my Spiderman impression, hanging off the side of The Frog for what felt like a very long time, turning the pump on and off and shouting for Pip to turn the hose on and off as well as jump on board to flush the loo - without rocking the boat so much that I fell in. Oh! That reminds me. A successful pump out is only normally achieved with a good boat rock when rinsing out with clean water. I wonder why I have only just remembered that. Needless to say, on this occasion we made do with getting most of our waste out. There was no way I was going to tip The Frog from side to side when I was already arm-achingly desperate to get to the end of the process!

So there you have it. The joys of the pump out. For balance, I calculate that we must have pumped out forty to fifty times on our various adventures. As I am not citing any other horrors here, you can work out that, all in all, the process is not that bad!

CHAPTER 6: GOT A LIGHT MATE?

As I write, I realise that there is so much background information the reader needs to really appreciate the tale of Our Year on The Frog, that it's very easy to get distracted from the main thread. This happened in the last chapter. So let me remind you of where we are up to. Pip and I have just left Gayton Marina and have had a pump out before heading off to meet Neil and Jackie, our boat movers.

I will clarify one more thing before I describe the cruise to meet Neil and Jackie. Most boaters use a guide book to help them plan their travels. There are various options available but by far the most popular is published by HarperCollins and is called *Nicholson Waterways Guides*. There are several versions covering most of the waterways in the UK. They are an excellent reference resource. Not only do they map the course of the waterway but they also give invaluable supporting information showing, amongst other things, navigational challenges, water points, pump outs, marinas, pubs and shops. They also give a short description of the more significant places you visit - like any good Travel Guide. Throughout this story, I will refer to 'Nicholson' or simply 'the guide' and it is this publication I am meaning. Ours are well-thumbed as they were always on hand near the helmsman, warning of upcoming hazards and opportunities or reasons to moor. They were also used extensively in the filming of our Vlogs and the writing of our Blogs - ensuring we were accurate in naming or numbering bridges and locks, as well as other locations. I am sitting with one open next to me right now. They were our bible and we would have been lost without them. Only the most seasoned boaters did not use a Nicholson, or some equivalent guide, to plan and check their route. Thank you HarperCollins!

Back to Neil and Jackie. We left the pump out wharf and headed north up the Northampton Arm to the first winding hole and our very first turn! This went surprisingly well, having been warned by the marina team that the hole was quite small and could be easily missed if you were not paying attention. The turn was certainly not 'three point', they rarely are in a narrowboat, but we ended up facing in the right direction without grounding or hitting anything. This, after all, is the main objective of winding.

We cruised back past the marina, waving confidently and cheerily to the team - thinking, this narrowboating lark is a piece of cake. It's only a short distance to the end of the Arm and we soon met the Grand Union Canal proper. A boat was coming from the West and I let it pass (not least because I did not want any observers) before I attempted the left turn and negotiated Bridge 48. That went well and we cruised on in a south easterly direction, under Candle Bridge and past the imposing Blisworth Mill before entering the wooded area just before the Blisworth tunnel. A few bends later and we were facing the entrance to the 3075 yard triumph of engineering.

It's important to set the scene in a bit more detail here. Blisworth is the third longest open to navigation tunnel in Britain. It's wide enough for two boats to pass (just), which is essential as a crossing typically takes about twenty to twenty five minutes and with Stoke Bruerne at the other end, this is a busy stretch of the canal network. For the metric amongst you: 3075 yards is 2811 metres. That is one and three quarter miles. It's not surprising therefore that the tunnel is pitch black in the middle.

So, here we are. Our first trip on our lovely new boat and we have been cruising for less than an hour. When I see the tunnel entrance I turn on the headlamp and ask Pip to pop down to the bow to check it. She does and it's not working! I frantically switch it on and off at the helm but to no avail. It is not going to cooperate. Pip comes to the stern and we discuss our options. Can we turn around? Not a chance. There is no winding hole and the canal is too narrow for that to be considered. Can we moor? Yes but then what? If we can't turn around, are we not just delaying the inevitable? Not only that, our boat movers will be arriving into Stoke Bruerne, on the other side of the tunnel and that is where the locks are (important for their 'training run'). So, we agreed - we had no option but to tackle the tunnel with no headlight. Pip would stand at the bow with her iPhone torch switched on, (other mobile devices are available) and shout back directions when (not if) I strayed towards a wall.

I never liked traversing tunnels on The Frog. What is unclear is if this was a natural aversion, in bred in some way or, as I think more likely, an acquired aversion, linked, most strongly, to the 12th July 2019 when I went through the third longest tunnel in Britain in almost total darkness listening to shouted instructions from poor old Pip, fifty seven feet away.

How did it go? Not great. I mentioned earlier that a normal transit through the tunnel would take twenty to twenty five minutes. Ours took forty five. It started badly with me hitting the right side wall with the chimney! I misjudged the height of the tunnel as I tried desperately to keep right. To say I was stressed was an understatement. My mind was working at a ferocious rate as I tried to get every ounce of light onto my retinas whilst listening intently to Pip. Ever the purist, Pip started relaying her instructions in nautical terminology as follows: 'Port, a bit more to port. Starboard, starboard more. Straighten up etc.' The last thing I needed was the added complication of 'translating' Pip's directions into everyday English. I snapped and my language reflected my stress levels: 'Just say F***ing left or right'. Poor Pip. She was also feeling a huge responsibility, as whether we hit the tunnel wall or not rested almost entirely on her directions to me. They needed to be accurate and timely. Not only this, the tunnel was very damp and, every few metres, water cascaded onto the boat from above. As the cratch cover was off (the cratch cover is a canopy, normally canvas, that sits on top of the well deck. The cratch is simply the structure that supports it) when the water cascades happened, Pip had no choice but to jump back inside the cabin of the boat. The result was that, at times, we were plunged into complete darkness even at the bow!

About halfway through another boat came up behind us. This did not help. Not only did it disorientate me further (at least when it was pitch black at the stern of The Frog I could make out vague shapes at the marginally better illuminated bow. Now the light difference was reduced by the headlight of the boat behind, making it more difficult to see anything at the bow. Conversely, the headlight behind me was not strong enough to light our way - the 'considerate' boater keeping a polite distance from the clearly novice helmsman in front of them. When we finally left the tunnel I moored and apologised to the people behind for their slow transit. Like all good narrowboaters they were desperate to reassure me that 'it was not a problem'. When I explained what had actually happened they said we should have pulled over and let them through. We could then have followed them and 'used their light' to get through more quickly. If kicking myself would not have meant me falling overboard I would have done it.

Pip and I made up and comforted each other. We agreed that this was not an experience to repeat and was certainly not a great start to our boating adventures. A phone call to Gayton had an engineer come out very quickly and fix the headlight. It seemed the wiring had got crossed over somehow. Any more explanation would need an ounce of technical understanding, which, we have already established, I don't have.

Anyway - back to the tale: we had made this maiden voyage to meet up with our amateur boat movers who were driving up to Stoke Bruerne the next day. We went to the pub that evening to drown our sorrows and avoid the need to cook. The Boat Inn is a really picturesque thatched building sitting right next to Stoke Bruerne Top Lock. It was busy that night as the British Grand Prix was on at Silverstone (about 10 miles away) and there were media and race spectators alike all congregating and talking about the race. It felt a million miles away from the four mph of the Grand Union (or one to two mph if you try to tackle the Blisworth Tunnel with no lights).

Next morning Neil and Jackie arrived as planned. Neil, remember, is an accomplished yachtsman but has never handled a narrowboat. After a short tour of The Frog, we agreed that I would take the Frog down the seven locks of the Stoke Bruerne flight and wind at the bottom and Neil would bring her back up as far as the mouth of the tunnel - which we would need to tackle again today - this time with lights.

The descent went well. Neil's only observation was just how long everything took - especially on a busy summer weekend on one of the most popular stretches of the Grand Union. He was very attentive and watched everything I did in order to prepare for taking the helm. Pip showed Jackie how to operate the locks (more about this below) as it would be her responsibility when they began their long trip down to our marina in Newbury. We eventually reached the winding hole. This was only the second time I had turned the Frog around - the first being the day before on the Northampton Arm - and today there were a lot more boats and gongoozlers around. (note: a Gongoozler is a boat watcher. A member of the public who likes to wait on towpaths - particularly at locks - and watch 'the action'. They are normally very unobtrusive and can even be a great help. Many times during our Odyssey, Pip and I would ask a gongoozler to help move a heavy lock gate - or even close one after us so we could jump on board and continue our journey more quickly.) That day, however, I just felt the eyes of an expectant crowd watching as I approached the winding hole.

I have already described the 'dark art' of winding. What I have not yet explained is the tendency of the Frog's bow to always pull to the left when reversing. I haven't explained this yet because, as I am telling the story chronologically, I had not yet discovered this endearing quality myself. Today I would! What does this tendency mean? Well, in short, it makes winding in a winding hole on the right bank a lot harder than one on the left. This is because after your first forward turn towards the bank you then need to engage reverse gear and move your stern out into the canal ready to go forward again and continue the right turn. Remember, narrowboats can't really be steered when in reverse as the rudder is rendered almost totally ineffective as the propeller is not directing water across it (which it does when you are cruising forwards). What you don't want to happen then, is for your crazy narrowboat to start 'undoing' your previous right turn by sending the bow back to the left. The Frog does this and not just slightly. It was also quite a windy day and I think the wind direction was also serving to magnify this newly revealed reversing 'quirk'. The effect was so severe that after my reversing manoeuvre I was almost facing in the same direction as when I started - much to the gongoozler's amusement. So what is the remedy? Power! The only way to counter the effect of the reverse is to turn even more sharply when going forward and the only way to achieve that is to up the revs, significantly on a windy day, whilst jacking the tiller over. Unless you have a bow-thruster of course (see my earlier description and understand why I was already getting thruster-envy.)

A short aside and another embarrassing anecdote: I have already described how a narrowboat is steered. It has a rudder at the stern, below the hull, across which the propeller sends a stream of water when in forward motion. The rudder is attached to a tiller above deck (or, very rarely, a wheel). When the tiller is moved left or right the rudder moves in the same direction and pushes the stern of the boat - again in the same direction. If you can picture this in your head you can appreciate that this means the bow of the boat must be moving in the opposite direction. So you always push the tiller in the opposite direction to that which you want the bow to turn. It sounds complicated, but the brain is a wonderful thing and it soon becomes second nature.

What I did not appreciate (and still did not for some time into our odyssey) is that many narrowboat tillers have a 'sweet spot' within which it works most effectively and turns the boat as you wish. On the Frog, this sweet spot is an arc of about 90 degrees from a midpoint position on the starboard side to a similar position on the port side. So what? I hear you say. Well if you think about what I am trying to do in Stoke Bruerne, and on many more occasions subsequently, it would have been really helpful for me to understand this feature of The Frog. When you are struggling to turn a boat I have already said that power is the answer and the phrase I think I used was 'jacking the tiller over'. What I now know is that this is only partly true. Power is needed, but the tiller needs to be moved with precision to the limit of the sweet spot and then held there. This would have given me maximum turning ability. If you push the rudder all the way to one side, then the stream of propelled water passing over the rudder, rather than turning the boat sharply, simply divides around the now 'flat' rudder. The net result is the boat goes almost straight ahead!

I only found this out when moored at Napton on 22 October 2021 - having owned the Frog for over two years and having been on our odyssey for nearly a month. We had by this time traversed the end of the K&A from Newbury to Reading, travelled up to Oxford on the River Thames and struggled up the tight-bended South Oxford Canal - hitting a few banks on the way. Not to mention our trip earlier in the year down the K&A to Bath and back. My frustration at the Frog's seeming inability to deal with tight bends led me to call out the RCR (River Canal Rescue: the equivalent of the AA/RAC on the road). The engineer was brilliant. Not only did he confirm very quickly that there was nothing at all wrong with the Frog's rudder and tiller but, through simple questions and watching my reaction, he also managed to uncover my total ignorance of the 'sweet spot'. He did this in a very uncondescending way and claimed it was a 'common misunderstanding amongst new boaters'. My embarrassed face must have looked like a beetroot and Derek's 'numpty' reference echoed in my ears. I was not too proud to admit my shortcomings, however, and that moment was a turning point in my helmsmanship; better late than never!

So back to our tale. When showing Neil how to wind on the Grand Union, of course, I was completely unaware of the sweet spot on the Frog. As a result, as well as applying lots of power to try and sharpen my turn, I also did indeed 'jack the tiller over', all the way over, and, as a result, my turn was anything but sharp. I was turning - but very slowly. I then decided I needed a 'longer run at it' so I reversed further across the canal - so far in fact that I buried the stern of the Frog into the opposite bank and surrounded Neil and I in the branches of a very large Buddleia. I don't think the gongoozlers cheered at this point but I do remember a lot more mobile phones pointing in our direction. Finally, after about a twenty point turn, we were facing back towards the Stoke Bruerne locks and it was Neil's turn to take the helm. I am not sure whether my poor boat handling was reassuring to him or made him think that the task ahead was going to be even harder than he already thought. I was too embarrassed to ask him! However he felt, Neil showed no sign of being fazed by the task ahead. Clearly his yacht handling experience was coming to the fore and he proved a steady hand on the tiller. We climbed the seven locks without incident and I only took control of the tiller as we approached the Blisworth Tunnel for the second time. What a difference a headlight makes. We cruised through the tunnel in twenty five minutes (almost half the time of our earlier passage) and were soon cruising sedately into our mooring back at Gayton.

When I reflect on what happened next I can only have enormous respect for Neil and Jackie. They followed through on their promise and boarded The Frog in early August to begin the long journey to Newbury. Apart from the brief practice run at Stoke Bruerne they had never handled a narrowboat before and had certainly not spent any length of time on one. Now they were facing a trip of one hundred and twenty nine miles that would take over nine days even if they cruised for seven hours every day at the speed of an experienced boater…….and they were alone!

Jackie kindly shared her iPhone 'Find My' application with us - which meant we always knew where they were. It quickly became apparent that the trip was going to be a lot longer than the nine days the Canal Planner predicted but I was not surprised. I have already alluded to Neil's assiduous approach to tackling new situations and to be honest both Pip and I were grateful for it. It really did not matter how long the journey took. What was far more important was that Neil and Jackie felt safe, had a good time and that The Frog made the journey without major incident.

Following our debrief with the intrepid pair, I think 'good time' would be stretching how Neil and Jackie felt about the boat move. It had clearly been very hard work and, throughout, they were carrying a heavy sense of responsibility. However, I can honestly say they really did a great job and Pip and I will be eternally grateful that, some sixteen days after leaving Gayton, The Frog was safely moored outside Ham Manor Marina in Newbury. Understandably, Neil and Jackie approached Emma and Derek to ask for help to take her into her berth. It was in this way that Derek met The Frog for the first time and used his highly developed boating skills to tuck her snugly into a mooring near the marina entrance. This will not be the last time Derek handled The Frog for us in the marina (more on that later) but for now it felt great to know The Frog was safe in her new home. Thank you Neil and Jackie.

CHAPTER 7: HOW DOES THAT WORK AGAIN!

Remember, we chose Newbury as it is 'only' three hours from our home in Cornwall. We didn't waste any time jumping in our car and driving up to see the Frog in-situ, as well as starting the process of kitting her out with more of the things we would need to start cruising. At that point we were planning to start our odyssey the following March, 2020. It's important to remember that, at that time, Corona was still just the name of a bottled beer you drank with a slice of lime (or a fizzy drink we had in the 1970s). We had no idea what lay ahead!

Back to our naive planning. It was clear from our experience in Gayton and the feedback given by Neil and Jackie, that The Frog's electrics needed a good seeing to. However, another problem took priority. We arrived in Newbury one very wet day in September and I was very concerned that the well deck (the seating area between the bow of the boat and the front doors) was about two inches deep in water with no obvious way of draining it out. This felt like a serious design fault to me. We quickly erected the cratch cover to stop any more rain getting in and I spent the next twenty minutes panning the water over the side using a small bowl. In the middle of the deck there was a small hole but it seemed to be superfluous as no water was running into it. I left The Frog and walked around the marina 'checking out' the other narrowboats to see how their well decks were holding up in the rain. It was only by doing this that I realised The Frog was almost unique in having a well deck that was below water level. Most of the other boats I saw had a high step out through the front door taking you up onto a well deck that was higher than the internal floor level of the boat. In these boats, on either side of the hull there were two holes cut that simply allowed the water in the well deck to drain away. Clearly, this was not an option when your well deck floor level is below the water line. I was really puzzled. As I remember it, this was the first time I got the disapproving 'Tch Tch' from Derek. I asked him to take a look at the flooded well deck. He asked me how it drained (I am convinced that it was a test and that he knew exactly how it worked). I shrugged my shoulders and realised how pathetic it sounded when I said: 'I don't know". "Didn't you ask anything when you bought this b£$$&y

boat?" On the face of it, having spent the amount of money we had, this was a fair question. I maintain to this day, however, that this was a classic case of: 'you don't know what you don't know'. The previous owner had passed away, remember, and whilst we asked an employee at Gayton to give us a tour, 'how do I avoid a flooded well deck?' was not on the list of things he showed us.

Derek went straight to the inside of the front door and lay on the floor. He opened a small door directly beneath the front doors themselves (in my defence a door that could be easily missed). This revealed a black plastic bowl full of water and a device called a float switch attached to a pump. Leading into this bowl was a pipe connected to the seemingly redundant hole in the well deck I spotted earlier. Derek stuck a screwdriver down the hole and water started to run into the bowl. On reaching a certain depth the pump kicked into life and started pumping the water out through a very small hole in the flank of our bow. Who would have thought it? Well Derek, obviously. I was in awe of this design ingenuity. Mystery solved, I thanked Derek and he mumbled something under his breath which I was probably best not hearing!

Back to the electrics; we knew that the inverter had seen better days and it was also a recommendation in the survey that we have the electrics properly reviewed by a trained electrician. We also had in mind buying solar panels. We had seen these on other boats and thought they would be a good way of supplementing the power generated by the engine to charge the batteries. You will already have worked out that I am a technical vacuum so I did not, and still do not, fully understand the intricacies of the electrics on a narrowboat. I have explained above what an inverter does and I think I will leave it there. Derek and Emma have a really good friend called Peter who specialises in boat electrics and in particular fitting solar panels. We asked if he could take a look the next time he was visiting. We liked Peter very much. He was a really amiable man who knows a great deal about his subject (and boats in general) but is really tolerant of those who don't. The electrics on a boat are a complicated set up and Peter accepted that I really didn't get it and must have explained how the inverter worked ten times over our relationship! Thank you Peter.

His first step was a thorough review of the whole system. There was good news and bad news. Yes solar panels could be fitted easily however, not only was the troublesome inverter kaput, but so were all the batteries. The final bill for replacing all these and fitting the panels was over £3000. We readily agreed to the work being done. The prospect of living on board, away from a marina, with anything but a reliable electric system was not something I was prepared to consider.

Peter replaced the batteries (with Rolls Royce Marine batteries - only the best for The Frog) and the inverter, but It was not until the following spring that the panels were finally added. This was our fault. We wanted to maximise the storage onboard and we had seen roof top storage boxes on some other boats. We asked Peter to mount the panels on new, specially built, boxes designed for the roof of the Frog. We employed a carpenter to make them from scratch. We were very pleased with the final look of the boxes and when the panels were added they looked even nicer. I will talk more about the boxes when we are on our Odyssey - and most of it is not positive - but in the spring of 2020 we were happy with our very expensive acquisitions.

Derek and Emma lived on site during the season in a lovely widebeam boat moored in the marina, not far from The Frog. So we saw a lot of them both as they passed by, enroute to and from the marina office. That said, I was still becoming paranoid that Derek was watching us for his own amusement. It was uncanny that he always seemed to be on hand when something embarrassing happened. A good example of this was when Peter was fitting the new inverter and checking the electric system. He called me to the stern and asked me what I wanted to do with the tumble dryer. Before I had noticed that Derek was at that moment walking past I blurted out: 'What tumble dryer?' Derek didn't need an invitation - he stopped and folded his arms with a smile on his face. He sensed something entertaining was about to happen and, for him, it probably was. In tracing back all the wiring Peter noticed that in a hollow area just in front of the tiller position and directly behind the head of our bed there was a tumble dryer. It was facing the top of our bed and was behind two cupboard doors that were clearly unusable as our bed was securely screwed in place in front of them - rendering the dryer redundant. Peter and I scratched our heads but Derek smiled knowingly. He was half amused that yet again there was something fairly fundamental about our new boat that we did not know and half self-satisfied that he had worked out what had happened. He explained that when she was built The Frog probably had a bed that was laid across her beam (sideways) with the headboard on the port side and the feet on the starboard. This is not unusual. It allows you to fit a wider bed into a confined space. However, it does mean that every morning the hinged tail of the bed has to be folded up onto the head of the bed to allow access to the steps leading to the tiller position at the stern (and vice versa at night when you want to go to bed). A process that was not to everyone's liking. Our now great friends, Mark and Katherine, on their narrowboat 'Double O' had this layout in their bedroom. Derek continued: a subsequent owner must have disliked the original design and had turned the bed through 90 degrees and in so doing had 'trapped' the tumble dryer in its otherwise accessible cupboard. This made sense. The boat had only had two previous owners. The couple who had her built (who obviously requested the traverse bed design) and the elderly gentleman who had sadly passed away leading to its sale to us. He lived near Gayton marina and clearly did not worry about losing the use of the dryer. And as he was not a 'live-aboard', he did not see the need to free up the valuable space the dryer was taking up so he just left it in place. As Derek was close by and enjoying the spectacle of my further embarrassment, I decided I could kill two birds with one stone: 'Derek, would you like the tumble dryer for the marina laundry?' He stopped smiling, coughed and accepted my gracious offer. I like to think my quick thinking staved off further eye-rolling from our host and at the same time we got rid of the dryer - freeing up enough room for what would become our folding bike store.

Another vital piece of preparation was our need for good Wifi. We knew that we intended to record our odyssey in a series of Vlogs and that it was important we could upload the finished products without relying upon the mobile data on our phones. We also had a small, smart telly in our lounge at home that would fit perfectly in the corner of the Frog. For this to work properly - good Wifi was a must. My work colleagues had also bought me Apple TV as one of my leaving presents (very generous of them). We did a lot of research, the most useful of which was watching a Vlog from *Foxes Afloat.* The two, new-to-boating, owners of The Silver Fox (Colin and Shaun) had recorded not only the building process of their new Bickerstaffe narrowboat (other boat builders are available) but also their preparations for living aboard. We watched the episode that explained their Wifi set up, how it worked and why they had chosen it. Knowing they would be making similar, and probably greater, demands on their system to those we would make on ours, it made sense to copy their approach. We were not proud. We bought a Huawei router with a hard wire connection to an aerial mounted upon a magnetic pole placed on the roof. We asked electrician Peter to drill another hole through the TV aerial inlet at the front of the boat which we knew was already covered by a plastic hinged housing and would be protected by the cratch cover in the worst of the weather. We inserted a '3' data only SIM for which we paid £26 a month. We chose this network as it seemed to offer the best nationwide coverage. Throughout our trip we realised there would always be days when we had no coverage, whichever network we chose. We just wanted to minimise these and we were pleased with our purchases.

I will finish this chapter with one anecdote about my head and its contact with The Frog. Within the space of three days I twice hit my head so badly that I drew blood and saw stars. The first occasion I walked too quickly from the tiller position down the steps into the bedroom. I did not notice that the sliding hatch was still half closed and planted my forehead on the leading metal edge. Many expletives and lots of tissues later I stopped bleeding. The second incident involved our new boxes (which is why it sprang to mind). They were fitted with 'stay up' hinges so the lid could be opened and both hands used to access the contents of the box. At least that was the theory. The problem was the hinges worked fine, unless the boat rocked or the wind blew. The first time I realised this, I was standing on the gunwale with the lid fully open putting something into one of the boxes. My weight on one side of the boat combined with a gust of wind made the lid slam shut. It would have been painful if the box lid had simply hit me. However, in the centre of each lid is a metal catch used to lock it when closed. This was very sharp and, unfortunately, I was standing directly under it when it fell. I will forever bear a 'Harry Potter' scar on my forehead! This was not the last time Pip and I would curse those boxes - but more on that later.

CHAPTER 8: CRUISING AND BRUISING

As well as turning the Frog into our new home we also wanted to get more acquainted with handling her and the K&A would be the ideal place for some much needed practice.

However, our first challenge was simply leaving the marina. Unlike Gayton, which was an expansive marina with lots of turning space, Ham Manor was small and had narrowboats moored directly facing each other across a narrow stretch of water. The exit to the marina was to our right and not far away. However, we had boats moored either side of us. This meant, in order to leave, we had to go forward and turn sharply to the right - trying hard not to hit the boat on our left side or those opposite. Needless to say, my first attempt at this was a disaster. It is important to remember that, at that time, I still did not understand the vagaries of the tiller 'sweet spot' described in an earlier chapter and I still believed that maximum turn came from shoving the tiller over as hard as I could. I was also very considerate about other boats and their owners (who, in many cases, were sitting on board their precious possessions and watching with a mixture of amused fascination and fear).

I must have tried five or six times to make the turn without hitting the boats in front (the boat to my left I'm afraid was getting a fair old bashing from my stern already and I really didn't know how I could avoid this) when I heard a call from Derek on his way to the office: 'Use your mooring line!' I had no idea what he meant by this and just turned and shrugged my shoulders - a gesture designed to display both a complete lack of understanding and submission. Derek took the hint and jumped onto the boat next to us, walked down its gunwale and jumped aboard The Frog. He immediately took the tiller (he clearly didn't feel the need to ask - and I wasn't complaining). He then took the stern mooring line and threw it around the mooring pin on the bow of the boat to our left. He wrapped the line around one of our stern mooring pins a couple of times and kept the loose end in his hand. He put the boat into reverse and pulled tight on the mooring line stopping the boat from moving backwards. As a result the bow swung to the right and was now pointing in a much better starting position than we were before.

Our stern was rubbing against the neighbouring boat but Derek was unconcerned. He noticed the look on my face and sensing my discomfort simply said: 'Boating is a contact sport - there's a reason the hulls are as thick as they are!' He would develop this point with me on several other occasions. One day when I was fitting fenders to the hull of The Frog he shook his head disapprovingly: 'They cause more trouble than they're worth. Why do you think the hull is made of steel? It's not like she's a 'yoghurt pot' (a disparaging reference to any fibre-glass vessel but, particularly, river cruisers who have the nerve to share the waterways with 'real boats'. We were to learn on our travels that this was a sentiment shared by many narrowboaters.)

Anyway I digress. Back to our manoeuvring in the marina. We were making progress but the job was only half done. It was a very windy day and we were now drifting sideways towards the boats moored on the other side of the marina. Derek seemed unperturbed. It was his marina after all! He is simultaneously telling me that he can handle any boat in any conditions through years of experience, whilst stepping sideways onto the bow of one of the, occupied, boats we were now rubbing up against. Once again he performed the mooring line process and jumped back onto The Frog and put her into reverse. We pulled the moored boat slightly out of position as we did so but our bow, yet again, swung around and was now facing the marina exit. Genius! I was incredulous - not only in awe of the handling skill Derek displayed but also the seeming cheek of not respecting any boundary when it came to other boats. "Don't worry about that" he said "There will be many occasions when you need to jump onto another boat and many times when they will need to do it to you." He was right. Thankfully it did not happen that often on our odyssey but, when it did, most boaters were fully understanding of the need to invade each other's space. A really good example is when mooring was limited and you needed to double up (moor alongside another boat). In these circumstances, I don't care what Derek says, it is courteous (and expected) to use your fenders to minimise deliberate contact with the accommodating boat. It is, however, inevitable that you need to walk across the other boat when going 'ashore' and when reboarding.

We are now facing the exit and Derek stays on board until we get to the narrow opening leading onto the River Kennet (forming part of the K&A at this point). He does this partly because he wants to jump off onto the, then, very close bank at the moment we leave the marina but also because entering the river is also a developed skill. Because it is a River, the Kennet has a flow moving right to left across the entrance to the marina. This means as soon as the bow of The Frog enters the stream it starts to drift downstream (to the left). This is pretty inconvenient, to say the least, as we want to turn right and head towards Newbury town centre. So Derek keeps hold of the tiller until the last minute and swings the stern around to just (and I mean JUST) miss the left hand bank at the exit. He then jumps off and hands the tiller (quickly) to me. The Frog is now partly pointing upstream and Derek shouts for me to keep the lock on in order to counter the stream. It works and we managed to get into the middle of the stream. I will admit, at this point, that this was the last time I managed to do this so well. On every subsequent exit I managed to end up heading for the far bank and the overhanging trees. On these occasions, as his workshop is near the exit, Derek could often be seen standing with his hands on his hips and shaking his head as he heard me go into reverse and then rev hard, in forward gear, to try and swing away from the bank. Once again my lack of understanding of the tiller sweet spot did not help.

Another reason we had to leave the marina was to pump out. The nearest pump out station was at Newbury Marina - about half a mile away from Ham Manor Marina but the other side of Greenham lock - our first on the K&A. We managed the lock and felt positive as we chatted nonchalantly to a family on a rental boat that joined us on the ascent (the locks on this canal are all double width). We left the lock after the hire boat as I knew I was mooring soon and I did not want the extra pressure of another boat behind me or to inconvenience them. I realise now that this sounds pathetic, but in the very early days 'hovering' on The Frog never felt easy. I have also described the challenges of reversing so I did not want to overshoot and the stream of the Kennet was constantly pushing the bow one way or another, so I was very conscious of the long term moored boats on the approach to the marina. Luckily the landing point was clear as I arrived so I slipped in without incident and tied up.

We were helped by a lovely lady who topped up our diesel and completed the pump out. I was relieved as I had yet to do this myself and wasn't sure exactly what to do. I watched closely to see the process she went through. This was well worth the twenty pounds we paid - not only for a job well done but also for the invaluable lesson.

We moved off towards the centre of Newbury, cruising past Victoria Park and under the wide bridge that carries the A339 over the river and past the lovely Newbury Wharf with its pretty tearoom. The River bends slowly to the left and then to the right and up ahead we could see the beautiful Newbury Bridge beyond which is the town's lock. This part of the river is really picturesque. The old buildings of the town centre dominate the approach to the bridge with the Lock Stock and Barrel pub particularly adding colour, noise and the curious eyes of its customers sitting outside. Thankfully, the lock traverse goes well and the river opens up into a lovely wider section passing another park.

We cruised on and had another new experience - a swing bridge. All boaters MUST carry a British Waterways key (now more accurately called a Canal and Rivers Trust or CRT key). It has a simple 'Yale' look but it has many uses: unlocking swing bridges - manual and mechanical - opening CRT bin stores, toilets, self service pump outs, water points etc. It's almost impossible to function on the network without this key, so it is not surprising that most boaters have at least two. We had three.

The swing bridge at West Mills in Newbury is mechanical. This means it operates electronically and the CRT key is used to activate it. Luckily, this bridge is only for pedestrians, so it was a nice one for Pip to break herself in on. The sequence starts with the insertion and turning of the key. An alarm immediately sounds and two lights flash as you press the 'open bridge' button. Two barriers drop down at either end to stop any impatient pedestrians jumping onto the moving bridge. The process is quite slow and as waiting pedestrians gather it can feel a bit intimidating. Some onlookers seem to like the diversion and spectacle of the bridge opening process, whilst others, probably those who live nearby and for whom the novelty of watching the bridge swing has long faded, seem less tolerant. They look at their watches and pace back and forth. Not only did the bridge take a while to open but we still had to move The Frog through. It is best practice to moor up on the bridge landing point but, in normal conditions, it is not necessary to tie up fully and the boat can be controlled on its centre line - which is held by a crew member on the bank.

I realise at this point that I have not explained the various ropes (or as they are more accurately called, lines) that a narrowboat typically has. It is not complicated: there is normally a bow line and a stern line. These are used primarily for mooring. I will talk more about mooring later. Most modern narrowboats will also have at least one centre line. This is attached, as the name suggests, to the centre of the boat - normally in the middle of the roof. The Frog had two (not unusual) with the idea being that one can run down the port side of the vessel, back to be within easy reach of the helmsman - whilst the other runs down the starboard side. That way it does not matter which bank you are pulling into, the centre line can be reached and thrown ashore (or picked up by the helmsman whilst he/she jumps ashore) very easily and without worrying about catching on the roof mushroom vents (so called because of their shape). Centre lines are used primarily for temporary holding of the boat on the bank - for example, when waiting to enter a lock or go through a swing bridge. They can also be used for extra security when mooring in windy or strong current conditions or where either a stern or bow line cannot be fixed. You should never moor on just a centre line, however, as the drag of passing boats will naturally pull your bow and stern away from the bank.

So at West Mills you can now picture me holding The Frog on the centre line waiting for the bridge to open. When it finally did, I gently pushed off the bow, laid the centre line back on the roof of the boat, climbed aboard and headed slowly towards the bridge - again very conscious of balancing my desire not to hit the narrow bridge channel with the pressure of not wanting to annoy the locals by going too slow. All goes well and Pip reverses the bridge opening process and we are soon on our way. Much more on swing bridges as we embark on our odyssey - they seemed to create a few problems for us.

On this trip out we went as far as Hamstead bridge winding hole where we turned and headed back to Newbury. It was a round distance of about eight miles but included five locks that we ascended and then descended on the return trip. Invaluable experience. We were still cutting our teeth and would not venture too far until we felt more confident. Over the next few months, before winter fully set in, we did the same trip a few times. The furthest west we travelled was to Kintbury (a beautiful village that I will say much more about when we undertake our trip to Bath the following summer).

On one such return trip we took Billy, our grandson, to moor overnight on the canal side just outside of Newbury. He loved not only the thrill of being on a boat with Tronny (the family name for Pip) and Grandad but also the chance to get his hands 'dirty', helping with the locks and the swing bridges. On the way back he even took the tiller. We have some lovely footage of our then seven year old grandson with a look of concentration on his face that was clearly driven by the strange concept of pushing the tiller the opposite way to the direction you want the boat to go. A few times his attention would lapse as he saw a heron or an interesting log on the canal side and we would head straight for the bank. Overall, he took to it really well and the times I had to nudge him back on course became fewer and fewer.

Pip's brother and his family live in Reading - about twelve miles along the Kennet from Newbury. One of their favourite pubs is the Rowbarge at Woolhampton, about five miles east of our marina. We wanted to get more practice on an unfamiliar part of the system and so meeting up with Rob and Sue for dinner gave us the perfect chance to do this. Woolhampton is also a lovely village straddling both the river Kennet and the old A4 Bath Road.

On this trip we descended seven 'new-to-us' locks, of which the most interesting was Monkey Marsh. Measuring over one hundred feet in length it is one of only two turf locks on the K&A. A turf lock is one that has no retaining walls. Instead, the lock, as the name suggests, is flanked by earth and whatever is growing in it. A timber framework has been built within the lock to delineate the channel that boaters should stay in. This type of lock takes a much longer time to fill - not only because it is so big but also because the water can spread much wider than in a classic brick or stone lined lock. It can also soak into the ground to a certain extent. To protect the foliage growing on its banks, a turf lock should always be left empty. So, if you are ascending through the lock, you should always leave the bottom paddles open before you pull away. This is usually an absolute no no! Canal etiquette and best practice are that locks are left with all their paddles firmly closed. An exception is made for any turf lock and it can also be an instruction on some standard locks, with the aim of easing the pressure on the lower gates. If it is, the instruction will be clearly marked on the gates - so always look out for it before moving on. Monkey Marsh lock is so significant that it is listed by Historic England as an ancient monument. We tackled it a number of times before our odyssey started and never tired of it.

We had a lovely meal with Robbie and Sue and moored overnight at Woolhampton. The next day we set off with some trepidation. In order to wind we had to cruise on a further three quarters of a mile to Frouds Bridge Marina. This meant tackling Woolhampton lock and the road swing bridge straight after. The lock is not difficult in itself but it is made harder by its co-dependence on the swing bridge. Just after the lock there is a strong weir on the right hand side. Depending on the flow, the weir has a significant drag and this means it is not advisable to hover anywhere near it. A sign at the lock explains that you should not leave the lock exit until the bridge below has been swung so that you can cruise straight past the weir and through the open bridge without stopping. Always one to follow instructions, I waited in the mouth of the lock and Pip went ahead to operate the swing bridge. Unlike in Newbury, this was a road bridge (the first we had encountered) and whilst it was only a B road it seemed to be a busy link between the A4 and villages to the south. Pip was nervous about setting the bridge but she plucked up her courage and inserted the key. The bridge took much longer than the footbridge at Newbury to open and cars were soon starting to queue on both sides. As boaters, we are entitled to our right of way, but Pip could not help feeling guilty about holding everyone up. Not only that, at that time we had not yet invested in walkie talkies and as the bridge was not visible from the lock exit it was not possible for me to know exactly when it was open. I stayed longer than I needed and Pip was, understandably, getting more embarrassed with every new car joining the queue. Finally, I realised the gate was open and came out of the lock exit thrusting hard to make the sharp left hand bend before the bridge and to avoid being dragged sideways by the weir. I narrowly missed the bridge support and moored up on the centre line just after - feeling very sorry for Pip. She closed up as quickly as possible and raised a hand in acknowledgement to the now twenty plus drivers affected and ran down the tow path to the safety of The Frog.

It was this experience that convinced us we needed to invest in walkie talkies so that we could communicate with each other whilst cruising. We splashed out (forgive the pun) on two Motorola handsets which were more expensive than many but they had a longer range, they floated and they were waterproof. These last two features would prove invaluable on more than one occasion as I developed a habit of dropping them into the canal!

Our longest practice cruise east took us a further seven and a half miles to the outskirts of Reading and a pub called the Cunning Man (near Burghfield Bridge). Can you see a theme developing here? This time we met with Robbie and Sue and their family and stayed the night moored directly outside the pub. When we were mooring up we saw a familiar boat approaching. When we took possession of The Frog in Gayton, the boat moored next to us was called 'That's Amore'. She was a lovely narrowboat, slightly shorter than The Frog and with a cruiser stern. The owners had not long taken possession and were intending to live aboard in the summer and travel back to their place in Tenerife in the winter. They left Gayton before Neil and Jackie brought The Frog south and when we said goodbye that was the last we thought we would see of them. The boat is so distinctive, however, and we were pleasantly surprised to see her cruising up the Kennet looking for a mooring. On our odyssey we saw her a further three or four times - the last being at the start of the Llangollen Canal in April 2021. It was always a pleasure and a reminder to us of just how intimate the boating community is. Something we would really value on our adventure.

I remember the return trip from Burghfield to Newbury. Robbie joined us on board as we cruised on to the winding hole below Southcott Lock. I turned the Frog (in the wrong place as it turned out (there is a small indentation in the bank before the actual winding hole, which I mistook for the turning point.)) Still I got around and we started back. We cruised back through Padworth lift bridge at Aldermaston and moored to join Sue and Kathryn (their daughter) at The Butt Inn for lunch.

It is worth commenting further on the Padworth lift bridge. We would go through it three times on The Frog - twice on this trip and once more when we began the odyssey. It is a VERY busy road (the A340 Basingstoke Road which joins the A4 after passing directly through the village). The bridge is actually controlled by the nearby Atomic Weapons Establishment (AWE) - responsible for the UK's nuclear deterrent. Their control of the bridge is understandable as there are times when certain movements to and from the establishment will dictate that the bridge mechanism is switched off to avoid any potential delay on the road. Pip hated this bridge - primarily because she knew she would inconvenience an awful lot of drivers whenever we used it but also because it was so big and so slow to operate. In addition, she knew it had a reputation for breaking down. We met a boater near Bath who was a professional boat mover. He had no time for road users and, unlike Pip, was deliberately as slow as he could be at every bridge raising/swinging. He told me of an occasion when, as a sole boater, he had raised Padworth and taken his boat through. Having laboriously (and unnecessarily) tied up all three of his lines on the bridge landing point he then ambled back to the bridge controls. He pressed the 'Close Bridge' button but nothing happened. He tried again and several times more - without success. By this point he had been joined by a few curious drivers whose inquisition was quickly morphing into anger. He phoned the emergency AWE helpline only to be told they were too busy to come out and the bridge would have to stay how it was until they could. The boater hung up and walked back to his boat. He revelled in describing the desperate drivers, apoplectic by this point, insisting that he could not leave until he had 'sorted his mess out'. The boater shrugged and said there was nothing he could do and maybe they should consider getting a boat. Brave words when you can only cruise away at four miles an hour. I asked him what happened next: 'Dont' know and don't care!' On reflection, it is probably attitudes like this that made life more difficult for boaters like Pip and I trying to rub along with our fellow travellers still on wheels.

Anyway, once we finished a (very late) lunch we said our goodbyes to Robbie and family and headed back towards Newbury. This trip was in the autumn of 2019 and the nights were starting to draw in. We were still some seven and a half miles from 'home' at about four pm. It was a murky day and after passing back through Woolhampton we concluded we would not make it to Newbury before dark and we started to look for a place to moor. This is when we first realised that the K&A has some disadvantages that are not immediately obvious. We could not find anywhere to moor. There was a great deal of 'empty' bank to choose from, but under the water the sides of the canal rose sharply and prevented us getting anywhere near the edge. Not only would this mean using a gangplank to reach the tow path but what usually happens is The Frog would drift slightly on her lines overnight and effectively 'run aground'. This is not an issue in itself (a barge pole and some engine thrust would free us in the morning) but Pip is really sensitive to any slight angle whilst sleeping. She senses it and it keeps her awake. So mooring like this was not an option.

We continued cruising as the light faded and it got darker and darker. The bulrushes near Monkey Marsh were really overgrown on both sides. This created a very narrow channel that I would have had to negotiate in the semi darkness if we pressed on. Just before the narrowing, we saw Long Cut Swing Bridge and I made a decision that we would moor on the landing pins for the bridge for the night. This would inconvenience any boats using the bridge so it is usually not something we would consider. However, I was pretty confident we would be the last boat along here tonight and as long as we were up and ready to move by eight in the morning I did not think there was a risk. So it proved. We had a secure mooring and woke to the beautiful setting of a mist covered canal disappearing into the distance through the bulrushes and on to Widmead Lock.

We finished the trip back to Newbury and all I then had to do was negotiate the marina entrance - which is actually angled to face upstream (the same direction we were cruising). This meant to get in it from the side I was approaching from would be pretty tricky. I planned to continue on to the winding hole at Greenham Lock, turn and approach the marina from the other side - which I had done on our last cruise east. At the last minute, however, I changed my mind. This is never a good thing when boating where everything takes a lot longer and is a lot harder than you think. It is always a much better idea to have a plan and stick to it. Maybe I was getting overconfident but, whatever the reason, I found myself trying to turn The Frog sharply to the right to go into the Marina. The bank outside the marina entrance was filled with permanently moored boats as it was also owned by and was, in essence, an extension of, the marina. A particularly nice, shiny, black widebeam was the closest vessel to the entrance and with the current taking our bow, we were now heading straight towards her. Sensing the danger I guess, her owner appeared on the well deck with folded arms and a disapproving look on her face. This was really not helping. I throttled hard and pushed the rudder to the right in an attempt to miss the widebeam. I did but as a result I was then heading, at speed because of my increased throttle, straight towards the metal flashings protecting the sides of the marina entrance. I hit the far side, hard, and we bounced sideways. At least this meant we were now pointing into the marina. I looked to my left and - yes, you guessed it, Derek was standing outside of his workshop shaking his head and throwing it backwards in an animated tut. He walked over to check the flashing I hit. I was relieved to see that it was undamaged - unlike my pride. I would not try that again!

Derek's mood did not improve when I asked him for yet more help. I have explained already how our toilet operated - it had a macerator with a poo tank. The Frog still had its original toilet in place and it had obviously seen lots of previous use. It was just after this latest trip that we found out just how 'used' our toilet was. Pip has given me permission to talk about her digestive 'challenges' - which will help set the scene. Never one to be very regular, Pip's digestion is made even more erratic by change, strange toilets, excitement, different foods - in fact anything really. Suffice to say, she had not used the loo for some days - until the end of this trip. When she had finished her ablutions, she flushed - only for the loo to emit a strangled gurgle and fill with brown water. She flushed again and watched the water move closer to the top of the pan. It was at this point she shouted for me and I, knowing my limits, went to fetch Derek. We knew that in a previous life, Derek had operated a hotel boat - so dealing with a broken toilet was not new to him. He took one look and told us we needed a new macerator and that he would fit it - but only after we had emptied the bowl. Ever the gentleman, I volunteered to carry out this task. Derek not only fitted a new macerator but also noticed that the narrow pipework leading to the poo tank was also looking very fragile and changed all of this. We were very grateful as the consequences of a broken soil pipe would have been disastrous!

We relayed this incident to Pip's daughter, Rachael, who, at the time, lived in a large motorhome in the US. She has similar digestive challenges to her mother and, upon hearing the story of our blocked loo, suggested a solution. A few days later we received a red cross package - all the way from the US - containing a long, plastic POO KNIFE! Rachael swore by it and Pip kept it hanging by our loo on the Frog and, without going into unnecessary detail, made good use of it on our odyssey.

We previously owned a static caravan in Cornwall and we knew the importance of 'winterising' the boat if we were not going to be living on or cruising on her through the worst of the winter. As autumn ended we started preparing. The most important thing was to ensure we avoided any internal water leaks (keeping the boat warm and well insulated) whilst also keeping her ventilated to avoid the development of mold. Derek gave us a great idea. He suggested we not only keep some of the windows cracked but that we also constantly run a dehumidifier. He recommended a desiccant model. These work well in colder temperatures and are often smaller and lighter, as well as lasting longer. They also generate a small amount of heat which would be enough to avoid the risk of freezing pipes. We had to ensure we bought one with a hose attachment. The unit would then sit on the side of the kitchen and the water extracted would run straight down the sink and not into a tank which would obviously overflow. We would also need to ensure the electricity was topped up.

I have to admit it did feel strange to lock up and walk away knowing that a dehumidifier would be running on board for a couple of months unchecked. But we trusted Derek and we were right to. When we returned in early February The Frog was clear of any mold and our water system was intact. We set the dehumidifier to the highest humidity setting. That meant it only started extracting when the air got above a pretty high humidity. This saved electricity but was still sufficient to avoid any mold.

CHAPTER 9: FINAL PREPARATIONS?

I retired in October 2019, so we were planning to start our odyssey in the spring of 2020 and finish in the autumn of 2021. In that way, we would have been cruising for about eighteen months but have had two summers and only one winter! Unfortunately, 2020 had very different plans for all of us.

We returned to the marina in February and started to make what we thought were our final preparations. As well as the obvious cleaning and polishing, to keep The Frog looking nice, there were other bigger jobs to do. But whilst we are on the subject of cleaning….

Washing the outside of the boat tended to be my responsibility. Whilst in the marina we had a boat moored close to us on the left side but there was a bigger gap caused by the pontoon on the right. The pontoon, however, was not full length and finished about six feet along the hull. On one of our visits, in early 2020, Pip had gone on a shopping trip and I decided it was time to clean The Frog. I was using a hose pipe that was attached at the stern and was long enough to be pulled along the gunwale as I walked the full length of the boat. On the left side of course I was able to walk astride The Frog and its neighbour with one foot on either gunwale. This meant even if I did slip it was very unlikely I would fall into the water.

The other side was a different story. I set off walking down our gunwale and looked over to the neighbouring boat. Towards the stern I thought that I could straddle the gap between the two boats - like I had on the other side, so I stretched my leg out. It was quite a sunny day and a trick of the light meant that the gunwale of the boat next door was casting a shadow directly underneath the gunwale itself. My brain told me that the shadow was the gunwale and it was not until I stepped confidently over that I realised it wasn't! I was stepping into thin air. I went into the water very hard - mainly because I was not expecting to fall and had stepped so boldly that my knee slammed into the hull of the neighbouring boat, with my head doing the same just after. On the way down, my right arm was the opposite side of our mooring line to the rest of my body. As a result my armpit straddled the line but I was falling with too much force for it to hold me out of the water. The bruise on the arm and ribs that developed later would be testament to how painful this was. In the moment, the cold water and adrenalin meant I did not feel a thing.

Luckily I was under for only a short time and did not lose consciousness. I came up and grabbed the mooring line. I tried to pull myself out but with the weight of my sodden clothes and my inherently poor power to weight ratio (too many beers and crisps) I was unable to do so. I never was the greatest swimmer (I can swim but very inefficiently) so I started having ridiculous premonitions that I would never be able to get out and would eventually die here! I was, at this point, hidden between the two boats and was invisible to everyone else in the marina. A slight panic set in. Had it not, I might have thought to swim out into the middle of the marina so I could be seen by a fellow moorer - but it did and I didn't. Instead, I started to think about how else I could get out. Pip was not around, remember. After a couple of moments treading water I had an idea. I held onto the mooring line and swung my legs up so my feet were pressing on the hull of the neighbouring boat. Then I pressed my back hard against The Frog and started to inch my way up the side - a bit like a mountaineer would in a mountain crevice - only less athletically. Eventually, I was high enough to roll onto the pontoon and heave a sigh of relief. I lay for a while in dishevelled indignity and caught my breath. It was then I noticed that I had lost my father's signet ring which I wore constantly on my right index finger. My dad died in 2016 and the ring was an important connection to him. The pain and humiliation that I was feeling was nothing compared to my sadness at losing my dad's ring. I tried to find it on many occasions using our sea magnet (a strong magnet on a rope that every boater carries to retrieve things like windlasses if they are dropped in the water) and I even borrowed a large sieve-like shovel, that filtered anything on the bed of the marina, from Derek and Emma. I did not find it and regret the loss to this day.

Whilst we are on the subject of me taking an early bath: in August 2020, about a month before we finally set off, I was giving The Frog another wash and using the hose to do so. I had pulled the hose pipe along to the front of the boat walking down the gunwale and was then slowly working back towards the stern - washing as I went. We had just bought a new hose pipe that had an amazing quality. When not in use, it was small and easily stowed, however when active it grew to about twice its normal length and stiffened to increase pressure. That sounds familiar! What I had not noticed, whilst cleaning, was that the now turgid hose was sitting on the gunwale (I had assumed it had all fallen into the water). As I stepped blindly backwards onto it, my foot turned over and the next thing I knew I was, once again, surfacing and spitting murky marina water from my mouth. On this occasion Pip was on board and when she finally heard my pathetic cries she appeared and 'woman-handled' me up onto the path at the stern of the Frog.

Both of the above incidents would have been a lot easier had I known a simple and ingenious feature of The Frog. It turns out she has a small horizontal plate jutting out on both sides of her stern. These plates are not visible unless the boat is out of the water. They were added for one purpose: to act as a step for anyone needing to climb back onto the boat from the water. I only learned this part way through the odyssey when an RCR engineer pointed it out. I never fell in again so I never got to use them.

Pip thought it was hilarious that I 'kept' (her word) falling in (she has never done so). She even bought me a mug to recognise my ineptitude. It has on it an 'amusing' cartoon of two feet sticking out of the water with the words 'I fell In The Canal' inscribed underneath! Thanks Pip. To be fair, I wrote earlier that I also fell in when on a family canal holiday in 2004 and I suppose I should also mention a similar incident when on a kayak in the USA in 2015. So if the cap fits I guess I should wear it.

Anyway, back to our preparations. One of the less enjoyable tasks we needed to do was to clean the water tank. On The Frog it was a huge cavernous tank basically taking up the entire bow in front of the well deck. This was great when cruising as whilst it took a long time to fill, when it was full we knew the water would last longer than many fellow boaters and it would also help the stability of The Frog adding a huge amount of weight, a lot of which was below the water line. Cleaning it out was a rare but necessary task. We decided from the outset that water in the tank would only be used for showers, the loo and washing hands/cleaning teeth. We would not drink it. Our drinking water was collected separately in plastic bottles and was emptied into two filtering containers - one that was portable (and pourable) and one that sat in the cupboard. This second container was bigger so it held more water and had a tap at its base. Our system worked well and we never suffered any ill effects from drinking water on our travels. Nevertheless, we still wanted to clean the water tank out.

Some people use special sterilising tablets or solutions to wash through the tank and the whole water system. We did not like the idea of this and instead I climbed into the tank (yes, it was that big) and emptied it by hand using a small bowl and, finally, a cloth. In that way I could get all the grit and debris out. I did not use any other cleaning fluid as I did not want to introduce that to the water system and we were happy that I had cleaned the worst of the material out and that the tank was only going to hold water that would be flushed down the loo or heated for washing and washing up.

I mentioned our new electrical system earlier and in March we took delivery of our roof top boxes and had the solar panels fitted. I also mentioned a few problems with the boxes (in addition to the trouble of getting them onto the roof in the first place - they were VERY heavy and it took three men to do so). The first of the problems became clear very quickly. The boxes were tailor-made to fit our roof and we had some input into the design. For example, we wanted their base to be slatted so that air could circulate from below. However, we left the hinging mechanisms to the discretion of the carpenter. The boxes each had two lids so we could open either side depending on which side of the boat we were on. The lids were hinged in the middle of each box near their apex. I hope that makes sense. The boxes looked lovely and we could not wait to move our storage items out of the cabin and make use of the extra space on the roof. About two days later it rained. We thought nothing of it until we next opened a box to get something out. Everything in there was wet. The hinges were completely void of any waterproofing and rain ran right through the gaps where the hinges interlocked - something we did not notice before we paid what was a very hefty carpenter's bill. Luckily for us, B&Q was right next door to our marina, so off I went to buy some duck tape. I managed to find some the same colour as the boat but, even so, it did compromise the look of our lovely new boxes. The tape worked well initially but after a few weeks it started to lift and I seemed to spend the next eighteen months constantly replacing it. For extra peace of mind, we also ensured everything in the boxes was inside a waterproof bag. More on the boxes later as, believe it or not, this was not their worst fault!

By this time we had also used the same carpenter for some work onboard. We wanted an extra cupboard in the bedroom and to use the doors that covered where the redundant tumble dryer was kept. We now had two fold away bikes in this space (which we bought second hand) and as the access to them was from above, the doors behind the bed were superfluous to need. We asked the carpenter to remove them and use them in the kitchen to close off an otherwise open end of a counter to create yet more storage. I have to say he did a very good job on both these pieces of work.

The winter had taken its toll on the wooden rail around our stern. The wood here was Nigerian hardwood and it is not only beautiful but also very long-lasting. Over the winter, the weather had started to pull the varnish off and blacken the surface underneath. A few hours of sanding it back and the application of two coats of yacht varnish and I was really pleased with the result. This is how you can tell the quality of the timber; it looked like new and I felt like a master boat-builder.

Finally, when we took possession of The Frog, as well as the leather seats in the dinette area, the only other seating was a large leather Captain's chair in front of the woodburner. This made sense. The previous elderly owner was known to come to Gayton and sit in his 'man cave' watching television (as well as regularly polishing The Frog to keep her looking absolutely beautiful). A large chair like this would absolutely fit the bill. It was lovely, but a bit too big and anti-social (the person sitting in it would swing around to face the television and anyone else would be behind them in the less comfortable dining area). So we took it home to Cornwall and put it into storage. We did the same for a small cabinet, leaving an inviting space to fill. Pip investigated and found a maker of bespoke furniture for narrowboats. We specified our design for a click-clack bed settee that would fill the space perfectly - providing a more comfortable and sociable place to watch television, more bed space for future visitors and yet more storage.

It arrived in five boxes, each of which weighed a tonne. It rained heavily on the day it was delivered so we sprinted down the marina path with each box in a wheelbarrow and somehow managed to get them all into the dry before starting the puzzling job of assembly. We took photos periodically to show our hard fought progress and, much swearing later, we were really pleased with the final outcome. It had a lovely tartan design and the colours, which Pip chose carefully, matched the curtains perfectly. Pip is an amazing seamstress and she had made all the curtains, the headboard cover and a Frog themed quilt for our bed. She wasted no time in filling the storage underneath (with wool mainly as she's also an avid knitter).

CHAPTER 10: THE BEST LAID PLANS...

So, jobs done, we were ready to start our adventure! It's now March 2020 and as well as looking forward to my birthday at the end of the month we are also looking forward to getting underway. However, whilst back home in Cornwall we were becoming increasingly disturbed by news reports of a virus spreading slowly out of China and across the rest of the world. By mid March the number of cases in the Uk was growing and the death toll was starting to rise across the globe. We will never forget the seeming unreality of the broadcast in which Boris Johnson told us we were entering a lockdown from the 23rd of March. The world was suddenly a strange and frightening place and even the everyday things we did took on a very different feel.

Our cruise was clearly out of the question and the extent of lockdown meant we were even banned from just visiting The Frog, with only the live-aboards in the marina being allowed to stay.

Pip and I shared what I'm sure was the feeling of many across the country. We were entering uncharted water (no pun intended) and our thoughts turned to loved ones, and the hope that they kept themselves safe and to a determination to ride out the coming storm and get out the other side of what was now clearly a catastrophic global pandemic. Our odyssey plans were certainly put into perspective.

Initially, of course, talk was of a lockdown for a month or two. It soon became clear that this was just wishful thinking. Pip and I took a stoical approach to our isolation and thought about what we could do to both prepare ourselves for our very delayed adventures and, more importantly, strengthen ourselves against any infection. Pip has a long and detailed medical history, including compromised immunity and a benign brain tumour, so we decided that I would do all the shopping on my own (you had to go alone in the early days anyway), I would wear a mask (even before anyone was told we had to) and that together we would get as fit as we possibly could. We spent the spring and early summer of 2020 enjoying the lovely weather we were blessed with in the garden and walking the lovely lanes of east Cornwall. We established a few circuits and used Strava to record our times and set out almost every day to complete each walk faster than the last time. We lost weight, got tanned and, ironically, felt fitter than we had for a long time. The novelty started to wear off, however, and as we entered June we were excited by talk of a loosening of lockdown rules. We had already planned to begin our odyssey by cruising down the K&A to Bath before turning and heading back past Newbury and onto Reading and the River Thames. When the news came that a partial relief from lockdown was coming on the 4th July we did not need to think twice. We drove to Newbury with enough clothes to see us through a month or so afloat and on the morning of the 5th July we left the marina en-route to Bath.

CHAPTER 11: A LATE BATH!

So we were underway - well kind of. We knew that full lockdown restrictions may come back into place at any time and indeed there were many restrictions still in place in lots of public places. We agreed that we would make the most of the reprise and complete our K&A adventure ahead of leaving the marina altogether. That way, if things tightened up again, we would not have lost our mooring. We also needed to sell our house in Cornwall and only now could we put it on the market. Meanwhile, we did not want to sit around waiting for it to sell and we saw this trip as a chance to gain more invaluable experience. Not only could we practise our boating skills further but we would also really find out what it is like to live aboard for a longer period.

Remarkably, we left the marina without incident. I managed to manoeuvre out of the mooring and through the exit without drama or Derek's help. We were on the river and heading for Bath!

The first day we did not overdo it. We filled with diesel at Newbury Marina and felt that two locks was enough for one day. We moored in Newbury near West Mills swing bridge. We were near a park used by young people (I deliberately use a polite term) all of whom, it seemed, were carrying loud musical devices, the output from which they were generous enough to share with everyone nearby. Thankfully they did not stay out too late and we managed a good night's sleep.

The next day we stretched ourselves a bit further. When we were moored at the marina, we had kept up the long walks we started in Cornwall and one day we followed the towpath all the way to Kintbury. We had also cruised there. As a result we knew it was a beautiful village with great moorings and at least one fantastic pub. This is where we planned to spend our second night and possibly longer if the fancy took us. The village is popular with boaters and we managed to squeeze in quite a way down the canal towards Vicarage Bridge. We had shared a number of the later locks with another boat and it moored just ahead of us. The mooring rings were becoming more spaced out/absent at this point, so they used their own mooring pins on the grassy bank closer to the bridge. However, the space they had left between them and us was what many boaters call a 'Git Gap'. It's a bit like car drivers who park with a space between them and other parked cars that is not quite big enough for anyone else to park in between. On the cut, especially in popular locations where mooring is at a premium, consideration for other boaters is really important.

It wasn't long before another boat approached. It is good practice for a crew member to walk ahead and look for a mooring space, signalling or radioing, if they have walkie talkies, to the helmsman when a space has been found. On this occasion the 'scouting' lady on the towpath had misjudged the space and when her partner brought their boat alongside it was clear they could not get in. There was, however, more space ahead of the boat in front of us and if it moved up a few feet the new arrival could squeeze in. As we had shared some lock time together earlier, I offered to talk to the owner of the moored boat - who was by this time sipping wine and reading a book on his stern deck. I deliberately mentioned earlier that they had used mooring pins to tie up as this would make any move more of an inconvenience for them. I was very assertive in my approach, which can be paraphrased as: "We can fit another boat in the last mooring space if you can move forward just a few feet - I'll help you untie and pull you down". The eye-rolling, in response, was better than on any reality show I have ever seen and would have given Derek a run for his money. Clearly, this boater was not in a charitable mood, however, faced with my assumptive offers of help, he did not feel he could decline. Much huffing and puffing later we pulled the boat forward enough to let our new neighbours in. Our lock buddy never quite got over this irritating inconvenience and looked daggers at us until they left the next day. I have no time for this attitude. Although we were new to boating, we already appreciated how interdependent boaters are. We are a community who should look out for each other. In different circumstances, it can mean the difference between life and death (as we were to discover on our return trip a couple of weeks later). We saw the couple we helped that day a number of times on our odyssey - the last time on the Middlewich Canal in the north west (a long way from Kintbury). They never forgot our help and that always gave us a nice warm feeling and a real sense of what it means to be a part of the boating community.

Telling this tale of mooring woes has reminded me that, in an earlier Chapter, I promised to talk about mooring in more detail. I have already run through the various 'lines' or ropes used for mooring but I have not mentioned how these lines can be attached to the bank to actually secure your boat. Again, for simplicity I will limit my explanation to three distinct options.

Mooring pins: where there is no other method of securing your lines, a metal mooring pin is driven into the bank using a mallet (usually rubber or wood). These pins are typically about two feet long with a sharp end and a head (like a big nail). They should be driven into the ground at an angle - with the head facing away from the canal. This reduces the risk that the pin will be pulled out should your boat be moved by, for example, the drag of a passing vessel.

Armco chains or 'nappy pins': many boaters will cruise another mile to find armco rather than mooring with mooring pins. Armco is the metal barrier that is fixed to the side of some sections of canals and canalised rivers. Its main purpose is to protect the bank from erosion but it is great for mooring. It looks a lot like the barriers in the middle of a fast road, separating the carriageways. Across the middle of the upright galvanised sheets is a horizontal bar creating a gap through which a chain can be dropped or a 'nappy pin' hooked. The chain has a small ring at one end which is fed behind the armco and then threaded through a larger ring at the other end - creating a very secure mooring. The 'nappy pin' is so called because it looks a bit like a closed safety pin but with a break along one side. This side is dropped over the top of the armco and gravity does the rest. Even if the pin 'jumps', the bottom section should catch and stop it coming off entirely. Personally, whilst we had these on The Frog, we never used them. I much preferred the chain option and bought two as soon as we could. I remember seeing a nappy pin fall off the armco when a fast craft passed a neighbouring boat when we were moored at Hawkesbury. I ran over and told the grateful boater who then tied the pin to the armco to stop it happening again.

Fixed Rings or pins: at lock landings there are almost always fixed mooring pins to wrap your line around and some better mooring sites also have these. In my opinion, the preferable option for overnight stays are mooring rings. These are normally set into concrete and if you pass your mooring line through them and back to the boat it is not possible for a prankster to 'unmoor' you without cutting your ropes or climbing onto the boat.

Anyway, where were we? Oh yes, Kintbury. We stayed here a couple of days - primarily because at this time the pandemic meant the wonderful Dundas Arms public house was only opening four nights a week and then only in the garden. Pip and I wanted to eat here so we stayed until we could. In one of our vlogs we recorded the new online ordering system they had started using to avoid a member of staff having to come and talk to us until they actually brought us our food and drinks. This felt really bizarre but it worked and as the sun was shining we did not mind being outside in this fabulous garden overlooking the canal on one side and a small river on the other.

Whilst moored here we filmed our first proper Vlog: *Welcome to The Frog*. We were complete novices and looking back at it now we cringe at how we came across and some of the camera faux pas! This first video was created to give a guided tour of The Frog as well as introduce Pip (or Pippa as she is called on the network) and myself. We felt quite self conscious during the filming - we were not used to being in front of the camera. The Vlog was posted and within the first week we had over one hundred and twenty views. Not exactly viral. However, the viewers posted lots of comments - all constructive and many very positive. Most were boaters or with an interest in boating. Some were abroad, either expats or foreign nationals who were drawn to what they saw as a unique and idyllic aspect of British life. We were starting to build a following and that felt like something we would be able to develop further when we started our long cruise. It was also a very welcome additional contact with other humans in those Covid times.

The next day we headed off. I remember it was raining slightly as I tried to pull away from the bank. There was clearly something wrong. The propeller was making an awful sound and we were barely moving. I put The Frog into reverse and then back into forward gear - but nothing changed. Finally, I pulled back into the bank and tied up again. This was the first time I was going to use the weed hatch at the stern of The Frog - there would be many more. I guessed that something had become wrapped around the propeller (prop) and the only way to access this (other than going into the water) was by taking off a metal plate that sat in the engine compartment directly above the prop shaft. I removed the keys from the ignition to ensure the engine could not be turned on while I was working and stuck my hand into the dirty water to try and feel what was causing the problem. It was immediately obvious. The bank here was prone to erosion and the CRT had lined it with a black webbing material (a bit like the matting gardeners use under chippings or bark to avoid weeds growing through). A loose piece had obviously drifted under the boat and when I turned on the prop it had caught and a large section had been ripped off the bank and was now wrapped tightly around the business end of our boat.

I pulled at the webbing as hard as I could. No joy. It did not move and it was so strong it would not tear either. The only way to get it off would be to cut it away. I started using a stanley knife. Whilst it was really sharp, it was so small it was making little headway on the hard-packed webbing. Finally, I went to the galley and, with Pip's permission, I took a bread knife from the drawer. It worked like a dream. The serrated, long edge was perfect for cutting through the offending material which quickly started to fall away. Having got it all off the prop I was careful to place it in a bin and not leave it floating in the canal (to potentially cause the same problem for another boater).

Delayed and wet, we finally headed off towards Hungerford. This pretty town is only about three miles away but we were not in a hurry and it looked like a lovely location to explore. On the way in we passed the boat that is normally moored next to us in our marina (the one I head butted when I fell in). Its helmsman was in the process of reversing past Hungerford Town Bridge to complete a winding manouvre before heading back to Newbury. They shouted over that a planned trip to Crofton had been cut short because the swing bridge at Hungerford church was broken. We stopped for water before finally mooring just past Hungerford Town bridge in what we thought was a brilliant location. The Beautiful tour boat, *The Rose of Hungerford,* was moored just behind us and we made a lovely sight together. I remember walking up onto the bridge and taking a photo through the summer flowers blooming in baskets at the roadside.

Hungerford is lovely but many of its attractions and shops were still closed. We made the most of our visit, however, and after a long walk exploring the town and checking out the broken swing bridge, we retired for the evening. My opinion of our lovely mooring changed overnight. Pip always wears ear plugs and I was glad on that occasion that she did. At about 1am, I was jolted awake by someone banging on the roof of the boat. This annoying intruder then moved to the stern, opened the metal exterior doors to the back deck and started to bash them against the sides of the boat. Their weight and movement on board was causing us to rock from side to side. I then heard two male voices - clearly drunk. One of our unwelcome visitors was berating the other for being a stupid w&$*£r. Well I agreed with him there! By this time Pip had woken up. Enough was enough. I walked into the bathroom and turned on the light en-route to the galley with the intention of going out the front door. However, turning on the light was enough. Our little 'friends', realising someone had stirred and was heading in their direction, scarpered very quickly.

Unsurprisingly, the rest of our night was pretty restless and we both woke bleary-eyed in the morning. I examined The Frog and was relieved that no harm had come to her. I then noticed the park bench a few feet away. This spot was clearly a gathering point for drunken youths after dark and we decided, there and then, that we would seek out a different mooring today. After breakfast we moved through Hungerford Lock and moored just above it amongst a number of other occupied boats. We learned a couple of lessons that night. In the future, unless we were right out in the countryside, we would always try and moor near one or more occupied boats. There is definitely safety in numbers with any mischief makers less likely to cause problems where they could be confronted by a few angry boaters rather than just the owners of one vessel. I also started to put the stern hatch cover in place every evening. This would act as a deterrent to anyone thinking it might be fun to jump onto the rear deck and it would also give some protection to the throttle mechanism (both from the elements and vandals). We continued the practice every night through our odyssey and never had anyone coming aboard again (except in broad daylight on the descent into Liverpool - but that is a tale for much later).

We moored in our new location for two more nights and I took the opportunity to use my new electric wax polisher to get The Frog sparkling again. We started the engine before I plugged the polisher in as I feared the high draw on the batteries was likely to trigger the inverter alarm. This had happened already when we used the washing machine on low batteries without the engine running and we realised we had to time the use of any high drawing electrical appliance very carefully to avoid a repeat. Ideally, we only used the washing machine when the boat was actually moving and the increased revs were helping to recharge the batteries. It was always a balancing act and we were still getting it wrong, on occasions, well into our adventure. We did know never to use an electric kettle and we only used the microwave when no other heavy appliance was on. It's greater understanding like this that made the trip to Bath an invaluable learning experience - exactly as we hoped it would be.

The moorings we were on were timed and after forty eight hours we had to move again. The swing bridge had now been repaired by the CRT, so we could not use that as an excuse to overstay our mooring limit. However, as we were expecting visitors (my step-son Ian, his wife Brittany and our grandchildren Billy, 8 and Lyra, 4), we did not want to move far. Instead we crept a few hundred yards towards the swing bridge and managed to moor on a fourteen day pitch right beside the beautiful Hungerford church. We took on our youngest crew members whilst Ian and Brittany went off on a visit. We would meet them again at Great Bedwyn two days later. Sleeping arrangements that night were interesting. Lyra and Billy were too young to sleep alone so we put them to bed together in our bed and then when we retired I made up the bed in the dining room and carried Billy out to sleep there with me. Pip shared our bed with Lyra.

The next day was July 11th - Pip's birthday. It was lovely for her to have Billy and Lyra there to share her present opening. I made breakfast and was insistent that we leave our mooring by ten. Pip was getting a little irritated by my nagging to get underway. What she did not know was that I had been secretly communicating with her sister Trish and family, who live in Wales, and had arranged to rendezvous with them at lunchtime just past Froxfield bridge. This was over two miles, four locks and two swing bridges away. Whilst this did not sound far, with Billy and Lyra 'helping' at the locks and swing bridges I knew it would take longer than normal - and I knew Pip would not be in any hurry (why would she be - it's her birthday).

As it turned out we made Froxfield by about twelve thirty - thirty minutes ahead of schedule. I insisted we moor, despite Pip maintaining that it was too early for lunch and being even more puzzled why my earlier insistence that we got underway had now turned into a very laid back 'life's too short' attitude. Luckily, the surprise guests turned up pretty soon after and I could stop the pretence. Pip was delighted and so were the children when they spotted that Trish had made an amazing carrot cake for Pip's birthday. The afternoon was spent cruising slowly down to the really sweet village of Great Bedwyn (just over two miles and six locks) with Dave (our brother-in-law) taking the helm. At Great Bedwyn we visited a park to wear out the grandchildren and then returned to The Frog to finish off the cake in very short order. Oh, by the way, this was also the day that we first smelt the suspicious odour that suggested we had a poo tank problem (see CHAPTER 5).

We said goodbye to Trish, Dave and family and were joined the next morning by Ian and Brittany. They left their car and helped us cruise onto Crofton - about two miles and four locks - the first time Brittany had been on a narrowboat. Ian took the helm and when we reached Crofton he ran back along the towpath to retrieve the car and collected his family at Crofton. Pip and I were now alone so we went for a walk to explore the local area.

Crofton has a very impressive pumping station which houses the oldest working beam engine in the world still carrying out its original function: drawing from Wilton water and feeding the canal at Crofton Top Lock. The concept of having enough water is a new one in this story that I need to explain. Most canals are not natural waterways. They were built by the great industrialists with most being developed in the late eighteenth and early nineteenth centuries. Unlike rivers, which formed naturally and have natural water supplies, canals usually do not and have to be fed from other sources. In many cases a canal was deliberately built near to a natural river (or a natural river was canalised to ensure its water levels did not vary wildly). Some canals, because of their location, have to be fed from a reservoir. A good example are the higher reaches of the Rochdale Canal - which are notorious for running low on water as a result. It follows, therefore, that, on a canal, water is a precious commodity that has to be looked after - especially at lock flights where the very usage of the locks themselves moves gallons of water from one part of the canal to another and always in one direction (the water is not 'put back up' when a boat comes the other way). Only by looking after water can we ensure there is always enough to take the traffic using the canal and ensure no part of the network runs dry causing catastrophe for any boaters using it at the time.

What can cause a water shortage? Obvious natural events like droughts are the most common causes of reservoirs and rivers running low. A good example was the summer of 2022 (well after our odyssey had finished) when drought affected many water authorities. When this happens it is understandable that priority is given to drinking water and less to filling canals and, over that summer, Pip and I read many on-line warnings from the CRT of waterway closures due to a lack of water. We were really glad we were not out there again and our hearts went out to the many boaters affected.

Water shortage can also be caused by poor maintenance leading to leaking lock gates and sluices or even a failure of these. An extreme example happened in September 2020 on the canalised river Avon in Bath. A sluice failed and the channel effectively emptied, leaving many boats stuck in the mud and, even worse, some were capsized by their own mooring lines and lost forever along with their owner's possessions. An awful event and one no one wants to see happening. Even more dramatic are breaches. This is where a fissure in the canal bed leads to a significant leak with often very dramatic results. We detail a number of these in our vlogs and I will reference specific examples as this account records our travels.

Water can get into canals by 'naturally' flowing from a water source like a river. A really good example is where the South Oxford Canal joins the River Cherwell at Shipton Lock. Here the lock is diamond shaped to ensure that as much water as possible is 'captured' from the river and brought into the canal itself every time the lock is used.

In other cases canals are fed from rivers or other water sources using pumps - like the one at Crofton. They are always ingenious feats of engineering and often beautiful to look at. Again when we come across significant examples on our travels I will write about them.

Where were we? Oh yes - moored at Crofton. I remember this evening really well. The weather was fabulous and the sunset was amazing. Pip and I had walked up the canal earlier and seen a live example of water wastage in action. Someone had left a lock paddle open and water had filled the pound below and was overflowing into the next lock at a very high rate. This is water that could have been used later when a boat was actually using the locks. Another boater told us he had closed the paddle now and it would stop running soon but how much water had been carelessly lost? It is easy to point fingers at rental boats when these things occur. To be fair, it is often holidaymakers, who may not be used to the many tasks you have to think through when using a lock or who may just be carried away with the joy of being on holiday, that cause these problems. However, it is not always the case. We all make mistakes and careless owners can also contribute to water loss.

Water usage and protection is a never-ending challenge on the network, which is why following canal etiquette is so important - especially at locks. When approaching a lock, if it is in your favour (if you are ascending, the lock is empty or, if you are descending, the lock is full) it is your lock to use. If another boat coming the other way has arrived before you, their first responsibility is to look ahead and see if another boat is coming the other way. If it is, they should moor up and wait for it to use the lock (ideally lending a hand with the mechanism). In this way the water being 'moved' on this occasion will be used to move two boats - theirs and the oncoming one. They should NEVER 'turn' the lock (empty it for them to use if ascending or fill it if they are descending) when they see a boat approaching from the other direction. That would be a blatant waste of water and is frowned upon by all boaters and CRT volunteers. Naturally, if there is no boat in sight you are not expected to wait until one appears before turning a lock. Your responsibility is, simply, to make sure there is no obvious lock user coming the other way.

If the lock is a double width and you are a narrowboat, where possible you should always join another boat in the lock. This is not only good for water usage but the respective crews will also share the workload. This may not always be possible and you are not expected to 'wait around' interminably until another boat comes along. The watchword is use your commonsense and save water whenever you can, being careful to shut all gates and paddles when you leave unless special CRT notices tell you not to do so (like at Monkey Marsh lock as detailed above).

Lesson over - until the next one! So we are moored at Crofton. Pip and I continue our walk along a footpath beside Wilton Water until we reach the village of Wilton itself. It's a beautiful Wiltshire village - thatched roofs, with not a straight line in sight. It seemed like everybody was lucky enough to live in a chocolate box cottage - an observation that we will make many times throughout this lovely county. Just outside the village stands the wonderful Wilton Windmill. It's the only working windmill left in the historic kingdom of Wessex and it still produces flour to this day. It was built in 1821 after a number of watermills became unviable when the building of the K&A lowered river water levels. Its heyday lasted about a hundred years until mass production methods rendered it redundant. Luckily for us, it only fell into disrepair and was not pulled down. In 1976 it was restored to working order by volunteers. On this site you can also see a lovely granary, built on a foundation of stone 'mushrooms' that allow air to circulate under the building to help avoid dampness affecting the grain within. This windmill is an example of the sights we would never have seen had we not bought The Frog and there will be many more before we finish our odyssey.

Our stop at Crofton was also when we phoned Derek for advice about our overflowing poo tank. The next morning we knew we had to reach Pewsey to pump out. I won't repeat the tale of the pump out here but the journey to Pewsey wharf included some lovely cruising which is worth detailing. However, before we move onto that, while we were moored here we were struck by a further observation. The canal is accompanied along much of its route by the railway. Rail engineers obviously found that the easiest route for them was that previously identified by the canal builders. At Crofton, the railway sits elevated above the canal and passing trains are an impressive, if noisy, sight as they roar past. Historians will know that it was the railways that finally spelled the end of the canals as a viable way to carry goods and raw materials across the country.

Back to our journey. The canal has been slowly rising all the way from Newbury to Crofton. The flight of locks here sees the canal climb a further sixty one feet in just seven locks. They are hard work, with some very old lock mechanisms and heavy gates taking real muscle power to move. We had set off early that morning to get to Pewsey as soon as we could, so we were cruising alone and there was also no sign of the CRT volunteers who often help out boaters here. It was our own fault so we fatefully battled on. Crofton Top Lock (55) was reached at last and we stopped for a coffee before heading off again towards the Bruce Tunnel.

From our experiences already you will know I am not a big fan of tunnels - but the Bruce Tunnel is different. To start with, it's only five hundred and two yards long and it's perfectly straight. This means you can see the other end clearly the whole way through. It is also double width and lovely to look at. It was built between 1806 and 1809 using a combination of brick and Bath stone. On one end it has a plaque giving thanks for the support given to the navigation by Thomas Bruce, 'Earl of Ailesbury'. Ironically, the tunnel was only built because the Earl insisted that a tunnel and, not a deep cutting, be used to take the new navigation through the hill sitting just south of the hamlet of Durley. This would have added considerable cost to the construction of the canal but, without the Earl's permission to cross his lands, the canal may never have been built.

Our cruise continued past the pretty Burbage wharf and Wootton Rivers (a village we vowed to visit on our return trip) and by lunch time we had reached the pump out at Pewsey. I have detailed the 'tricky' process I then had to go through in a previous chapter so won't repeat it here - suffice it to say, having an empty poo tank was a relief in so many ways!

Our final destination for the day was a further three and a half miles but the extra distance was worth it. Honeystreet and The Barge Inn are must visits for most boaters and we were no exception. On the day we arrived a music festival was in full swing and we were very lucky to find a mooring. I remember the gap was literally inches longer than The Frog and the only way we could squeeze in was to draw alongside the gap and use the mooring lines to pull her in sideways. We made it and settled in for the night - or at least we would have had the music festival not continued into the wee small hours. We did not mind, however. It felt great to be surrounded by the sound of merriment and happy people after the many months of lockdown.

Having cruised so far the day before, the next morning we decided to take it easy and targeted All Cannings for our next stop. All Cannings is another beautiful village with a little shop, which we used to top up with a few necessities. We had missed our customary daily walk the day before so this was a chance to get a few miles in along the towpath and into the village. We love walking the canal tow paths. Assuming they are in good condition, there is nothing like having the canal and other canal users as constant companions. We also liked to walk ahead of our next day's cruise to check out places to moor, potential hazards and places of interest to capture for our Vlog. Today, the weather was bright and clear and a lovely walk was in prospect, however a family of swans had other ideas. Mother, father and several chicks were 'taking in some rays' right in the middle of the towpath. We could not pass without moving them on - and they were not planning to go anywhere. The presence of chicks also meant that both parents were not too happy to see us approaching. The ability of a swan to break a human arm is a well known urban myth but, at that moment, I didn't fancy putting it to the test. Pip immediately got her phone out as she realised this had the potential to be YouTube gold. At the very least, I would look like a numpty in my hilarious efforts to coax the swans into making way for us. At best, I would be attacked!

When we watch the resulting clip back we still fall about laughing. I was clapping my hands, saying shoo and edging slowly closer to the dominant adult swan sitting closest to me. It started hissing and if swan looks could kill I would have immediately collapsed into the canal. At one point Pip tried to escalate the drama and asked 'what would happen if you rushed them?' - my reply was simple - 'I would get bitten quicker.' The hold up took about ten minutes - mostly because I kept retreating every time the swan reared up and turned to face me - which it did several times. Eventually, they got the point and waddled lazily to the canal edge before slipping gracefully into the water. We continued our walk. On reviewing our vlog (Exploring the K&A) I am reminded that that evening the same swan family came up to our bow to share the contents of the box of swan food we had on board. The cheek of it!

The next day we decided to stay put and use our folding bikes for their maiden outing. Unfortunately, when we put them together we realised they had two flat tires and we had no pump. One element of preparation we obviously overlooked. Luckily, we spotted some bikes on the roof of a nearby widebeam and having borrowed a pump we were soon on our way - heading for Devizes. The town was about six miles away - which doesn't sound far until you remember we had single gear bikes, with very small shopper bike wheels and a route with several steep hills. We found it hard going and got off many times to walk. What made us feel even worse was a brief meeting we had with an eighty five year old riding a fantastic Bianchi multi-geared, derailleur bike. We got chatting because we had taken a wrong turn (and secretly fancied a rest) and he gave us directions to get back on track. He was so fit it made Pip and I feel really inadequate. He was a living breathing advert for the benefits of cycling and all credit to him.

We made it to Devizes and headed straight to a bike shop for a pump and riding shorts for Pip. Then we headed for the canal wharf and the wonderful Caen Hill flight, which we would be tackling in the next few days. Caen hill is one of the longest flights of locks on the network. It carries the canal up and down a two hundred and thirty seven foot climb in the space of just two miles and has twenty nine locks in total. Sixteen of the locks (the flight proper) take the canal up the steepest section and have very small pounds between them. Today we just wanted to walk the flight and check out the mooring points at the top (near the wharf) and more importantly, at the bottom, where we would want to stop for a rest. More on the flight later.

On our return trip to All Cannings we decided to take the canal towpath as an alternative to the road route we had got lost on. The path out of the town was lovely - wide, tarmacked and smooth. This lasted for about a mile but once we were out in the country, conditions changed radically. The weather had been dry so at least there was no mud. What there were plenty of however, were tree roots and potholes - both of which would have been tricky for a mountain biker on a machine with highly engineered suspension. On our little shopper Bugattis, (yes - like the sports car (the name being the only thing they had in common)), with no suspension whatsoever, we were destined to suffer five miles of bum-numbing hell! What made it worse was the bell on Pip's bike was loose. She was ahead of me and every time she hit a bump her bell sounded and I knew I was about to encounter the same bone juddering obstacle. Needless to say, we were very happy to round the final bend and get back to The Frog for a well-earned rest and a cup of tea.

The next day we headed off on our cruise to Devizes. The route of about five and a half miles took us past Bishop Cannings and through several swing bridges. It was a windy day. In hindsight, probably the first seriously windy day we had faced and one that should probably have been sat out rather than cruising. We had gone through swing bridges before, of course, and it was this all too little experience that led me to feeling cocky. I decided not to follow our normal swing bridge routine (pulling in, jumping off and holding The Frog on the centre line until the bridge was fully open and only then moving off). Instead, I dropped Pip on the towpath and stayed on board - reversing out into the centre of the canal. Or rather, trying to reverse out. What actually happened is the 'natural' bow swing that happens when I backed up was exaggerated greatly by the wind. I had never experienced anything like it. The boat weighs about twenty tons and yet in the path of these gusts it felt just like a sailing dinghy - skimming across the top of the water. Unlike a dinghy, however, I had no sail to swing about and easily change direction.

Moored on the far bank was a trade boat owned by a blacksmith. Our bow hit the side of the trade boat and scraped along its hull. There was no-one on board and as I did not cause any visible damage on the other boat, I heaved a sigh of relief and finally managed to pull away and get through the swing bridge. My troubles were not over however. Having pulled in to pick up Pip I pulled away from the landing pins only to find I was once again heading across the canal straight towards a fibreglass boat moored just after the bridge. This was very worrying. It's one thing to hit another steel hulled narrowboat, it's quite a different thing to hit a 'yoghurt pot' and possibly breach it! Luckily for me, this one was inhabited and its owner sprung into action. He ran to the bow and lent over the side moving a very large fender around to protect his hull from my approaching bow. I slammed our boat into reverse and managed to slow down enough so the impact on the moored vessel was minimised. All I then had to do was pull away and straighten up to face down the canal. Don't forget, at this point I still thought 'more tiller was better tiller' and I was pushing the rudder hard to one side to try and counter the wind (now I realise this was an ineffective thing to do). I was also not confident enough to use my engine fully and it was the owner of the 'target' boat who put me right on this - in no uncertain terms. 'You need more f*****g revs!' he shouted. I pushed the throttle forward really hard and the propeller responded accordingly, pushing me forward at great speed. Fortunately, my hand must have inadvertently pulled the tiller back towards the centre enough to hit the sweet spot and we swung towards the middle of the navigation. I throttled back and straightened up - thanking my would-be victim for his colourful guidance.

We cruised on, past Devizes marina. By this point we were on the outskirts of the town in a cutting that gave us shelter from the wind and made very pleasant cruising. The canal was lined on the off side with the back gardens of a mixture of houses - most of whose owners clearly valued the benefit of being canalside. Decking abounded - as did privately moored narrowboats and other smaller craft. The canal straightened out after London Road Bridge and we were soon passing under Cemetery Road Bridge and approaching the moorings opposite the wharf. As we got near a group of teenagers in kayaks came off the wharf and into the middle of the canal. I blew my horn and started frantically signalling with my right arm that I was intending to pull into a mooring on the right hand side in the hope that the kayaks would move left and not get trapped between me and the bank. Thankfully, despite their obvious inexperience, all the kayakers managed to get out of my way and we moored safely.

Our day was not finished however. I remember the sun was shining and the boat was not - so I gave her a polish. The other priority was gas. Our oven and grill both used propane gas, two metal canisters of which were held in a small cupboard at the stern. One was connected and the other was a spare. Our spare was now empty and needed to be replaced. I googled suppliers and found one in the middle of the town - just under a mile away. I picked up the canister and thought that whilst it was a little heavy, I could easily carry this to the supplier. I have concluded that I am not very good at chess because I am not very good at thinking ahead and the gas bottle incident is an example of this failing. I reached the shop with no problem. What I forgot of course, is that I would then need to carry the FULL gas canister back to the boat. It weighed about twice as much as the empty one - which seemed bizarre - after all it was only full of gas! I could carry it, but only about twenty paces before the pain in my hand meant I was forced to put it down. The journey back to our mooring took forever. I finally reached the wharf entrance and noticed that the final approach to the boat was downhill. Being both bored and tired of carrying it, I put the tank down and turned it on its side. I was smart enough to stand downhill and control the canister as I let it roll towards the boat. Even then I almost fell backwards (which would have seen the canister drop into the canal). Pip watched, aghast, convinced the gas was going to explode at any moment.

All chores done we wandered into town to meet Pip's sister, arriving from Wales by bus. Trish was joining us to help take The Frog down the Caen Hill flight and to spend a few days afloat. The next morning we set off early for the flight. We did not want to be the first boat down as all the locks would be set against us until we passed a boat coming in the other direction (all the locks are emptied overnight by the volunteer CRT lock keepers to remove unnecessary pressure on the lower, smaller gates). Equally, we did not want to miss the chance to buddy up with another boat. Our timing seemed to be good and after completing a couple of locks alone, we met up with a holiday boat that was moored up with its occupants having a quick coffee break before starting the descent. We agreed to buddy up.

Pip's confidence at handling The Frog was developing fast but at this point she preferred to operate the locks and leave me to handle the tiller - particularly as we were going to enter many locks 'in tandem' with another boat. I have already explained that the twenty nine locks on the Caen Hill flight are quite close together - with sixteen being very close indeed. This meant if there were no boats coming the other way, the quickest way to move from one lock to the next was 'in tandem' - or side by side with another boat. This required both helmsmen to stay at roughly the same speed and to steer the same line as they move from lock to lock. Contact with the neighbouring boat is not considered an issue and it was often easier to steer slightly towards your partner so that each boat was gently pushing the other - ensuring the tightest formation and less likelihood you will not fit through the upcoming gates. It would be very tempting, and indeed may seem to make sense, to have your fenders down when entering the lock in this way. However, best practice on a narrowboat is to have all fenders up whenever you are using a lock - even if you are going solo. Fenders can get caught on lock gates, overhanging walls, the boat next to you and may even mean you get stuck in the lock. The most likely outcome, however, is that the fender rope snaps and it falls into the water. As I explained earlier in our tale, fenders are really just for mooring purposes. (I have just watched the Caen Hill section of our Exploring the K&A Vlog and noticed my front starboard fender is down. Pip reminds me that at that time it was simply tied in place and balanced on the gunwale when it was put up. I must have knocked something and made it fall back into place. That's my excuse anyway).

With Pip, Trish and the holidaying family on the mechanisms, we made good time over the first few locks. When we were part way down the sixteen close locks of the flight 'proper' we started to see boats coming in the other direction. Entering locks in tandem is clearly not an option where you are passing oncoming boats. Instead, we switched to the: one out, one out, one in, one out, one in, one out one in, one in method of passing each other. Picture both sets of gates open with two boats in one lock facing the two boats in the next. The boat nearest the bank in lock A comes out and tucks into the small 'layby' cut into the side of the pound - designed just for this purpose (one out). A boat from lock B comes straight across and takes the vacated spot in lock A (one out, one in). The second boat from lock A then cuts across and takes the newly vacated spot in lock B (one out, one in). The second boat in lock B then comes across and fills the empty spot in lock A (one out, one in). Finally, our first boat leaves its temporary mooring and takes the final slot in lock B (one in). Get it? It's actually a lot easier to do than to write about - trust me!

We make it down most of the full flight in about five and a half hours and moor up for lunch near Lock 24. Refreshed, we set off and soon reached Lock 22 at Foxhangers. This is effectively the last lock of the extended Caen Hill rise and is situated next to Lower Foxhangers Bridge (146) and just before the Foxhanger Marina. A lot of people hire boats out of this marina and, unlike many others, the rental company here brings its hirers along to Lock 22 so they can see it in action. Which is a really good thing to do. Such a party arrived just as we entered the lock so I thought we had better do everything correctly. As we were alone in a double lock I put the centre line around a central bollard and slowly released the line as the boat dropped in the lock. I thought this was the sensible and right thing to do! The Foxhanger's employee was highlighting, positively, everything we were doing to the interested hirers - with the exception of my rope work. In fact he went further and said: 'Oh - by the way, never use your ropes when descending in a lock as all it does is wear the rope out!' He had a point. Ropes can be useful when ascending in a double lock alone, as that is when you are most likely to be buffeted by incoming water. When descending, water is leaving the lock so you are usually fine to drift in the middle. The only exception may be a lone boater (cruising with nobody else on board) holding his craft tight on the side of the lock.

That night we moored at Semington and strolled along to the Somerset Arms for a well-earned drink. We met an old work colleague of mine who lived in the village and so ended a tiring but rewarding day and our first experience of the beautiful Caen Hill. It really is a wonderful feat of engineering for which John Rennie (canal engineer) should be rightly honoured. The innovation did not stop in the eighteenth century. As well as the many ongoing repairs needed to keep the locks operational, in 1996 a new pumping station was built at the bottom of the flight near Foxhangers. Remarkably, every night this pump sends over seven million gallons of water back to the top of the locks to ensure all the pounds are replenished for use the next day.

After breakfast the next day we set off for Bradford On Avon. I suspected this was going to be a challenging day. Bradford is a very popular location for boaters. It's pretty and has a lovely lock at its heart. It is also blessed with a number of pubs near the canal - sitting either side of the quaint Bradford Lock bridge - built from the unmistakable Bath stone which looked even more golden in the summer sun.

There are no locks from Trowbridge to Bradford, so we made good time on the cruise. We were approaching the village at about lunchtime - a strategy that was deliberate. Mooring is limited on busy sections of the canal. If you leave your arrival too late you can struggle to find a spot. By arriving around lunchtime we have given the overnight moorers time for a late breakfast and to up pins and move off - leaving a space for The Frog.

We were still some way from the lock and approaching a sharp right hand bend near Underwoods Bridge (171). The canal narrows here and it is a blind bend. The on side was full of moored boats and on the corner apex I saw a large black widebeam - with its occupants enjoying lunch on its cruiser deck. It was moored badly. Mooring on a bend is never ideal as your bow and stern protrude much further into the channel than normal. When the boat is a wide beam, the problem created is even worse and I had to swing out wide to pass. I sounded my horn as the law of sod dictated that there would be a boat coming the other way in the, now, very narrow channel. There wasn't one boat coming - there were two - both hire boats and both clearly ignoring the etiquette of slowing down as you pass moored boats. Neither seemed to know where their horn was so I only knew they were coming when they loomed into sight! Luckily I was only moving slowly but I still needed to stop quickly. I put The Frog into reverse and, as I had now come to expect, the stern veered to one side heading for the trees. I pushed the throttle forward and steered hard to starboard, in an attempt to get out of the way of the convoy coming the other way. The Frog was now heading straight for the widebeam so I jerked the tiller the other way and managed to miss it by a few inches as the holiday makers flew by - oblivious, it seemed, to the stress they had just caused. The occupants of the widebeam watched on and I got the feeling that this was not the first near miss they had witnessed that day. We were, it seemed, all part of the lunchtime entertainment.

We finally arrived at the lock in Bradford and I tied up to allow Pip and Trish to jump off with their windlasses. As expected, the lock was busy, with two boats just entering the bottom gates. I have explained the principle of gongoozlers already and at Bradford they were out in force. Thankfully we got through the lock with no embarrassments and we exited the bottom gates to see a mooring spot right below the Canal Tavern pub, just past the lock landing pins. I couldn't believe our luck; this was a prime spot! It seemed our lunchtime arrival strategy had worked yet again.

We tied up, and had lunch. That afternoon we walked into the village and visited the amazing Bridge Tea rooms, dating from 1502. I don't think the building had a single straight line anywhere on it. The roof looked like it was about to fall in and the facade was full of stone mullioned windows with glass so old that it had started to flow south. It was beautiful - as was the cake we were served up inside. Well worth a visit. On the way back to the boat, we detoured via the Tithe Barn, a fourteenth Century monastic structure maintained by English Heritage. It's one of those places where you are both amazed and delighted at its survival. I was in awe of its scale and the evident construction skill in a building with such a modest purpose.

The next morning we decided to stay put on our great mooring and I took the opportunity to add another coat of varnish to the wooden rail on the stern. I'm glad I did. From here I got to be a gongoozler myself as boat after boat approached the landing pins for the lock. Many were rental boats with varying skill levels in evidence. Most pulled in and moored up with no issues. Late in the morning, however, things got a bit more challenging for them. A rental widebeam (yes they do hire out these enormous craft to people with no boating experience) came out of the lock and pulled into the landing pins. The crew members who had operated the lock came on board and I was waiting for it to pull away and continue its journey. It didn't move. Instead, two other crew members (there must have been six or eight people on board) went into the pub and came back with a tray of drinks for all. The drinks were in glasses so I guessed, correctly, that they were going nowhere until they had at least finished this round. Meanwhile, a rental narrowboat had cruised past us and was looking to moor on the landing pins before going through the lock. Realising he could not land easily, the helmsman went into reverse and ran aground on the far side of the canal. Eventually they poled themselves free (pushing into the bank with one of the long barge poles every narrowboat has for this very purpose) and managed to push their bow up to the final pin of the landing point and tied up - waiting for the lock to become free. All we needed was another boat to come along for there to be a big problem. It didn't take long! It was another rental narrowboat with a very worried looking lady at the helm. Her gender was not relevant - her facial expression was! She was facing a very narrow canal, a large, closed, lock gate and a lock landing point filled with two other boats. She could not go alongside either without blocking the canal. I could see she was starting to panic so I shouted to her to throw me her centre line. I grabbed this and pulled her across until she abutted the bank and the stern of The Frog and I held her there until the lock gates opened and she was able to join the other narrowboat in the lock.

At that point I lost my temper. The drinks were still being downed on the widebeam and they showed no sign of moving off. I marched over and with as much indignity as I could muster demanded to know what they thought they were doing: "These are the lock landing pins. You can't stay here. You are creating chaos. I've never known anything so selfish." They apologised and said they were just waiting for someone to join them and this was the only place they could find to stop. I corrected them: "But this is not a place you can stop" and stomped back to The Frog. A few minutes later they untied and moved off. Unfortunately for us, they moored some way down the canal and bad timing the next day meant we ended up following them for a large part of that day's trip. Cruising behind a rental widebeam on one of the busiest parts of the network is not something I would recommend to anyone. We were not glad to see the back of them until we were - if you see what I mean!

The next day we said good-bye to Trish. Pip and I continued on towards Bath alone. The next section of canal has lots of lovely features. Just west of Bradford is the Avoncliff Aqueduct. The canal has a ninety degree turn to the right before it enters the aqueduct that carries it over the River Avon itself. The aqueduct is really impressive - another Grade II listed engineering masterpiece of John Rennie. Underneath it, we found another lovely pub - the Cross Guns - in what must be one of the most scenic locations of any inn on the canal system. Outside, its gardens drop all the way down to the river's edge and you can enjoy your drink looking up at Rennie's magnificent erection (cheap joke).

The aqueduct finishes with a further ninety degree turn - this time to the left - as the canal picks up its roughly east-west course.

As we are talking about Avoncliff I will jump ahead to our return trip. When we came back this way Pip and I were still alone on board. The weather had deteriorated and, having crossed the aqueduct, we decided to stay put and hunker down. We moored just on the Bradford side - about one hundred and fifty yards from the sharp bend of the aqueduct itself. It was raining so we got out our books and settled in for a quiet afternoon. After about an hour of relative tranquillity the peace was shattered by a very loud bang. The Frog lurched sideways and there followed a hideous scraping sound. I jumped up, ran to the bow and, opening the cratch cover, stuck my head out to see what was going on. By this time a rental narrowboat was slowly moving backwards away from our hull (which was now sporting a scratch, covered with remnants of paint matching the distinctive livery of the hire company). In the well deck a very apologetic old man was waving his hands at the helmsman. He explained that they had literally just picked up the narrowboat and started their holiday. They did not know the canal and the inexperienced helmsman approached the aqueduct at a speed that would have made it impossible to negotiate the ninety degree bend whatever the traffic. However, at that moment a widebeam was coming off the aqueduct in the other direction. He had panicked and decided that rather than hit a large, oncoming craft head on, he would prefer to 'glance' off the side of a smaller, stationary, boat!

If this had been on the road I would be reaching for my phone to record the licence number and insurance details of the offender. On the cut it's different. Remember Derek's assertion that boating is a 'contact sport'. Well here was living proof he was right and apart from giving the hire boaters a piece of mind and (fruitlessly) calling the hire company to suggest they give better guidance to their new hires, there was nothing else we could do. We loved the Frog and incidents like this were painful but had to be taken on the chin I'm afraid. There would be other similar incidents on our odyssey.

Anyway, back to our 'out' journey towards Bath. After Avoncliff the canal has two largely straight sections passing past Freshford and Limpley Stoke. On the right, Conkwell Wood provided a beautiful backdrop as we followed the course of the River Avon flowing gently off of our port side. At Dundas the canal crosses the Avon again with a very similar aqueduct to Avoncliff. Dundas is a busy wharf with lots of moored boats watching the traffic passing by. The ninety degree right hand exit is directly in front of the wharf which, when we passed, was two deep in boats making it tricky to negotiate if anything was coming the other way. We were still following our widebeam 'friends' and that was the only time I was glad we were. They were stopping for nobody - ploughing a course for us to follow with oncoming boats pulling in sharply to get out of their way.

We moored that night in a pre-arranged location near Bathampton Swing Bridge (182). The next morning we were meeting my stepson Mark and his girlfriend - who were joining us for the final section into Bathwick and our next night's mooring at Sydney Gardens. Mark has not been on a narrowboat for about sixteen years, since a holiday we had together in 2004 (the one where I fell in). On that trip he took the helm most days and he had lost none of his ability. The canal here is very busy with moored boats and oncoming traffic is a constant challenge. Keeping a straight line through narrow gaps and controlling the boat when you temporarily have to 'hover' is not easy.

Bath needs no tourist blurb from me. It's always worth a visit even when it's pelting with rain - which it was the next day. My daughter, Charlie, was due to join us but the rain meant we stayed on board which would have been a covid risk had she come - which was very sad as I had not seen her for some time. We spent the night hoping that tomorrow would see a dry start to our return trip.

Thankfully we woke to the sun. I took the Frog through Bath No.1 Tunnel and under the two footbridges before facing Bath No. 2 Tunnel with its slight bend. Both tunnels are really no more than long bridges but they are arguably the most attractive crossings on the cut. They both have buildings upon them - including the former canal company's old headquarters, Cleveland House. Both have ornate entrances on their Sydney Gardens facade with a carved face on each. No. 1 Tunnel has a representation of Hafren, a water nymph associated with the River Severn, whilst No. 2 Tunnel has a depiction of Old Father Thames. So, together they are a reminder of the two major waterways the canal was built to connect. Gaining permission to dissect Sydney Gardens with a canal was not easy and the beautiful (and very expensive) stonework here was clearly part of the deal to ensure that the ornate gardens were not compromised by the new canal.

Just after No. 2 Tunnel is the winding hole and I swung The Frog around in one go - helped, it has to be said, by the wind coming from the south west, pushing the bow around in the right direction for a change.

Our return trip took place through the hottest temperatures of that summer. I particularly remember passing through Trowbridge one lunch-time and desperately seeking out a mooring under some trees to try and cool us down. The heat also made the return trip up the Caen Hill flight more challenging. We did not have Trish with us so Pip and I would be doing the locks alone unless the volunteers were out to help us. The night before the flight we moored by Lock 25 - about four locks up from the start of the climb. This positioned us well to have an early start the next day. We knew, from our descent, that the locks are always emptied every night so they would be 'in our favour' unless another boat passed us and went ahead. We got up very early - both to ensure we were the first boat through and also to ensure we did as much of the flight as we could before the hottest part of the day. The downside of leaving when we did was that we had no partner boat to help with the work. This was unfortunate but if we had waited, we risked two 'buddy' boats coming along together and, understandably, going up as a pair - leaving us to reverse all the locks before we could follow.

The early climb went well with Pip and I swapping roles (she had become much more confident on the helm by now) and, thankfully, we were joined by a volunteer before we hit the sixteen locks of the flight 'proper'. By late morning we were moored for a coffee just above lock 44 - a well-earned break before we finished the climb back to Devizes wharf and our mooring for the night.

I mentioned Wootton Rivers on our out-journey and that was our next significant stop on the way back. We took the time to explore the village and snapped numerous photographs as each cottage seemed to be even more cute than the last. Eventually, we inexplicably found ourselves in The Royal Oak pub, having dinner and a well-earned pint (or two). Don't know how that happened!

We liked our second mooring in Hungerford so much that we used it again on the way back but not before we negotiated Hungerford Marsh lock 73. On all our travels I only saw three locks with a swing bridge across them and this was the first. The bridge had to be swung before the lock was used, for fairly obvious reasons, but when you are ascending it is actually possible to enter the lock without doing so. Your problem will come as the lock fills and your roof starts pressing on the underside of the bridge. If you keep filling the lock you would sink! On this leg we were descending (we actually came through the lock the other way when Billy and Lyra were helping Pip - they were fascinated by the notion of a swing bridge over a lock and Billy loved the potential 'danger' element involved in getting it wrong).

Whilst we are on the subject of 'getting it wrong', the very next morning it almost went very wrong for a rental boat that was moored nearby. It was quite early and Pip and I were eating breakfast whilst moored between Marsh Gate and Hungerford locks (locks 73 and 74). We noticed that a 70 ft hire boat behind us was pulling their pins and were obviously about to leave. I was keen that we share the lock with them, as it was in our favour. I jumped up and started preparing to go. Pip followed and as the holidaymakers entered the lock we shouted for them to keep the left gate open and we cruised along to join them. Pip and a young lad were operating the front paddles to empty the lock (we were descending). The helmsman on the hire boat was concerned about being too close to the front gate so he reversed slightly. Unfortunately, he was not paying attention and was enjoying telling me all about his holiday. As a result, after his small reversing manoeuvre he had not used any forward throttle to stop the boat drifting. I noticed that he was now heading dangerously close to the rear gate of the lock.

This was significant. At the foot of every pair of top gates in a lock is something called a Cill. It is normally a stone lintel but can be wood or metal. As the foot of the bottom gates are obviously lower than the top it follows that when the lock is empty, the Cill is part way up the wall at the top of the lock. This makes it VERY dangerous and is probably the most common reason narrowboats sink on the network. If you are not paying attention, as the water level drops in the lock, your stern can get stuck on the Cill. As the water drops further the front of your boat will tilt forward, your bow will go under the water and you will flood.

I interrupted the helmsman and told him he was over the Cill and that he should move forwards quickly. By this time the paddles were fully open and the water level was dropping fast. He pushed the throttle forwards but he did not move. His stern was now firmly stuck on the Cill and it was clear the boat was already starting to tip forwards. I screamed at Pip to put the paddles back down. Thankfully, she read the situation immediately and shouted at the young lad on the other side to do the same. Rightly Pip just took her windlass off the paddle and let it fall on its own. This practice is normally frowned upon as it can damage the mechanism but it is the quickest way to close it. Meanwhile, back at the stern I realised I had my windlass in the back cabinet of The Frog and that we were not yet so low down that I could not get off. I grabbed the windlass and jumped off. I jammed the windlass onto the top paddle mechanism and started frantically raising the paddles to let water back in to refill the lock. Another of their crew followed my example and opened the other side.

It was not long before the hire boat straightened up. It wobbled slightly as it started to float again and I told the helmsman to throttle forward. Thankfully, the boat moved off the Cill. Just at that moment a head appeared out of its back hatch. A very disgruntled 'chef' holding a frying pan with a half cooked egg in it had a puzzled look upon their face: "What the hell is going on?" I left it to her very shaken helmsman to explain.

We really had been very close to a disaster and Pip and I were also both a little shaken as the adrenalin still pounded around our systems. The hire boat pulled in for water just after the lock and we cruised on, relieved that we would not be sharing the next lock with them.

The last leg of our trip to Newbury was uneventful but away from the canal things were moving apace with our house sale. We had received and accepted an offer - an important step in our departure plans. At that point we were a long way from being free from the grip of Covid but we did not know that. We naively hoped that from August 2020 onwards we would see further relaxations in restrictions. In reality things stayed pretty much as they were for the next month but we approached the end of September, and the completion of our house sale, with a determination that we would start our long delayed odyssey as soon as we could.

CHAPTER 12: THE PLANK

Our house sale was completed on 23rd September. Remarkably, it took two removal lorries and nine crates to take most of our worldly possessions off to storage in Gloucester and Pip and I had a hectic last day finishing our packing and cleaning before we said goodbye. In the few days leading up to our departure we had slowly said farewell to our friends in the village - mostly over drinks at the Kings Head pub.

Our packing was made more complicated by the need to work out what needed to go into storage and what was coming with us on the boat. It was a tricky balancing act. We had to work out exactly where everything would go on the boat and, more pressingly, what we could fit into our car. By the end of the day our poor Prius was crammed to the roof and, just before we left, I remember squeezing our toiletries into the only free space I could find.

We were very tired and were pleased we had thought ahead and booked a night in a country pub about halfway to Newbury. The prospect of unpacking anything other than our toothbrushes was just too much for us. We had a lovely meal and chatted excitedly about our adventures to come. It felt very liberating. We no longer owned a house and most of our daily essentials were sat in the pub car park. We had a good night's sleep, a hearty breakfast and set off in bright sunshine towards Newbury and our new life!

When we arrived it took many wheelbarrow trips from the car to The frog to unload everything we had brought. We spent the day rearranging all of the storage and putting away all the clothes and other things that made us feel even more at home. When we were finished I remember standing on the stern and looking into our bedroom. I was overcome with a feeling of happy optimism (unusual for me) and I resolved, in that moment, that this was going to be a great adventure!

For the next few days we cleaned and got The Frog ready for our departure. There were a few important chores we had to complete in Newbury. First we had to sell the car. We drove into a local dealership and after a little haggling the deed was done. The dealer was about a mile from the marina so Pip and I walked back - feeling further unburdened. Next we needed to buy a new gangplank. The one on the frog was metal and, in my view, poorly designed. When we had used it on our K&A trip it always felt wobbly and insecure. It was also not very long. On our travels, we had seen many other boaters simply using scaffolding planks for this purpose. We googled a builders merchant. The nearest one was two miles away - without a car. Again, my failure to plan ahead and do things in the right order was in evidence. Maybe we should have bought the plank and then sold the car. This brilliant hindsight was not helpful.

The walk back from the builders merchants was hilarious. The plank, uncut at that point, was almost fourteen feet long. Pip and I held one end each and set off - negotiating bends as best we could and trying to ignore the many 'witty' comments of 'to me, to you' from passing motorists. Pictures of Eric Sykes sprung to mind (for readers of a certain age). Those of you who have not seen his brilliant film, *The Plank,* please google it. It's very funny!

Ironically, our biggest challenge was crossing the river Kennet over a very narrow footbridge, with twisting ramps giving disabled access. We could not turn very sharply and had to lay the plank across the walkway, duck underneath it in a manouvre that felt like an assault course. Finally we made it back to the marina and I got to work with my saw, cutting the plank to the eight foot length we needed. I donated the remaining six feet to Derek's 'useful one day' wood pile.

It's now Monday 28th September. We had arranged flu jabs ahead of our departure so we both got the needle and popped to Tescos for our final big shop. All this took longer than expected. When we got back, Pip did three loads of washing but we were too late to use the laundry drying room. Do you know what a Chinese laundry looks like? We did and it would not be the last time our tiny living space was criss-crossed with hanging damp clothes and bed sheets.

The next day we would leave. We had a short term plan. The Cratch Cover had seen much better days and needed replacing. We got advice from Emma to use Kinver Canopies who had a great reputation for creating fabulous, made-to-order covers. We called the company and agreed we would cruise up to Stourbridge, where they were based, so they could measure up and create the template needed. Luckily, this tied in with our general objective of 'going where most of the waterways were' - that is north, starting with the River Thames and then the Oxford Canal.

It was the morning of Tuesday 29th. We woke early, excited and slightly nervous (well very nervous actually) about leaving the safety of our marina and heading off. Pip got out the camera and took some photographs to capture key moments like me pointing out our new 'frog' tiller pin and me unplugging the mains electricity shoreline - which felt a bit like cutting an umbilical cord with the realisation we would never plug back in at this marina again.

We sought out Derek and Emma to say our goodbyes. In conversation, I mentioned that whilst we were heading east towards the Thames, I was planning to leave the marina and head west - an easier manouvre and one which I had done on all the previous occasions I had cruised east. We would then cruise half a mile to Greenham lock and wind before heading back past the marina. Emma said this was a big detour and that I should simply leave the marina and turn east immediately. I reminded her that the exit to the marina 'pointed' west (she obviously already knew this) and, having had the bad experience of trying to turn directly into it the last time we cruised to the east, I was nervous. Emma asked me how easy I actually found it to go out and head west, with the current on the river pushing me downstream. She was right. I have already explained just how tricky this was. At this point Derek chimed in: "To turn east, all you need to do is stick your nose out into the stream and let the current take you. It's easy!" I became a bit suspicious. Knowing that this was our last day in the marina, was Derek just looking for one final incident to entertain him: me struggling to turn east and hitting the moored boats in the process? After our chat I walked over to the entrance and scoped it out. The river was definitely wide enough for the manouvre and the stream was reasonably strong today. I decided to give it a go.

Before I describe our departure I will say one final thing about Derek - who has had a pretty bad press up to this point. Overall, it was obvious that his grumpy demeanour was much much worse than his 'bite' - in fact there was no bite. His help and advice throughout our time in the marina was invaluable and he certainly knew boating inside out. If he was ever frustrated by our ineptitude, we probably deserved it and I would hate to leave you with the thought that he was an ogre. The truth is far from it. Thank you Derek for all your support and guidance.

I took The Frog out of her berth without incident and headed for the exit. As usual, Derek was standing outside his workshop and looking on. I took a wide arc to the right of the exit and tentatively pushed our bow out into the river. Derek was shouting instructions. I turned hard to port and then went into neutral - letting the current complete the turn for me. The Frog's nose swung round to the left and when we were fully out I went back into gear and took back control. It worked like a dream and whilst I am pretty sure that Derek did not clap, I felt as good as if he had!

Our Odyssey had begun!!

CHAPTER 13: GOODBYE NEWBURY!

Right outside the marina is Ham Lock - our first challenge. We had tackled it twice before so it should not have been a problem. Just to the left of the lock is a wide weir. Today, following recent rain, the stream was stronger than I had seen it and I completely misjudged the lock entrance. We were heading for the weir and The Frog was not turning to starboard despite my efforts to get her to do so. I quickly went into reverse and managed to bring her back past the entrance and got in on my second attempt. Not exactly the encouraging start to our travels I was hoping for.

We cruised on to Monkey Marsh (remember this is the turf lock I detailed earlier). Sat on a nearby bench was Chris. He was reading, but as soon as he saw us approaching he jumped up and pulled a windlass from his bag. He helped us through and told us he loved canals, and this lock in particular, so much that he quite often came down to read and help boaters through. He told us all about its significance and was largely the source of all the information I have already shared with you. If the network was filled with people like Chris then our travels were going to be a joy!

Earth and bump! The next lock was Colthrop. When we arrived it was empty and we needed to fill it to descend. We opened the top paddles and waited and waited and waited. When a lock fills, you know you have reached the point where the water in the lock is the same level as that of the canal as the lock gates slacken and, sometimes, they will even swing open. At the very least you should be able to push them open with ease. This didn't happen. I looked at the water level in the lock and could see it was about an inch below the wet mark that indicated where it had previously been. I walked to the bottom gates and for the first time noticed the huge amount of water that was rushing out of the lock through a gap in the lock gates. The gap had either been caused by erosion over time or a slight misalignment of the gates - possibly caused by a boat hitting them. Either way the water coming in through the top paddles was no longer enough to compensate for that being lost here. The lock was never going to fill properly unless I did something. It was then I remembered talking to an old boater who had told me about how he had dealt with a similar problem. I went back to The Frog to fetch the longer of the two barge poles. I walked out onto the gates until I was astride the point where they met. I turned the pole until it was vertical and slowly lowered it inside the lock so that it partly plugged the gap between the gates. The water pressure was enough to keep it in place. I asked Pip to go back and try the top gates again and after a few minutes she was able to move one of them. Once one gate was open I was able to remove the barge pole and finish working the lock.

Locks and other assets on the network wear out and, all too often, they can cause long term canal closure if not dealt with promptly. So our next job was to phone the CRT and tell them of the problem we had just had. Hopefully, they would be able to get out soon and at least carry out a temporary fix until the gates could be properly repaired. We finished our first day cruise back at Woolhampton and we met up with Robbie, Sue and Jackie and Neil, our brilliant boat movers, for a 'start of Odyssey' celebration at The Rowbarge.

The next day we had intended to stay put as the forecast was for torrential rain. When we woke, however, it was only overcast so we decided to make the most of this respite and head off. As we pulled out of the mooring I stopped and let another boat pass us. It was the first time we saw the wonderful *Coo-Ee Too*. The live-aboard owners, Kathie and Geoff, had her built and had started their adventure almost a year before. As I write, through social media we know they are still out there and still loving their life aboard. Kathie had seen our Blogs and recognised the boat name. We shared the lock with them and stayed together until Aldermaston where they stopped for water. We exchanged details and were pleased we did. Not only were they really nice people but they went up the Thames ahead of us and their ongoing reports on conditions over the coming weeks would prove invaluable.

We reached Towney Lock and Pip realised she had left her windlass back at Aldermaston. She loved it and, whilst we had others on board, she was really upset. As we approached Towney we saw a familiar face on a bicycle heading up the tow path. We had first met Ken at Dundas aqueduct on our return journey from Bath. He had read the Blogs and also watched the first few Vlogs. He had rushed out of his boat and shouted to us and we had a conversation as he walked along the towpath towards the aqueduct. We really appreciated his enthusiasm and, now, we really appreciated his presence. We told him about the windlass and, after he had set the lock for us, he jumped on his bike and headed back to Aldermaston. Bless him. We went through the lock and tied up awaiting his return with the errant windlass. We thanked him profusely and, again, exchanged details. Ken lived on a Dutch barge that was at least one hundred years old. We followed him on social media from then on and realised just how active he was in tackling the CRT and helping to keep his beloved K&A in good order. Another saint of the waterways.

The expected rain finally came in so we moored at Sulhamstead swing bridge, completely alone and on a very isolated part of the canal. It was getting cold so I took twenty minutes to light the fire and then realised I had overdone it with the amount of coal. We were roasting. All these little bits of learning helped us get into a great routine as winter came on. For a few months, I never let the fire go out and got skilled at stoking it up each evening before shutting down the air vents meaning it slowly burned through overnight. In the morning we would wake to a cold bedroom but a lovely warm main cabin. My first job of the day was to empty the ash tray below the fire, top up the coal and open it up before making Pip a cup of tea and going back to bed. In this way, by the time we had breakfast the boat was really toastie again.

It's October 1st and we set off early with Pip at the helm. She kept control all the way to Burghfield where we met Robbie and Sue before going to theirs for dinner. Pip was great at the helm. She was a bit spooked by a sluice at Theale swing bridge and almost missed the landing pins. She also misjudged one sharp bend and my diary says we did some 'hedge trimming'. But overall she was growing in confidence, which would auger well for our adventures ahead. Today she passed her first oncoming boat. This may sound like a small thing but on a narrow canal even this felt like a challenge to her.

CHAPTER 14: LOG FLUMES AND FLOODS!

The next day we had intended to take The Frog through Reading. We had really been looking forward to this part of our trip. The River Kennet flows right past the pedestrian area outside The Oracle shopping centre and gives a unique view of the centre of the town. For this reason Robbie and Sue both wanted to come onboard for the ride. Unfortunately, the weather was atrocious, with Storm Alex bringing both rain and high winds. We ended up finishing the next Vlog and posting it before spending the day at Robbie and Sue's, catching up on laundry. Tomorrow we really do want to head off as we are worried by all this rain and what it was doing to the River Thames.

Saturday saw us waking to more rain but a prediction that it would stop by mid-morning. We contacted Robbie and agreed that we would set off from Burghfield at about eleven. I was filled with mixed emotions. On the one hand I really wanted to take the next step on our adventure but on the other, the awful weather and the prospect of joining the Thames was daunting and my nerves were jangling! I tried not to show Pip how I was feeling.

My first job was to attach the anchor. On the canal network, where there is at most a mild current, anchors are not needed. On the River network they are an essential safety item. Rivers are strewn with weirs where land levels change significantly. At this point, part of the river is diverted into a narrow channel where a lock allows boaters to negotiate the change in level in a controlled way. The majority of the river, however, continues on a different, much wider course and tumbles, often violently, over a weir. Cruising along a deep and powerful river is fine as long as your engine does not fail. If this happened on the canal you would simply push your boat to the bank and moor up. On a river, especially one like the Thames after heavy rain, this would not be possible. Engine failure would result in you being at the whim of the current, pushing you sideways towards narrow bridges, into overhanging trees or underwater hazards or, if you are really unlucky, towards a weir. So anchors are not for mooring and they are usually deployed only once, in a crisis, to stop your boat before it reaches one of the many hazards that could mean you saying goodbye to your vessel, your worldly goods and, at worse, your life!

So I searched and searched and couldn't find an anchor anywhere. Derek's face came to mind again and I have to say I really did feel like a numpty this time. We knew we would need an anchor and had simply assumed The Frog had one. I even swore to Pip that I had seen one in the rear compartment. Obviously I had not. I rang a marina that was situated just where we joined the Thames. They had one in stock so as soon as Robbie arrived, alone (I think Sue was put off by the cold and rain - I don't blame her) we set off.

We met another boat at the first lock going in our direction and this helped us through the remaining challenges on the approach to Reading. They had also been through Reading before and understood the traffic light system that controlled entry to The Oracle (the channel here is too narrow for boats to pass and traffic lights ensure boats don't meet in the middle).

The rain was pouring again and I was getting soaked at the helm. The water level was rising all the time and when we reached Fobney lock (105) it had almost reached the height of the metal walkway that was the landing point as we left the lock. A powerful weir brought water in from the left, under the walkway and another, on the right, brought the river around the lock. This was the first time I realised my morning nerves were probably justified. We pulled away from the lock and the stream felt the strongest I had experienced so far (we were moving with the water flow). The approach into Reading was through a pretty, residential area and lovely back gardens lined the river. I could hear Pip and Robbie chatting about how attractive they were as I struggled to keep The Frog in the middle of the River. I throttled right back but we were still moving at what felt like a high speed and handling was made harder as I was sending less water over the rudder (the faster you go, the more responsive the tiller normally becomes and the easier the boat is to handle. However as we were moving with the water flow, I had the double whammy of moving fast but with less control)!

We eventually reached the Inner Distribution Road bridge, which sat right in front of a sharp right hand bend and County Lock (106). I approached the bridge too fast and once again I was heading for the weir next to the lock. At this point I think it must be Holy Brook (a tributary of the Kennet) that joins the river - tumbling over the weir as it does so. It was in heavy flow and, whilst the weir looked really impressive, it was also terrifying when you were heading straight for it. I turned sharply and managed, with a slight bump, to get into the lock. I jumped off and walked down to look at the entrance to The Oracle. I wish I hadn't. The water coming over the weir was adding to the already heavy flow of the main river and all this water was then being squeezed into an ever narrowing channel giving the feel of a log flume. A log flume that we were about to negotiate!

When we got the lock gates open, Robbie walked down and pressed the button that would turn our traffic light green and, presumably, turn the one at the other side of The Oracle red. Our buddy boat set off first and I noted they kept to the right as they moved away from the lock - so avoiding the worst of the flow. I did the same but was still alarmed at the speed I was doing. Thankfully as we moved away from the weir my speed dropped a bit but the tight bends in the middle of the shopping centre still made avoiding the walls on either side hard to do. Gongoozlers were out in force and we were greeted with lots of waves from little children and enthusiastic adults alike. I tried to smile and look like I was having a nice time.

At the end of The Oracle, the river bends left and then sharply right under what is laughingly named High Bridge. It's beautiful and I have subsequently admired it from the road above on many occasions. That day, however, it felt like my nemesis. It is very low (especially at its edges and even more so as the river was in semi-flood). It's also on a bend and, as I approached, I felt the current pulling us to the left. I corrected and aimed for the centre of the arch as best I could. When I look back at the Vlog footage (taken by Pip at the bow) it looks like a perfect manouvre as we cruised through with no problems. In reality, the stern was swinging violently to the left and heading for the wall. I worked the tiller hard and managed, just, to miss the very unforgiving brickwork. It was difficult as, if I overcompensated, I risked turning the bow straight into it. We ran about thirty metres parallel, and perilously close, to the wall until I finally managed to ease us away. We cruised on - with Pip and Robbie blissfully unaware of the drama on the tiller!

The final lock on the Kennet is Blake's Lock - with its distinctive wheel paddle controls - which Robbie and Pip enjoyed using. Two bridges later we floated out onto the Thames. By now the weather had improved and the river looked glorious. It is so wide compared with the narrow canal. We had all donned our life jackets (another must when you are river cruising) and we immediately sought out the marina to buy our new anchor. We saw an opening with a few boats moored and headed into it - tying up at a pontoon in front of what looked like an abandoned chandlery. I looked in the window, however, and saw it was well stocked. We were still firmly in the grip of Covid so I was not that surprised when an old gentleman came to answer the locked door and asked me what I wanted. I could see an anchor just inside the door but it was enormous and not right for us. I asked the vendor for a river anchor and a length of rope. He immediately dragged the big anchor I had seen across to the door and started searching for some rope.

'We are only on a narrowboat'. I protested.

'New to the Thames are you? ' he replied. The look on my face gave him his answer. He went on: 'This is a river anchor and when you have twenty tonnes of metal under you, caught in the current and heading for a weir, you will see why you need this anchor!'

He looked like Old Father Thames himself and I trusted that he was sharing genuine experience and not just some old wives tale sales patter. Having parted with far more pounds than I was expecting, I dragged the anchor, its chain and a long rope across the pontoon and back to The Frog. Twenty minutes later it was attached to the helm mooring point and I felt more assured. At this point Pip looked at the Nicholson and realised the marina we had spoken to was actually slightly upstream of the confluence with the Kennet and we had actually stumbled across the wrong place. Hey ho!

We had lunch and then headed off towards Caversham - where we dropped Robbie before tackling our first Thames river lock and paying the additional licence fee needed to cruise the Thames. As we approached the lock I got my first experience of a Thames weir. It was enormous and, because of the recent rain, fast-running. I headed well to the left where I spotted the small blue sign pointing to the lock entrance. River locks were like nothing we had seen on the Kennet. They were huge, electronic and, thankfully, manned. Their size was a reminder to us of the dimensions of the other craft who used the river. We passed both bow and stern mooring lines around a bollard and waited to be lifted. Once we were up, I paid the £70 licence fee for seven days cruising on the Thames and we headed out back onto the River proper.

Not far from the lock we passed under Reading Bridge and immediately pulled in to moor by Christchurch Meadows. We were planning to stay here for the night but storm Alex had other ideas. We woke up the next morning and it was still raining. We had CRT warnings enabled on our iPhones and we were not surprised to see that the route we took yesterday was now closed. Another boater/walker posted a picture of Fobney lock where the water level was now above the metal walkway we had seen the day before. I can only imagine what the weir at County Lock was like.

Worse news was to follow. We could see the water level outside rising and the Environment Agency updated their online warnings to post 'red boards' for this section of the Thames (in fact most of the Thames). Red boards meant 'No navigation' and were only ever ignored by very experienced boaters. I was definitely not in that category and having checked with our insurance company we were told that our insurance would be rendered void if we tried to cruise in these conditions. It seemed we would be in Caversham for a bit longer.

Pip and I went for a walk that morning and our nerves did not improve as we took note of both the rising water flow and also the flood poles positioned on the bank of the river. These poles had markings that told you, at a glance, how deep the water was at that point (remember, these are on the bank). The measures went as high as nine feet - well above the height of The Frog. At that level, the river would have flooded the entire meadow we were moored next to. We could only hope that the rain would stop soon. On our first walk we doubled back to the lock and stopped to talk to the lock keeper of the day. We asked how long he thought the red boards would remain in place. He held out his flat palm and pointed to a crease that ran width-ways across it. He then pointed out the number of much smaller creases that 'fed' into it. He explained that the 'main' line was the River Thames and the many other creases were its large number of tributaries. He went on to tell us it would take days for all the rain that had fallen to find its way into the various rivers that feed the Thames and then into the river itself. In short, don't hold your breath! He did reassure us that our seven day licence was academic in these circumstances and that we could stay on the river until we were able to move again. In the end we stayed for nine days. What a start to our Odyssey.

That afternoon Pip and I became very concerned by a tapping sound in the bedroom and lounge. It was irregular but quite loud. Pip posted a question on a boating forum and got some amusing and some concerning replies. They ranged from your water pipes are 'farting' right through to you might be taking on water. We naturally became a little anxious at this last one. I racked my brain and finally I had a thought - what do the bedroom and lounge have in common? Both these hull sections have fenders outside dangling into the water. On the canal, with no flow, they do not move. On the river, with heavy flow they did. I popped out and pulled them up onto the gunwale. The noise stopped immediately and we were hit with a rush of amused relief!

There were some upsides to our forced visit to Caversham. We walked every day and explored Reading itself including the famous Gaol (temporary home to Oscar Wilde), the Abbey and the beautiful Forbury Gardens. We also walked out to Mapledurham - following the course of the River to the next lock. Mapledurham has a wonderful stately home with gorgeous grounds and out-buildings. The movie, *The Eagle Has Landed*, was filmed here. The lock, here, was enormous (even bigger than Caversham). At that time the water level was still really high (above the mooring pins) and its gates were firmly padlocked. We would not be going through here anytime soon.

The second day of our mooring in Caversham became a red letter day for us when we would meet a couple who will be lifelong friends. A lovely narrowboat called Ange de L'eau or water angel, had moored just behind us. When we came back from one of our walks we were approached by a very tall man who said he was just off to do some shopping but wanted to introduce himself. His name was Wolfgang and he explained he was German and that, for the last eight years, he and his lovely wife, Marlene, had spent their summers aboard Ange de L'eau, cruising the UK's waterways. They explained that they were heading back to their winter moorings on the Grand Union Leicester Line and were now worried as they had a deadline to catch a plane back to Bremen. Wolfgang invited us for a drink that evening. We chatted and it soon became clear that he was the font of all knowledge when it came to our waterways. I don't think there was a waterway they had not traversed and he seemed to know every lock and the best mooring spots everywhere. It turned out their route to their winter berth was the same general direction as us - up the Thames and the South Oxford Canal - so we agreed, if timings allowed, that we would go together. Wolfgang was also a vlogger - in German - and he was interested to both share his channel and watch ours. He was very encouraging in his feedback and we learned some filming techniques from watching his output.

The next day our electrician friend Peter paid us a planned visit. He wanted to check over the electrical installation he had put in and answer any questions. I have detailed previously my limited knowledge of how the electrics work and it was on this visit that I learned most of this. Peter tightened all the alternators, which had worked loose, and told me what each did. He then explained that we did not need to run the engine just to heat water. The Frog has a central heating system run from an Eberspacher diesel heater. It was a separate unit to the engine even though it is positioned in the engine compartment. It worked by burning diesel to heat hot water but we had assumed this was simply for the radiator. Peter explained it also put hot water into the water tank, under our bed, meaning we could use it instead of running the engine. This would only be useful if the batteries did not need charging, as that was our primary reason for running the engine - with hot water being a side product, but it was still helpful.

By day four we were getting concerned that our poo tank was going to get filled before we could move. We knew that on the island, just a few hundred yards ahead of us, there was a refuelling and pump out facility but we could not travel even that short distance with conditions as they were. Day six saw some amber warnings appearing upstream. This was a good sign but the section of the river we were on was still firmly red! It's now Saturday 10th October and we were not happy to move, Wolfgang and Marlene, who were worried about their flights, decided to risk it. They left and we kept in touch by text. That afternoon we heard that they had reached Mapledurham lock only to find it was still red-boarded, the gates were locked and the pins were still under water. When we met up a few days later, Wolfgang gave us a more lurid description of the terrifying trip they had that day. Not able to get through the lock or even moor up there, his first challenge was to turn his boat around in the teeth of the weir. Just below the lock the river bends and at one point he explained that he was out of control and drifting sideways towards a grassy knoll. At the last minute he managed to pull her around to face downstream. They cruised back about a mile and then, in desperation, moored on a private mooring - throwing themselves on the mercy of the landowner. Thankfully they were understanding and let them stay until the river calmed further.

On Sunday morning the weather was lovely and as the local warnings were amber we decided to cruise up to the Island to pump out and top up with water and diesel. The attendant had to do the pump out as our outlet was on the wrong side of the boat. This meant he had to feed the hose over our roof and then perch on the port gunwale above the still fast flowing river - sooner him than me. When we were finished we wanted to return to our mooring downstream but were obviously facing the wrong way. As I have said, the river was still flowing strongly. Our attendant, whilst young, was an experienced river pilot and he said he would help us turn around. He took hold of our stern mooring line and wrapped it around a mooring pin on the wharf. He told me to pull our bow out into the stream and then go into neutral. The river took our nose and swung us around. All this time the attendant held on tightly to the stern line ensuring we pivoted on that point rather than drifting out and across the river. At the last moment, when we were once again facing roughly downstream, he quickly unwound the mooring line and threw it to me to catch. I had to ensure I had it under control and on the boat (rather than trailing in the water) before turning the prop back on or I risked it wrapping around the shaft. Remarkably, it went smoothly and we were soon cruising back towards Reading bridge. The river is very wide here so turning again to face upstream before mooring was quite straightforward. The only challenge was having to jump off and hold the centre line as soon as I reached the bank to ensure the strong stream did not pull us backwards. I held her tight whilst Pip secured the bow and stern mooring pins. Finally, I re-pinned the centre line to give us some added security.

The next day we were planning to move off and catch up with Wolfgang and Marlene but, unfortunately, at nine-thirty, the Environment Agency website still showed red warnings at both

Mapledurham and Pangbourne locks. Pip received a message from Kathie and Geoff on Coo-Ee Too who were moored upstream at Goring. They told us the boards there were amber so I called the lock keeper at Pangbourne and he told me they are amber and that the web site will soon be updated. Pip and I looked at each other and reached for our life jackets - we were on our way. I put in one final call to Wolfgang and asked him how things were at Mapledurham. He said the weir was strong but passable. He told me he would prepare the lock so we could go straight in. He recommended I use full throttle as I pass under the weir to ensure I was not dragged sideways. Good advice but not what I wanted to hear just before we set out!

The river from Caversham to Mapledurham was moving reasonably quickly but we still made good time, despite cruising upstream. As we got closer to the lock, I noticed foam appearing on the surface of the water. This was my first indication of how fierce the weir was going to be. As we got closer we could hear the water cascading and I gripped the tiller slightly harder. I could now see the white water of the weir to my right and the river between us and the lock was becoming choppier. I remembered Wolfgang's words and pushed the throttle forwards. The bow of the Frog was now bursting through the waves. The tiller was jumping in my hand and I had to use all my strength to keep it facing forwards. At last we made the entrance of the lock and I had to throttle back very sharply to ensure we stopped before hitting the back gate! What a relief. I was so impressed with the performance of The frog and I think our slightly higher horse powered engine really helped us push through this tricky stretch of water.

We reunite with Ange de L'Eau and after a brief lunch we head off towards Pangbourne and Whitchurch lock. It is raining most of the way so you can imagine our surprise when we saw two gongoozlers high up on Whitchurch Bridge, crossing the Thames just before the lock. As we got closer we saw they were waving. Even closer and we realised it was Robbie and Sue - bless them. They had driven up to say another goodbye and watch The Frog in action on the Thames. We waved back and caught them on camera for our next Vlog.

The plan today was to get to Goring where Coo-Ee Too was still moored. The river above the locks was very calm and we enjoyed the expansive views the Thames offered. Beautiful houses lined the bank and there was always something to see. We cruised out into the countryside and on a sweeping bend we saw a commercial narrowboat heading downstream at speed. It had a second boat tied to its side and was being controlled by what I could only assume was a very experienced boatman.

Goring on Thames was our next lock and we wanted to moor overnight before we tackled it. The river here splits into three and tumbles over two large weirs and one smaller one. Below the weirs the channel is surprisingly narrow so the water is running fast. We approached the moorings with caution and spotted Coo-Ee Too with a space behind her. We pulled in but realised we did not fit. Kathie and Geoff sprang into action and pulled their boat forward slightly so we could moor. Like at Caversham, it was important to act quickly to secure our lines. Unlike Caversham, here there were mooring bollards and despite the faster moving water, once we were tied up, I felt happier than I had the previous nine nights.

Wolfgang was following us but unfortunately he misread the mooring situation and carried on too far, only stopping when he reached the lock landing pins - where, of course, he could not moor. I walked up and after a brief chat, I took his centre line to ensure that his boat did not drift out into the current as he backed up. Skilfully, Wolfgang reversed past the line of moored boats until we found a spot he could pull into. Meanwhile I was walking back down the towpath. As we passed each boat I had to ensure the centreline did not catch on their chimneys, mushroom vents etc Finally, he was safely moored and we heaved a collective sigh of relief.

Pip and I chatted with Kathie who had been moored here for the last nine days (like we had at Caversham). She told us they were very worried at one point as the water level rose well above the mooring pins. Thankfully, they never broke loose and the river slowly subsided. She also told us that just before we arrived another boater had fallen in when his rudder hit an obstacle under the water and his tiller spun around and knocked him overboard. You are taught, when on the tiller, to stand just in front of it (if your deck size allows you to do so). That way, if this happens to you, you do not suffer the same fate. Luckily for him, somebody saw him go in and as he was wearing a life jacket they were able to help him out using a barge pole. I looked down at the dark whirling water and imagined how it must have felt to be up to your neck in it.

It was still raining but Pip and I wanted to explore the sweet little town of Goring. Just off the river, up a little side street, stood Mill Cottage - former home of George Michael and where he passed away in December 2016. We walked past and up to see the weirs which were awe-inspiring. On the way back we saw another boat pulling in to moor in a very tight spot. It was raining hard and I noticed a lady in heavy waterproofs on the towpath pulling on a centre line attached to the mooring vessel. She shouted something to the helmsman and I recognised her voice. It seemed Emma and Derek were engaged in their other job of boat moving and were taking this boat back down the Thames to Newbury for a client. It was really strange to see them away from the marina. We said hello and goodbye before heading back to the shelter of The Frog.

CHAPTER 15: LOCK? WHAT LOCK?

The next morning was bright but chilly, with a steady north wind in our faces as we went through Goring and then Cleeve locks. We said a brief goodbye to Wolgang and Marlene, as they were planning to stop at Wallingford for food, and we headed for Days Lock with the intention of meeting up again that night. The river was beautiful with some stunning bridges and scenery along our route past Wallingford. Rowers were out in force but, unlike on the canal, there was room to spare as they sped past.

Benson lock was our next challenge and, as usual, as we got closer I started to see the tell tale signs of foam on the surface of the water. The lock and weir were nowhere in sight, however, as they were still around a tight right hand bend. We cruised out past the end of the tree line and saw the weir in all its glory. I scoured the river for the lock entrance, which I knew, from Nicolson, should be on the left. I could not see the usual blue 'LOCK' sign anywhere but I eventually spotted some mooring pins, which I assumed belonged to the lock, and headed straight for them. After a minute or so I realised that the lock entrance was actually even further left and I was now pointing straight at the weir! I reacted quickly and threw The Frog into reverse. I turned to port and knew that the natural strong flow of the weir would help us swing quickly. When our bow was pointing at the lock I engaged forward gear and upped our speed to counter the water flow and stop us swinging any further. We narrowly missed the right hand wall of the lock approach and, finally, we were in the sanctuary of the lock channel and could relax. That was close and a scare I did not want to repeat anytime soon!

Four miles further on we reached Days Lock and our planned mooring point. We stopped on a landing point designed for waste disposal and had a bite to eat. We looked ahead and spotted Coo-Ee-Too in the lock. Kathie told us later that they had been pinned to the landing pins by the strong weir coming from the left. They had to use a pole to push off and only just made it into the lock. I'm glad I did not know that before I approached it. They had seen us stop on the landing point so told the lock keeper to set the lock ready for us when they had left. This turned out to be a god-send. We set off after lunch and approached the lock at half revs. As we emerged from the cover of the left bank the weir current hit us hard and I was thrown right, towards the landing pins. I tillered right and went into full revs pointing our nose back at the weir. The Frog responded beautifully and we entered the middle of the open lock entrance - albeit at an angle resembling an aeroplane landing on a very windy day!

When we emerged there were no visible mooring spots (we were supposed to meet Wolfgang and Marlene here) so we continued on to the next lock at Clifton Hampden. We cruised under the fabulous Clifton Hampden bridge, a magnificent, Grade II listed construction with six glorious arches silhouetted against a still lovely blue sky. Just after the bridge, the river course stays left and I scoured the bank to see the entrance to Clifton Cut and the lock. We made the turn ok and after completing the lock we spotted some overnight mooring pins. This was a perfect location - tucked away in the sedate waters of the cut and having fixed mooring pins. Ideal on a river. We moored and walked along the footpath into the really sweet village and bought some goodies at the Post Office.

The next morning we waited for Wolfgang and Marlene to catch us up and then we set off for Abingdon together. We were now more than two thirds of the way to Oxford. We were always looking ahead to plan our route and the word online was that the water level at Isis Lock (the entrance to the South Oxford Canal in Oxford) were still too high, making it impossible to fit under the little footbridge that crosses its exit. At this rate we may need to continue further up the Thames and take the alternative Duke's Cut route across to the Canal. We would see.

En-route to Abingdon we passed the weir where the cut ends and really felt the push as we passed by. The same is true as we approached Culham lock. The moment is captured on our Vlog where Pip comments on the lurch she felt as we crossed the stream. Abingdon is a lovely town. The sun was shining and its beautiful stone buildings looked sublime framed against an azure sky. Less attractive was the prospect of mooring in the middle of the town. Kathie had told us that there was a mooring spot right in front of her but, once again, it was only about two feet longer than we were. What was worse, the approach to the mooring spot was under a low hanging tree and the wind was blowing hard. I caught the front of Coo-Ee-Too as I approached but at least they were friends and it is a contact sport after all. We headed into town for a haircut and food shopping. Tomorrow we will reach Oxford.

CHAPTER 16: DREAMING SPIRES AND LOW BRIDGES

Abingdon lock was memorable for two reasons. Firstly, we spotted Blue Sapphire, a narrowboat we met on the K&A in the summer and had shared a few locks with. Their owner always spent winter moored just above the lock and helped out the lock keeper from time to time. It was good to catch up. Secondly, the Environment Agency employee here was voted Lock Keeper of the Year in 2019. In my view, he should have won another award for the official looking notice on the lock side which read: *'The cooking of roast dinners, bacon, egg or sausage sandwiches is prohibited whilst in the lock. Please pass all items to the lock keeper for safe disposal'!*

We cruised on through Sandford lock. The current approaching here was strong but the river's strength was definitely abating. We passed through Kennington and under Isis Bridge (not the one mentioned above) before tackling Iffley lock. Upon leaving this lock we really felt we were on the outskirts of the city. The river widened and calmed and we were soon passing the confluence with the River Cherwell, just before approaching the beautiful Folly Bridge. The bridge is classic 'Oxford': built from cotswold stone and crossing the Thames in a series of arches. Our last challenge of the day was Osney Lock and we were soon moored up on East Street, just before Osney Bridge.

That afternoon Pip, Wolfgang and I walked into the City and found the start of the Oxford Canal. A short walk took us up to Isis Lock which would be our course if we came through the Sheepwash (a narrow cutting that links the river to the canal and is an option for us the next day). You may recall, I wrote earlier that when water levels were high, Isis lock can be impassable due to the low footbridge just after it. That day it looked like we would be able to get through. Wolfgang had been through here before and he pointed out the lock landing pins and the fact that the lock is around a very tight bend at the end of the sheepwash channel. He suggested that as I approached I should take the bend in two stages and pull into the landing pins before entering the lock. We walked back down through the sheepwash towards the river and I saw something that really concerned me. About half way along its short length, a wide railway bridge crosses the channel. Rusting away on one bank are the remains of an older swing railway bridge that obviously used to allow taller vessels through. I wished it was still in place but as the bridge was positioned just outside Oxford station I could understand why it was no longer practical. The clearance under the 'new' bridge worried me. Our roof boxes made The Frog a good foot higher than Ange De L'Eau and this was going to be a squeeze!

I was so concerned that the next morning I took my sea magnet and the length of rope it was attached to and walked back to the railway bridge. I dropped the magnet and held it just above the water level and tied a knot where it met the underside of the bridge. Back at the boat Wolfgang placed a barge pole on top of the roof boxes and I dropped the magnet down beside the Frog until it reached the water. When pulled taut the knot was about eight to ten inches above the boxes. It would be tight but we knew we would be able to make it as long as we took the chimney and TV aerial down.

Wolfgang volunteered to set off first and go through to the lock and message back how much clearance he had under the bridge. True to his word he was able to reassure us that, in his view, we would get through ok. Filled with trepidation, we set off. Our journey did not start well. I misjudged the turn INTO the Sheepwash channel and ended up almost hitting a narrowboat moored on the left bank. I had to reverse and swing again before getting through. This only served to add to my nerves as we approached the bridge. I have just watched the Vlog back, which shows us passing through the very narrow channel under it. The clearance was very tight and I had to duck to get through - but we made it.

Our next, immediate, challenge was the approach to Isis lock and the tight left hand bend. As we approached I noticed Wolfgang was standing on the bank directly ahead of us and he had his video camera in his hands. No pressure then! I am not sure if I simply forgot the instructions he gave me the day before or if I had just got such a boost of confidence after coming under the railway bridge. Whatever the reason, I didn't slow down. I swung the tiller to the right and we turned so sharply that my hand and the tiller were briefly buried in the foliage of the hedge on the right hand side of the bend. Remarkably, we made the turn in one and the Vlog contains Wolfgang's brilliant footage showing just how self-satisfied I was at my fluked entry to the lock. I cruised straight in and I reflect, now, that this was the first time I had taken The Frog into a single width lock (hence my head swinging from side to side as I try to avoid scraping down the wall - see Vlog 7).

I remember the palpable sense of relief I felt. We were finally off the Thames and the sedate Oxford Canal stretched out ahead of us. The troublesome bridge over Isis lock (bridge 243) was actually a beautiful wrought iron footbridge that is an iconic image on the waterways - well known to all boaters. It certainly looked good to me on the 15th October 2020 and we fitted underneath with no problem.

CHAPTER 17: A TIGHT SQUEEZE

The Oxford Canal links Oxford to Coventry (at Hawkesbury Junction) and was completed in 1790. It was designed by the brilliant canal engineer James Brindley, whose statue stands proudly in Coventry Basin. The canal is in two distinct sections. Oxford to Napton and, with a part of its course shared with the Grand Union, north of Napton to Coventry. The canal forms part of the original navigation linking Birmingham to London via the Thames and for fifteen years it was really important as the main artery of trade. Its prominence waned when the Grand Junction (now Grand Union) canal was completed in 1805. It is Pip's favourite canal and, whilst I prefer the Peak Forest Canal (of which much more later), I can see why she loves it. Along its course it has a lovely combination of long pounds, where the natural contours of the land were followed during its construction, and attractive lock flights, like Napton and Claydon.

So back to our journey; we have just passed through Isis lock and the sedate South Oxford Canal soon transformed into a busy, narrow and slow South Oxford Canal. The city is obviously a place a lot of people want to moor and they certainly did so along this stretch. In addition, there were a number of counterweighted lift bridges. Some out of use but others that needed to be opened. In all cases, where we encountered a lift bridge, the canal narrowed to only a lock width. This, along with the many moored boats, meant we moved pretty much at 'tick over' for the rest of the afternoon. My diary even says I was *'pining for the wide open River Thames'* - something I never thought I would write! At one point, we passed a rental company who had double moored their boats on the off side opposite another boat moored on the towpath side. This left a gap that was about four inches wider than The Frog.

One of the joys of our waterways is the variety it offers. The lift bridges here were smartly designed. Generally, they only carried footpaths and as such were small but still quite heavy. The clever counter-weighting, however, meant to open them a boater just had to pull on a chain. The weights did the rest. Vlog 7 has a great shot of one of these lift bridges opened by Pip. She then pans left to show me holding The Frog under the thundering A34. This contrast between the 'rest of the world' racing by and our waterway idyll would recur as a theme many times on our travels. It was moments like this that made us really appreciate life at four miles an hour on the tranquillity of the cut!

We passed the junction with Duke's Cut and moved onto Drinkwater's lift bridge (231). Just after passing through I noticed that my radio was missing. I moored and ran back down the towpath and quickly spotted its distinctive yellow colour and flashing light in the canal. I already mentioned that the walkie talkies were waterproof and floated - I forgot the flashing light that was triggered when the device was submerged. This made it really easy to find and I grabbed a bucket from outside a moored boat and fished it out. As expected, it dried out with no ill-effects.

Two more locks saw us reach the lovely canal village of Thrupp. The village featured in an episode of Inspector Morse (*'The Last Enemy'*). We went for dinner at the Boat Inn and ate in the 'Morse Room', where the ale came in a lovely pint glass with a narrowboat printed on it. The waitress kindly let us take one away for The Frog and it still has pride of place in our glass cupboard today. Later, we watched the Morse episode and wished we hadn't. Apart from the obvious interest of seeing our current location on film, the rest of the story was a bit pedestrian. John Thaw was as majestic as ever, however.

The next morning we left Thrupp. Wolfgang and Marlene went ahead and I am glad they did. When we departed we had to tackle the archaic looking Aubrey's lift bridge - another that is counterweighted. I noted that it was open and assumed it was permanently like this and cruised through - oblivious to the narrowboat moored up waiting to go through. The helmsman of this craft had moored, got off, opened the bridge, returned to his boat and was about to pull away when I 'steamed' through. Ouch! I apologised profusely and, unfortunately, lost my concentration. We needed to leave some rubbish in the CRT bins which are just around an almost ninety degree left hand bend after the bridge and, having let The Frog drift too far forwards, I was in no position to make the turn. Remember, I have still to learn about the sweet spot so my attempts to correct the turn simply meant I ended up being pinned alongside moored boats on the opposite bank. All that time I was also holding up the poor guy who was ahead of me at the bridge. Embarrassing!

Finally, we get away and head for Lower Heyford. Pip took a turn at the helm, her first time on the narrow canal, and she negotiated two locks really well. En-route we passed through Shipton Weir Lock (41). I have already mentioned this lock, which is our entry onto a short stretch of the River Cherwell. It is diamond shaped which helps to maximise the water drawn from the river every time a boat passes through it - feeding the southern reaches of the Oxford Canal with water as it does so. At Baker's Lock (40) the Cherwell courses off to the left and we approach the lock via a cutting and feel we are back on the canal proper.

We arrived at Lower Heyford in time to get lunch, explore the pretty village and complete a few chores. The only downside of this lovely spot is there is no TV signal and no wifi. Some may call this a bonus - and I felt the same until Pip beat me twice at Cribbage and moved even further ahead in our ongoing, very competitive, league (which she kept on her phone so I couldn't change the scores. She knows me well).

We talked with our travelling companions and agreed on the mooring point for the next evening. Wolfgang knew a great spot about a mile and a half short of Banbury - a cruise of over ten miles. That may not sound a lot but with seven locks and a stop for diesel and a pump out on the way it was going to be a full day.

This stretch of canal was beautiful even though it was an overcast day. A highlight was passing through Somerton Deep Lock (34). The lock, which rises twelve feet, is 'only' the 16th deepest in England and Wales but somehow its narrowness and the presence of a bridge (194), directly in front of it, made it feel cavernous. Pip took some lovely footage of the entry for our Vlog and I supplemented it from the helm. Deep locks mean big gates and I videoed Pip's attempt to close the huge lower gate - without success. I made the mistake of shouting for a 'big push'. These words would never be forgotten and Pip would throw them back at me, usually with a very sarcastic undertone, on many subsequent occasions! Luckily, Wolfgang came along just at the right time and his teutonic muscles were enough to get the gate closed.

We took a lunch time stop at Aynho wharf and then headed off towards Aynho Weir Lock where the River Cherwell 'crosses' the canal - creating a drag right to left as it does so. Luckily water levels had subsided and the lady at the wharf had already given us a heads up that the weir was behaving today. Pip took The Frog through the lock and the weir with ever-growing confidence.

A little further on we met a river cruiser (yoghurt pot) that had just come through Nell Bridge Lock (32). They were too tall to have their canopy up or to even have anyone at the helm whilst going under Nell Bridge (187). This meant they could not use the engines and when we arrived we saw them pulling her through the bridge using a rope. The crossing carries the B4100 and is quite wide and has no footpath access through to the lock. This meant they had to give their boat a big shove out of the lock and then grab the rope as her nose appeared - hard work.

I am now chuckling as I read my diary: *'The Frog was struggling on starboard bends today - very strange - and I had to put full power on a few times. May check the weed hatch tomorrow morning.'* We now know it was just me who had the problem.

Wolfgang and Marlene came over for a farewell drink as, the next day, they would continue their trip back to their marina, whilst we would stay in our mooring for another day to do some shopping and to explore Banbury. That evening, Wolfgang shared a huge amount of his knowledge about our upcoming route and pointed out the 'must sees' on the network. It really was a sad farewell the next day. We have only known them for a couple of weeks but our shared experiences have created a bond that we know will last for a long time. That is what boating can do - especially when your companions are just so bloody nice. As I write I am reflecting on their recent visit to the UK. They have now sold Ange De L'Eau and have purchased a river cruiser based in The Netherlands which they intend to cruise across to Germany. Our latest vlog on our YouTube channel captures three days of cruising we shared with them on *'Old Gilly'* on the beautiful waterways of the lowlands. They truly will be friends for life and I look forward to visiting them in Bremen at some point.

Following their departure, Pip and I walked into Banbury to stock up on supplies. On the way I bought some snow boots, which will be perfect for the deteriorating weather conditions and the very muddy towpaths we were starting to see. I carried our large rucksack the two and a half miles to Waitrose and Tescos and then made the mistake of filling it. The walk back was torture with a spaghetti squash bouncing on the top of my backside the entire route!

Banbury has great significance to all boaters. At its heart stands Tooley's boatyard and the Tom Rolt Bridge (164). The boatyard itself is historic. There has been a yard here since 1788 and it is now a scheduled ancient monument. As part of its history, in July 1939 Tom Rolt and his new wife, Angela, completed their renovations of a narrow flyboat *Cressy* in this very yard. The boat had been in the family for some years. His uncle, Kyrle Willans, had originally bought her as a horse drawn vessel and had added a steam engine. Tom's conversion was designed to make her suitable to live aboard, as that was exactly what he planned to do. He and Angela set off and headed along the Oxford Canal. Their four months initial voyage was captured in his book *Narrow Boat* - published by The History Press - which was an immediate success with readers and critics alike. Tom was a lover of traditional engineering and had an interest in cars, locomotives and the canal network. At the time of his voyage the network was at a pivotal point. It would be nationalised in 1947 and its importance as a commercial transport system was waning rapidly as both the rail and the burgeoning road systems grew in popularity. In short it was under threat and Tom joined others in founding the Inland Waterways Association - with the declared aim of protecting the waterways from closure. Direct action saved the Stratford Canal and momentum grew to keep other parts of the network open. Today, all leisure boaters owe a huge debt of gratitude to Tom Rolt and others like him. They really were pioneers, often traversing difficult waterways that had fallen into disrepair and, by doing so, ensuring they stayed open.

We left Banbury about midday and tackled the lock in the town centre and the lift bridge (which is operated using a windlass - the first time we had seen this combination) before cruising on to Cropredy. We walked around the sweet little village and popped into the stores sitting between Cropredy Lock Bridge (152) and Wharf Bridge (153). The coal we bought at Aynho (Excel) seems to be much better than our previous purchases and I overdo it when I build the fire that evening. It is so hot we have to open the front door and windows to cool down. Little did we know on this visit that we would finally say our goodbyes to The Frog in Cropredy marina - but that is all for much later. I will just mention the Brasenose Arms. This is a fantastic pub on the main road through the village and within staggering distance of the marina!

We note that it's due to rain on Wednesday 21st October so we set off early on Tuesday morning to make the most of the remaining good weather. It is worth a reflection here. When you are out on the network you really do feel much closer to nature in so many ways. There is the obvious ever-changing outlook as you cruise through beautiful countryside and remote villages. There is also the 'hunter gatherer' spirit that grows in you. We always had to plan ahead as we knew we would run out of water, food, space in our poo tank and eventually, diesel. We even ran out of coal on one occasion, a long way from a supplier and I had to get out the bow saw to collect and cut wood for the stove. So, what the weather was going to throw at us became an important consideration in our planning. Could we get to where we needed to be without getting soaking wet, snowed on or blown all over the place. This last one, in my opinion, was the most important. I could tolerate being cold and wet at the helm (I wouldn't like it, and unless we had to move, we probably would not) but cruising in a high wind can be really difficult and, consequently, embarrassing.

Back to Tuesday 20th October; whilst the sun is not going to shine we do know that it is not forecast to rain, so we plan a longish day of cruising. Beyond Cropredy we were faced with three individual locks before reaching the Claydon Flight, which climbs thirty plus feet over five locks in quick succession. It's on this section of canal that we first noticed little white metal posts with the letters D.I.S printed on them. They are positioned about one hundred yards either side of the locks. A little research told us that they are called Distance Markers and they were used by commercial boatmen to settle any dispute on lock usage. If two boats approached from different directions, then no matter how the lock was set, it 'belonged' to the boat that passed the Distance Marker first. Clearly, no consideration for water usage there! The system was obviously still open to dispute, as I am sure the argument simply moved from 'who reached the lock first' to 'who passed the Distance Marker first'.

Our progress was slow as I was still struggling to take right hand bends and I naively thought it was because I was going too fast. We also got a warning from a boater coming the other way that we are approaching an area with low water levels. This is the first time we were faced with a water level challenge and it reflected the fact that we were reaching the top of the Claydon plateau before descending into Napton. This is a high point on the Oxford Canal and explains why, despite the recent rain, the water level was still low. In addition, I had a bad habit of cutting corners - probably the result of my nervousness that we would not turn at all - and the water level is particularly bad on the inside of right hand bends. This is where silt builds up - as anyone who has 'O' Level Geography and studied Oxbow lakes will tell you.

By two o'clock the wind was getting up and we were tired. We were approaching Fenny Compton through the eponymous 'tunnel'. The parenthesis is called for here as the tunnel, which was built between 1775 and 1777, was taken down in about 1869. On any OS Map it is still referred to as a tunnel, as it is in Nicholson, so we were surprised as we approached it. What we actually experienced was a long, narrow cutting between two wooded banks with the occasional passing point cut into the bank. Luckily it was a quiet day and we did not meet anyone coming the other way.

At Fenny Compton we found a narrow spot to moor and pulled in. We decided to walk to the village and regretted our decision. Not only is it a long walk down a pretty fast and uninteresting road but there was little there when we arrived. I am sure I am doing the village a massive disservice and accept it is hard to get the feel for a community on such a fleeting visit. Maybe the dowdy weather also played its part.

After a day of working on the Vlog and cleaning the boat, we filled with water and headed for Napton. The sun was shining, as it always seemed to be for us on this stretch of canal, and we made great progress - helped by the fact that there were no locks for the first six miles. Pip took the helm for much of it and complained about the same turning 'issue' that I had. We arrived at the top of the Napton Flight, at Marston Doles, by about twelve thirty - but, unfortunately, so did five other boats ahead of us. We had no option but to sit it out and slowly pull The Frog down the bank until it was our turn to take the single lock (the first single lock descent we had made). I distinctly remember a hire boat coming out of the top lock that was unable to take the bend in the wind. It was 'trapped' against a house and garden wall on the far bank and the inexperienced helmsman seemed to have little idea how to get off. We could not help as we were on the other bank. The memory stayed with me, however, and when we were faced with the same manouvre about eleven months later I had a crew member on the towpath holding the bow line and helping to pull us around. I also put on high revs but only after the stern was fully clear of the lock exit - which extended for some distance and explained how the hire boat, and no doubt many others, had got into a pickle.

Back to our descent, which went really smoothly from then on. A stream of boats coming up the flight meant the locks were always being turned in our favour. We pushed on past possible mooring points and descended through eight of the nine Napton Locks until we found a brilliant mooring spot right above the bottom lock (8). I was really pleased with this as The Folly Pub (arguably the best pub on the entire canal network) is about two hundred yards away and was where we were due to meet my sister Helen and her husband, Graham, the following night.

We were now nearing the Grand Union Canal so as we were not cruising the next morning Pip and I walked the towpath the mile and a half or so to Wigrams Turn (or Napton Junction as it is more commonly known). I was slightly nervous (as I always was at that time about anything new) of what the junction was like, how sharp the turn and how narrow the bridge entrance were. I was relieved to see the canal was really wide at this point and walked back happy that the turn should go well when we encountered it. We walked back through the village, which was lovely, and paid a very expensive visit to the Village Stores. My diary tells me that in the evening I had a Chicken and Tarragon pie in front of a roaring log fire in The Folly with Helen and Graham - but I don't need my diary to remind me of that! It was one of the best pies I have ever eaten and was all washed down with amazing local ales. My diary also tells me that Leeds United (my team) had beaten Aston Villa 3-0 - so, all in all, a good day.

The next morning was windy, with a prediction of rain, so we decided, in view of our rudder 'issue', that we would not move. Instead, I opened the weed hatch to see if there was any obvious obstruction that may have been affecting the steering. I could find nothing so, in desperation, I finally decided I would make the call, I described in an earlier chapter, to the RCR. This was my eureka moment and after their visit, I finally understood the sweet spot and how to steer The Frog properly. I had only owned her for about fourteen months!

CHAPTER 18: EE IT'S GRAND!

Our RCR saviour having left, we flushed the loo and realised we needed a pump out. I'll spare you the detail but we knew we had to move off right away - despite the wind and rain! A few minutes research and we identified a marina at Ventnor on the Grand Union - about three miles and four locks away. En-route we completed Wigrams Turn with no problems and headed for the Calcutt Locks. As we started our descent I met a Leeds United fan and, together, we chatted/bemoaned our shared pain. It's always nice to talk with a fellow sufferer! What was interesting was he was a Leeds fan for the same reason as me: we have no connection with the city at all but we are of a 'certain age', which placed our influential childhood years in the early 1970s when Leeds made all other teams look very ordinary under the exceptional management of Don Revie.

That's enough of this self-gratification - on with the story. The locks at Calcutt are our first double locks since leaving the Thames and it was good to share the workload with another boat. The Grand Union is a lovely canal to cruise. It's wider than the Oxford and, in most places, straighter. It was built and developed over time. The first major development was the Grand Junction Canal, built between 1793 and 1805. It ran from Braunston in Northamptonshire (the very heart of the canal network) to Brentford and the River Thames and was built to compete with the already operating Oxford Canal. Later, it was extended to both Birmingham and Leicester in the Midlands and in the late 1920s a further Act Of Parliament authorised the creation of the Grand Union Canal. In the following decade significant improvements were made to introduce double locks in places where they were still single, to widen and straighten sections as well as upgrading some banks to reduce the risk of water loss and breaching. From the very completion of these works, however, the Grand Union's importance started to decline. If you like canal nostalgia, you should watch the film *The Bargee (1964)*. It stars Harry H. Corbett (of Steptoe and Son fame) and Ronny Barker (doing his usual great job as a character actor). Harry H.Corbett plays a 'born-to-the-water' Bargee, working the Grand Union from London to Birmingham with, yes you guessed it, a girl in every 'port'. Ronny Barker is his side-kick and Eric Sykes plays an annoying 'yoghurt pot' owner who keeps getting in their way. It's a bit like 'Carry On' in its attitude to women, however, so be warned.

Back to our journey: we arrived at Ventnor Marina and I have already detailed our dreadful pump out experience in Chapter five - the one with the flagpole and the wind (of the meteorological variety, I hasten to add). As we left the marina the skies turned even blacker and we decided enough was enough and pulled in to moor. As I took the centre line, the heavens opened and Pip and I got absolutely drenched in the few minutes it took us to drive in the mooring pins and secure The Frog. We were definitely here for the night!

That day the clocks went back and we realised even more that winter was looming. The time change also meant we woke early and set off again at about nine o'clock the next day. The sun was shining on a beautiful crisp day and our first task was to negotiate the fifty four foot drop over the ten locks of the Stockton flight. We met up with a lovely couple on their narrowboat *Ainsley.* Our companions were on a schedule and needed to get through the locks quickly. They were experienced boaters and worked the locks well but they were big locks with 'candle' paddle cranks that, in many cases, took over fifty turns of the windlass to raise. The cranks are called candles because they are long, metal tubes painted white with a rod running down through their centre. This rod is attached to the paddle at its base and as you turn the windlass, it rises up from the tube and resembles the wick of a candle. They were built in the 1930s renovation mentioned above and, alongside, you could still see the remains of the old single lock which, in many cases, acted as the lock bywash (a channel that takes water around the lock). The gates were also heavy - so Pip was in for a tiring day.

We said goodbye to Ainsley at Itchington Bottom Lock (13) and we moored briefly outside The Two Boats Inn for lunch. We set off to find a shop and my diary describes: ....*a dreadful convenience store with an Alsation the size of a dinosaur, sticking his nose into any orifice he fancied'.* Not surprisingly, we did not linger and, after bacon sandwiches, we headed off past the village of Long Itchington itself and through a beautiful wooded section, turned golden by the early touch of Autumn. We soon reached the top of the Bascote Locks (14-17) and their drop of twenty six feet.

These locks are also double locks with 'candle' cranks but locks 14 and 15 form what is known as a staircase - the first we had encountered. A staircase is where two or more locks are linked to each other with no pound in between. This means the higher lock(s) will empty directly into the lower lock(s) and it is important they are properly prepared before you try and pass through. We were descending, so the top lock obviously had to be full to allow us to open the top gates and enter. Before we could open the bottom paddles, however, it was important to empty the bottom lock fully so that it could be filled with the water leaving the top lock. When the water levels out between the two locks, we could open the bottom gates of the top lock and move into the lower lock - which we then emptied as normal having closed the top lock gates and paddles behind us. Hope that makes sense. Like many things in boating, it's probably easier to do than it is to describe! The most famous staircase locks on the system are at Bingley on the Leeds and Liverpool Canal. The Bingley Five Rise takes the navigation up nearly sixty feet in five consecutive locks over a distance of only three hundred and twenty feet - making it the steepest flight in the UK. It is potentially a dangerous passage, so CRT volunteers are usually there to help boaters through. We will tackle the Bingley flight the following June so I will write more about this magnificent engineering achievement later.

After Bascote, Pip and I were both feeling weary and as storm clouds were gathering again we decided to moor. Unfortunately, we prevaricated and for the second time in two days we got soaking wet, trying, unsuccessfully, to hammer mooring pins into the towpath just after Wood lock (19). We took shelter inside The Frog but we knew our pins were not secure. As soon as the rain subsided we cast off again and finally we successfully moored between locks 20 and 21 at Fosse Wharf (having completed yet another lock - a total of seventeen for the day). Needless to say, we slept well that night!

We woke and after the rain stopped we decided to complete the remaining three miles or so to a potential mooring spot in the heart of Leamington Spa. We were joined by another boat through the last three locks between us and our mooring. My diary says: '*The couple are from London and a bit snooty so we are glad to part company after the last lock*'. I have to say this is unusual. In all our travels on the network we rarely met anyone who we did not get on with - albeit we usually only spent a few hours with most of them. Until I re-read my diary, I had forgotten this couple. I now remember that they were only moving their boat because they were switching marinas. The journey, therefore, was nothing more than an inconvenient interruption to their preferred pastime of sitting on their boat in a marina, sipping G&Ts. I apologise for my acid comments but I really have no time for people like this. For us, part of the joy of boating was meeting new people with a shared passion for life at four miles an hour. We were there for them in times of need and, in most cases, know that they were there for us. I would have hated to be reliant upon this couple for anything. Rant over!

We moored between bridges 39 and 40, right beside a residential building for the local college. We knew we may regret this (students are not known for their early nights and quiet reflections) but there were other boats moored here and that is usually a good sign. We walked into Leamington Spa and fell in love with this pretty town. The wide high street has a Georgian splendour and Jephson Gardens is a lovely Victorian park, through which the River Leam cascades over an attractive weir and under an ornate wrought iron footbridge. The gardens are named after Dr Henry Jephson, who was instrumental in promoting the healing qualities of the local Spa waters, which attracted visitors to the town. We called into a tea shop on our way back to the boat and had *'the best Eccles cakes ever'* (diary entry). I am a real fan of this northern delicacy and have sampled many, so this was quite an accolade.

The next morning we filled with water at the slowest tap in the world and, eventually, cruised the three miles or so to Warwick. The approach to this historic town is really nice. We crossed the railway and the River Avon over two aqueducts before entering the suburb of Emscote. Just the other side of Warwick we would face the towering Hatton Flight of twenty one locks, which we did not want to start today. So we just completed the two Cape Locks (24 and 25) and found a great mooring point opposite The Cape of Good Hope pub.

I did not record this in my diary but I have just remembered a little incident that made me see red at lock 24. We were coming up the lock on our own. Two privately-owned boats approached the landing pins above the lock - clearly waiting to come the other way. They could see us in the lock and must have had at least six crew members across both boats. They held their crafts on the centreline and then.........did nothing! I have already explained how tough these locks are and Pip was busy, working hard, winding up one paddle, walking over the lock gate and winding up the other. To avoid me being banged around in the lock, she was opening the paddles in stages and had to walk across the lock gates a few times to do this. Finally, she had to open the heavy gates on her own - all the while being watched by the crews of the waiting boats. At one point she turned to me and spread her arms wide in disbelief. This is awful boat etiquette. I was exasperated for her so I called her on the radio and we hatched our plan. When the gates were open, I saw the two 'spectating' helmsmen get back onto their boats and pull slightly away from the bank. I stayed in the lock and pretended to be doing something under the tiller. Eventually, I stood up again, went into forward gear and started to leave the lock. However, I then kept knocking the Frog into neutral, with a puzzled look on my face suggesting there was something wrong with the engine but I was not sure what. I crawled, and I mean crawled, out of the lock and continued to move VERY slowly past the waiting boats. Meanwhile, out of the corner of my eye I could see the helmsman fidgeting with their tillers and struggling to hover their boats - keen to get moving into the lock. As I finally pulled past them I turned and shouted *'Thanks for your help'* and slid The Frog into Lock 25 at normal speed! Petty? Well yes, I guess so, but it felt really good at the time. This self-centred and discourteous approach to boating was, thankfully, a rarity on the network.

That afternoon we walked the mile to the town centre and were really pleased we did. Warwick is full of beautiful architecture and at its centre sits the Norman splendour of Warwick Castle. We visited the castle when we cruised the Warwickshire Ring in 2004 and we were keen to re-visit. Unfortunately, Covid restrictions meant you had to pre-book and we were turned away. We comforted ourselves in a local tea room eating Tea Cakes and Yorkshire Tea bread - if you haven't tried it.....

That night we completed the Oxford Canal Vlog and uploaded it. The next day became another red letter day for us. We had a magnetic sign on the outside of The Frog which showed our Blog and Vlog links as well as our Facebook and Twitter accounts. Lying in bed the next morning, Pip noticed a comment on the latest YouTube posting from a couple who had walked past us the day before and had taken a picture of our sign. It seemed they had spent that evening reading all of our blogs and watching all of the vlogs so far - in order. They said they loved the blogs and had spent the whole evening laughing out loud at our prat-falls! They were on their own narrowboat 'Jack 'n Janner' and were moored just up the canal, facing the other way. Pip sent a message back and invited them for a socially-distanced coffee and later that morning we met Val and Ade for the first time.

They are a lovely couple with whom we share many things - not least that they are also from the South West (they had a house in Plymouth). Their boat name reflects Ade's history as a submariner in the Royal Navy (Jack) and Janner is a term for anyone from the naval city. They lived aboard and rented their property to friends (who would also play a significant role in our story but much, much later). We clicked straight away and coffee turned into a suggestion of dinner at The Cape of Good Hope the following night. Remember, they were heading the other way so we had to make the most of this short time together. The meal was fab (I had a pie) and we said our goodbyes with a rosy glow on our cheeks.

Val and Ade are experienced boaters and when together we picked their brains in any way we could. One blindingly obvious suggestion was to leave all the cabin lights on when in a long tunnel (duh!) but Ade also said he had purchased a handheld halogen light that he used to supplement the headlight when in tunnels. We ordered one straight away and arranged to pick it up from an Amazon 'box' (other suppliers are available).

That night it was quite windy and I was woken by the boat moving a little more than I liked. I decided to go out and check the bow and stern lines. Having started at the bow I then headed for the stern. It was dark and I had not bothered with a torch. Big mistake! I had completely forgotten that I had, unusually, attached the centre line to a ring on the towpath. In the dark, I tripped over it and landed face down on the towpath. The beer I had consumed must have increased my tolerance to pain and, other than shock, I didn't feel a thing. The next morning however, my bruised knees and hands were an all too painful reminder of my nocturnal faux pas.

The weather improved, as expected, on Friday and we set off to tackle the Hatton Flight. There are twenty one locks in the flight and it takes the Grand Union up an impressive one hundred and forty six feet in about two miles. The locks, in their current form, are part of the 1930s renovation and beside each is the tell-tale evidence of their single lock 'predecessor'. They all have candle paddles and in terms of lock operation, in my opinion, Hatton makes the Caen Hill flight feel like a walk in the park. It is known, colloquially, as '*The Stairway To Heaven*'. This is probably just because of the significant height it climbs but boaters also point to the famous cafe that sits next to the Top Lock (46). They served the most indulgent breakfast baps I have ever seen and I am sure this also contributed to the celestial bliss many boaters feel on reaching the top of the flight.

Just before we left our mooring we chatted with a family on a hire boat who had pulled in to get water. They were heading for the flight and we agreed we would amble up to the bottom lock and wait for them to join us. This was their first time up the flight so they were glad of the company and the relative 'experience' of Pip and I. What a frightening thought! Having just re-watched our Vlog (8), I remembered that we got on really well with the family and we made good progress up the early locks of the flight. Part way up, we were also joined by a CRT volunteer and this sped up progress even more. Pip and I were sharing the burden of the lock setting - which meant Pip had to take The Frog into the lock beside another boat (something she had always been too nervous to do before). She did brilliantly and it helped us both to have a 'rest' on the tiller every few locks. We reached the top in about three hours. We moored under the cover of tall trees that line the canal at this point and we walked back down to the cafe for a well-earned breakfast bap.

Fully 're-fuelled', we pressed on past the Midland's Yacht club (a sign that would have seemed anachronistic had it not been surrounded by moored and dry-docked boats). We cruised under Ball's Bridge (58) and were on the approach to Shrewley Tunnel. At four hundred and thirty three yards or three hundred and ninety six metres, Shrewley Tunnel takes the canal right under the village of the same name. It was built between 1795 and 1799 and was originally on the Warwick and Birmingham canal, becoming part of the Grand Union in 1929 following the amalgamation of a number of canal companies. It is wide enough for seven foot boats to pass and has chains down its wall, similar to The Bruce Tunnel on the K&A, to help non-motorised barges pull themselves through. As we left the tunnel, we moved into a deep cutting which shows the engineering that was needed to cut through the hill, even before the tunnel was started. In addition, if you turn around at this point you can see a much smaller tunnel to the right of the main tunnel, set at the top of a rising footpath. This tunnel was used by the tow-horses and their handlers to walk through the hill and rejoin their boat on the other side (the 'horse tunnel' was actually shorter than the main tunnel and came out in the woods near the village).

Two and a half miles later we pulled in to moor at Turner's Green just before bridge 63. I remember Pip's assertion that she had found her ideal house. It was a beautiful old brick building, probably converted from an old canal warehouse. Not only did it look magnificent and have canalside gardens but it was also right next to the Tom O'Wood public house. Pip is easily pleased - well, she married me! This mooring was only about a mile from Kingswood Junction, where a short cutting allowed boats to leave the Grand Union and join the Stratford-on-Avon Canal. This was going to be our next step, but Boris had other ideas.

CHAPTER 19: CHANGE OF PLANS

It's now 31st of October 2020. Those with good memories will recall this was a significant date. It was the day when Covid cases had reached such a level that a, so-called, 'fire-break' lockdown was announced for a whole month, starting on the 5th November.

This was not what we had expected. We had hoped that restrictions would be loosened and not tightened, the further we got from the Spring/Summer lockdown. So this news was really disappointing. In March, we were in Cornwall, in our house, with all the benefits that had brought. We could walk the lanes, sit in the garden and do the many chores that came with having time on your hands. Now we were on a seven by fifty seven foot narrowboat in the middle of the country and we were facing all the new uncertainty a lockdown would bring, a long way from our friends and family. We were also realistic enough to assume that any lockdown could and, probably would, be extended into December and, possibly, beyond Christmas.

Our thoughts turned to practicalities. We reflected that we were only heading to Stourbridge to get the Cratch cover measured and replaced. What had suddenly become more important was finding a mooring for the winter. With the news that had just broken and in view of the CRT lockdown rules, we knew many boaters who were 'out' this winter would now head for shelter and we were concerned we would not find a marina to take us. We sat down immediately and scoured our Waterways map of England and Wales, looking for possible options.

We phoned a few and got the answer we expected: 'Sorry we are full'. Eventually, we phoned a marina near Leicester and were delighted they had a berth for us. We started to plan our route. By way of background, the winter is when the CRT carries out much of its essential maintenance, issuing notices when a waterway is going to be affected. We did our CRT research and reached the depressing conclusion that, due to planned works and closures on the network, we simply could not reach that marina. There wasn't even a realistic detour.

We went back to the drawing board and continued tracing our fingers down the Leicester Line of the Grand Union. We stopped when we read the word Crick. You may remember, from an earlier chapter, that Crick marina is where the Boat show is held each year - so it's a marina we knew. It is also the village where my sister lives and, at that point, there were no stoppages preventing us from reaching it. But this is Crick. Was there really going to be any chance we could get a mooring here? We phoned and spoke to Mark, the Marina manager, for the first of what would end up being many times. He was brilliant. Warm and welcoming over the phone and he gave us the reassurance we wanted: Crick could fit us in.

Our next job was to contact the cratch cover makers in Stourbridge. We still needed to change the ancient leaking one we had on the front of our boat and, thankfully, they agreed to come and meet us out on the cut to complete the templating. By this time we were only about thirty miles from them. In a van that was no distance at all but in a boat.......

As we were no longer going to cruise up the Lapworth Flight on the Stratford Canal, on Sunday 1st November, we decided to walk it. It is beautiful at any time of year. Crowned with Autumn colours it looked sublime and was just the tonic we needed after the bad news of the day before. On the way back, we sat on a bench and filmed the face to face section of our next vlog - announcing to our followers how our plans had changed. In short, we would now need to turn around at Kingswood junction and head back down the Grand Union towards Braunston and onto Norton Junction to take the Leicester Line up to Crick.

Our challenge was going to be lockdown rules and how they affected boaters. CRT had made it clear that during lockdown boats should not move EXCEPT for 'essentials'. We interpreted 'essentials' as: getting water, diesel, pumping out and getting to your allocated mooring! That said we did not want to take advantage and the rest of our tale will show that this lockdown affected us greatly and we really did only move when we had no option. Initially, of course, we had four days before the lockdown came into effect - four days to get as far as we could towards Crick. There was no time to waste so we walked back to the Frog and immediately brought her the last mile up to the junction before winding and returning back to our previous mooring - this time facing East.

CHAPTER 20: THE RACE TO BRAUNSTON

Kinver Canopies had agreed to meet us at 8.45 on the morning of Tuesday 3rd November in Leamington Spa. Early on the morning of Monday 2nd November we were sat at Turner's Green; nine and a half miles, one tunnel and twenty three locks away. Needless to say, we left early and for the second time in three days we went through Shrewley tunnel and approached the Hatton Flight. There was no other boat in sight and the wind was blowing strongly across the top of the locks. Because of the conditions, it is not possible for us to swap roles and poor Pip had to work eighteen of the twenty one locks on her own. Meanwhile, I was being buffeted around in the big empty locks. On reflection, I think Pip would have been fine at the helm but in the end, we did not swap until we reached the lower levels of locks 28-26 and the wind had abated. By the time we approached Warwick she was very tired.

We flew through The Cape of Good Hope locks and through the rest of the town and approached Leamington at about four o'clock. We needed to shop and use the tumble dryers at Morrisons (yes, a launderette in Morrisons) and, by the time we emerged, the light was fading very fast. We were half a mile from our mooring and luckily there were no moored boats on our way. I pushed the throttle forwards and only slowed down to take the last few bridges for fear of hitting them. We arrived just before it got totally dark and quickly tied up at the same mooring spot we used just a few days before. We spotted a Mexican takeaway about a hundred yards away and we were soon wolfing down one of the nicest takeaways we had ever eaten. It's funny how much nicer food tastes after a long and tiring day when you are starving.

The next day the man from Kinver canopies arrived and used huge sheets of paper to create a template of the cratch cover. It took about an hour and as soon as he had finished we headed off again. We completed the Fosse and Bascote locks and moored overnight back at Long Itchington just below the Stockton climb. En-route, Pip took the boat into all of the locks. Just below Bascote we were joined by a holiday boat - with a very concerned looking couple on board. Not only were they completely new to boating and very nervous but they were also upset that the lockdown was going to cut right across their holiday plans. We helped them through the Bascote flight and they were really appreciative - especially when they saw the two lock staircase. We would meet them again the next morning and complete the Stockton flight together, only saying goodbye when they pressed on at Ventnor, whilst we stopped for lunch. Calcutt locks lay ahead, along with Calcutt Boats (between Locks 1 and 2) where we filled up with diesel, water, coal and pumped out. I bought a few things in the chandlery and chatted with the team there about how the new lockdown was going to affect them. This latest development was, understandably, going to be less impactful than the income lost over the spring and early summer but, nevertheless, calling all their customers back to base had not been something they had relished. We pressed on to Wigrams turn and moored up straight after turning north east towards Braunston. We were, at last, on 'new to us' water but lockdown had started and we now needed to be really disciplined about when and why we moved.

We were running low on food, so the next morning after an exploratory walk along the canal to scope out our route, we decided it would be sensible to move closer to Braunston and the shops there. We had a very surreal feeling. The canal, like the roads, had become ghostly quiet. By way of contrast, it was a lovely autumn day. The sun was shining and the sky was a gorgeous blue. This section of canal is a contour navigation and we wound our way past Lower Shuckburgh and Flecknoe before it straightened out at Wolfhampcote. Just before reaching the iconic Bridge 100 (Bridge 100, I think, provides a farmer with access to the rest of their land. It is built of brick but it looks as if it has had its upper walls removed) we met Val and Ade heading in the opposite direction. We moored up for a socially-distanced chat and they reassured us that Braunston was quiet when they left a few hours before. We decided to complete the remaining couple of miles and moored just after taking the turn at Braunston junction, near the bridge that takes the A45 over the canal.

Over our odyssey, we would get to know Braunston really well, but this was our first visit to the lovely village that sits high above the two canals that brought its prosperity. It was once the home of the annual boat show and remains a much-loved location for most boaters. Now the Oxford and Grand Union canals meet to the west of the village but at one time they merged directly to the South - where the marina now sits. The Stop House is a historic brick building, built in 1796, and sits right next to the old junction. It was in operation until the end of the nineteenth century - collecting tolls from passing boats. Vessels were 'stopped' as they moved from one waterway to the other and there would once have been a stop lock, which not only forced passing boats to stop but would also have prevented the water from the Oxford flowing freely into the Grand Union. I have written about how different canal companies protected both their water and their trade in an earlier chapter.

There is quite a climb up to the village itself but the walk is worth it. The skyline is dominated by the impressive spire of All Saints Church and the main street is lined with a real mixture of old shops, pubs and houses. There is even a disused windmill. As you walk further east the pavement is set back from the road with a beautiful raised section. A stroll down Dark Lane, at the east end of the village, takes you back to the canal and the fantastic Admiral Nelson pub - sitting right beside Lock 3 of the Braunston Flight.

We were now in lockdown and as there was a convenience store in the village, we resolved that we would stay where we were until we had to move for water. The next day the sun was still shining so we walked up the flight to the entrance of Braunston Tunnel (more about the tunnel when we finally traverse it). On the way back, we stopped at a lovely canalside shop above Lock 1. On board, we had lots of Frogs of all shapes and sizes, but we were still missing one thing - a bucket. The little shop sold small colourful metal buckets painted with the Rose and Castle motifs typical of canal arts and crafts. We bought a dark blue one and placed our 'hanging' frog in it so that it just peered out over the top. We also bought some magnets so we could put the bucket on our roof without the fear that it would fall off. Pip also spotted the 'I fell in the canal' mug which I described in a previous chapter. Incidentally, you may be wondering why this shop was still open during lockdown; canal memorabilia could hardly be classified as 'essential'. The thing was they also sold sandwiches so they could class themselves as a food store. Whatever, the reason - we were really pleased that they were still open.

My sister, Helen and her husband Graham paid us a further (outside) visit and kindly brought our post (mostly wool and some business cards designed by Pip's sister Trish, for Pip's burgeoning 'Narrowboat Knitting' Etsy business). We walked back up to 'The Admiral' and bemoaned that the lockdown meant it was now closed. That evening I remember walking up to the fish and chip shop - which was still doing 'at the door' business. The walk back was interesting, as away from the main village it was completely dark. For 'safety' reasons I walked down the middle of the main road to ensure I did not fall into any ditches on the way - jumping to one side when any cars came.

The next few days were full of domestic chores. Most notable was our decision to walk and do a 'big shop' in Daventry - about five miles away. Much of the route was on the busy A361 and it had no footpath. We did not realise this until we were far enough towards the town that we did not want to turn back. We had a very scary experience lorry dodging and we were really pleased when we finally turned down a side road and headed for the town centre. Needless to say, with a full rucksack and fresh memories of the frightening walk in our minds, we took a taxi back to Braunston.

By this time, our water tank had about three inches of water in it - so we had to move. We filled up just past the A45 bridge and as we wanted to stay in Braunston we searched for another mooring. This stretch of canal is always busy with moored boats - including a number of trade boats (selling anything from coffee and beer to canal art). There is also a hire company who moor their vessels two deep along the main drag by the eighteenth century pumping house. One boat is permanently moored beside the Stop House. It's a cafe called *The Gongoozler's Rest* and it has a brilliant reputation. Unfortunately, lockdown meant it was closed so we would not be able to sample its wares on this visit. How many times will I be writing that? Unable to find a mooring, we had no choice but to start climbing the flight. We went through three of the six locks and stopped, just above the Admiral Nelson, in a relatively small pound between Locks 3 and 4. There were no other boats around us but it was such a pretty spot with the bushes in the hedgerow opposite turning a beautiful golden red colour.

That afternoon Pip spotted mold in both the bin cupboard and the pan cupboard - where we also keep some food. The difference in interior and exterior temperatures is creating a lot of condensation and we started to think of ways to mitigate the problem. To start with we used our electric dehumidifier, as well as some free-standing ones we had bought in B&M for a pound each. They are simply plastic containers half-filled with foam balls that sit between two permeable membranes. They seemed to work, as the next day we noticed that water had appeared in the bottom section. We concluded that these efforts were not enough to cure the mold and that we needed to do something to help insulate the boat further. More on this later (bet you can't wait)!

The next day we planned a walk back down the canal towards Napton, until we reached bridge 102 and then south to walk back through the villages of Flecknoe and Wolfhampcote. My poor planning once again meant we didn't really think through just how far this was and by the time we had finished we had covered nearly eight miles. The villages were lovely (I would go there again) but after also washing the outside of The Frog we were both very tired that evening.

Cleaning continued the next day and I have just rewatched the 'educational' section of our Lockdown Reflections Vlog, the one where I swept The Frog's chimney for the first time (sounds like an episode of Friends). Such were our boredom levels by this point that we got very excited about the increased draw we saw on the newly swept fire. Sad but true.

That night, Pip was looking at messages on social media and noticed that the pound between locks five and six (two pounds above us) had been almost drained of water because somebody had left a paddle open on Lock 5. I went out in the dark and checked our ropes and noticed the water level was definitely up where we were moored. This incident highlighted to us how vulnerable we were being tied up in a small pound between locks. If the same issue occurred at Lock 3, below us, we would be in trouble. At best, we would be grounded or have our ropes snap under the tension caused by falling water levels. At worst, in extreme circumstances, we could even capsize. Either way we had a fitful night and agreed we would move the next morning and head off through Braunston Tunnel.

CHAPTER 21: A SLOW BOAT TO CRICK

It's Friday 13th and we question if this is the ideal day to move again. We both agreed, however, that we did not want to spend another night exposed where we were. As we were preparing The Frog to move off, I spotted a man with a windlass in his hand walking up to Lock 4. I asked if he was on a boat climbing the flight. He said no, but he was helping the Fuel Boat through. Fuel boats are really helpful at all times but during lockdown they were a godsend to many boaters. They typically carry diesel, coal, wood and gas. Some also have a few chandlery items on board. I asked if we could join them on the climb (some fuel boats need more space in the lock). Luckily we were fine to go along - which would make the lock work a lot easier for Pip. The boat was owned by Jules Fuels and I can only estimate its age as some time in the early twentieth century. It was powered by an ancient (but beautifully kept) diesel engine that chugged away with a rhythm I could have listened to all day. The helmsman not only had a tiller to operate but also a wheel and a series of levers that controlled the drive (don't ask me how.) The climb of the last three locks was a pleasure and in Lock five we even bought two bags of coal - which cheered up the fuel boat helmsman no end. I have just searched for Jules Fuels online and took time out to watch a YouTube video recorded in November 2021 (a year after we shared the locks at Braunston). It shows the boat at work, bringing vital supplies to boaters all along the canal network, in all weathers.

We reached the top of the flight and marvelled at the quaint Top Lock cottage and the helmsman on the Fuel Boat asked if I minded if he left the lock first (and therefore entered the tunnel first). Of course I said he could and when we reached the tunnel entrance I understood why! He entered the tunnel without slowing down and, as far I could see, did not put on his headlight. Clearly he had traversed the tunnel so many times he didn't need to do either. He was a very skilled boatman and he disappeared into the darkness with us following much more slowly behind with the headlight and the newly purchased handheld lamp fully on.

Braunston tunnel is over two thousand yards (one thousand eight hundred metres) long. It was opened in 1796 and has a slight 'S' bend near one end, caused by soil movement during construction, which made it vital that I paid attention all the way through. Whilst the tunnel is wide enough for two boats to pass, lockdown meant it was very unlikely we would meet anyone coming the other way - and so it proved. Despite this, my diary says I did not enjoy the tunnel. About a third of the way in I even experienced a slight feeling of panic - which I had no choice but to quickly suppress. It seemed, no matter how hard I concentrated, we kept drifting to the left - even touching the wall at one point. I thought this was something to do with the slight kink and it was not until we had almost reached the exit, and I came close to ploughing into the left hand wall, that I realised the kink was actually only in one place. The other incidents were clearly just a reflection of my poor boat-handling skills!

We emerged into a dimpsy November morning - made worse by the many trees lining the canal at this point. We moored immediately and walked into Daventry to stock up with food again. The two mile walk there was fine but coming back with a full rucksack was very hard work! We moved off and searched for a suitable overnight spot, ideally nearer to other boats. We found a nice mooring near Bridge 10. Just ahead of us was Norton junction and the start of the Leicester Line (our route to Crick) but lockdown meant we had to stay here a few days until there was a genuine need to move again.

The next few days are spent exploring the local countryside. We took a walk down the Grand Union to the bottom of the Buckby Flight and Whilton Marina. Whilton was one of the marinas we visited during our boat search. Old records we found on board also confirmed that the previous owners had actually bought The Frog out of Whilton. Boating really is a small world. When we reached the marina, we left the towpath to pick up a B road and headed south west towards Norton village itself. After a quick look around the village we took a further turn, this time to the north, and our route eventually intersected with the canal back near our mooring.

The next day we walked again - this time to the village of Welton. Not far up the Leicester line is Welton Hythe Marina - which is the winter home of Ange D'Leau (Wolfgang and Marlene's boat). They had told us how sweet the village was so we were keen to explore it.

On our Vlog we captured the welcome sign at the entrance to the village. Next to it was another claiming the village was twinned with Cape Town. Clearly they have a developed sense of humour in Welton.

When we got back we checked our water levels and started planning our next move accordingly. We thought that there was no accessible tap at Norton (this was my fault as when we first arrived I was sent off with the water bottles to fetch drinking water. When I reached the junction I headed for the bin enclosure - which was towards the top lock on the Buckby flight. Here I also found a water tap and assumed it was the only one around. In actual fact, there is another just around the bend at the start of the Leicester line). So, armed with this erroneous information, we thought we needed to go all the way to the Watford Flight of locks to fill with water (pumping out at Welton Hythe Marina en-route). Pip did some research and discovered that the flight was locked and that passage would have to be booked with the CRT. At this point we did not know why and assumed it was to do with Covid restrictions. We phoned the marina and booked a pump out for two days later. We decided not to book the flight as the CRT told us they would need a definitive day and time and, at that point, we were not sure how quickly we would need to move again.

To help in our planning, the next day we walked the four mile round trip along the towpath to check out the marina and to see the flight for ourselves. As we set off on our recce at the junction we crossed a tall wooden footbridge that takes the towpath over the Leicester Line. The bridge is right next to a really sweet cottage overlooking the sharp turning off the main Grand Union. To get to the cottage you have to use the same footbridge and I'm sure the lucky inhabitants must feel like they are on a little island idyll. The magic was broken only by their little Jack Russell terrier doing a great job of seeing off all-comers (as they always do). As we descended from the bridge Pip pointed out the other water point which I had previously overlooked. In my defence, it was very small.

On our walk, the canal almost followed the course of the A5 (Watling Street, the famous Roman Road), which passed over our heads at Watling Street Bridge (5). Welton Hythe Marina looked nice and its entrance was wide and accessible - phew! I concluded that I could swing The Frog in and turn sharply to face back out onto the canal before reversing onto the pump out point. That was a relief and showed us once again the benefit of these little sorties to plan our route. To our right we could hear the hum of heavy traffic getting louder - interspersed with the occasional thunder of a passing train. Just before the flight, where the M1 comes very close to the Canal, we spotted the famous Watford Gap Services through some trees and decided to go and explore. You will not be surprised that there was not a lot to see here and I guess this anecdote goes to show just how bored we had become during lockdown (the fact that it was open made it a bit of a novelty). My diary entry reads: '...*the services were really small and dreary*'.

Finally, we reached the flight and it became clear why the CRT did not allow boaters to use them on their own. It has seven locks - four of which are in a tight staircase in the middle. They are narrow and deep and, in total, they rise over fifty two feet in just a few hundred yards. They would be a challenge to any but an experienced boater. It would also be an issue if two boats approached from different directions at the same time. So the booking regime allowed the CRT to not only keep boaters safe but to also control the flow of both water and boats. More on the flight later when we actually ascend it.

Just before the first lock there was a water point and above the top lock there were CRT bins. The village of Crick was only two more miles up the canal (three miles cross-country - the Crick Tunnel had no footpath through it) and we concluded we could walk to the shops when we needed food. Whilst there were no other boats in sight (not surprising with the need to book the flight) we decided that we could moor just before the water point until we needed to pump out again.

The next day we set off. It was dry but overcast when we left our mooring but the day was immediately made more colourful when a kingfisher flew across our path and perched on a neighbouring boat. I was really pleased that Pip caught it on video - which is not easy to do - and it is now in our Slow Boat to Crick Vlog (Number 10). I made the sharp turn onto the Leicester Line in one go - much to my amazement and delight - and I reflected once again on the benefit of knowing how my tiller actually worked!

We stopped immediately and filled with water. The tap here is VERY slow and it was about ninety minutes before we were on our way again. We retraced our steps of the previous day, but this time on the boat and we were soon approaching Welton Hythe Marina. The manouvre to get alongside the pump-out goes well and we chatted about Wolfgang and Marlene with the attendant. It seemed they were both well-known and well-liked. Why was I not at all surprised? We were filled with diesel and I commented to Pip in the Vlog that we had achieved our optimum state: full of water, full of diesel and empty of poo. These little triumphs kept us going through the darker days of lock down! It was not long until we reached our new mooring and we tied up for the afternoon. We felt like we were in the middle of nowhere. In reality, the A5 is just through a small group of trees and beyond that is a main railway line - whilst to our right we can hear the M1 only a few hundred yards away.

The next day we walked the three miles to Crick. It was a lovely walk. We climbed up the flight and along the towpath to Kilsby Road bridge (8). Here we turned south east and headed down the Kilsby Road towards the village of Watford. After a few hundred yards, we turned left onto Watford Road and, after crossing a cattle grid, we found ourselves on what felt like an unadopted road with sheep grazing freely on either side. We continued and crossed a further grid before the lane became steeper and we began the climb up to the outskirts of the village.

We explored Crick and then headed for the Co-op to get some provisions. I have let my sister know we are near but she is working at the Doctor's surgery today so, after a short circular walk, we took a taxi back down the A5 to a Caravan showroom that sat right next to the lock flight. A short walk through some trees and we were back to The Frog. The taxi fare was ten pounds so we immediately decided we would get a Tesco delivery the next time we needed food.

The days passed slowly and we looked for chores to do. We had a socially-distanced (in the garden) visit to Helen and Graham who kindly gave us some old insulation board which I cut to shape to line the bin cupboard and pantry. We noticed the difference immediately as the new surface stayed warm and did not attract moisture. We also cracked open the skylights more often and kept the fire burning at a higher temperature. Again, both actions seemed to help to reduce the condensation.

The following day was lovely, but cold, so we decided to take a walk over Watling Street and, by footpath, up to the village of Ashby St Ledgers. Not only is the village really attractive but it is also historically significant. At its heart is a lovely Manor House. Buildings have been on this site since Norman times and in 1375 the house was passed into the Catesby family. After the Battle of Bosworth (1485) it was confiscated (the Catesbys were clearly on the 'wrong' side), but later it was returned to the family. Keen historians will recognise the name Catesby. The family were staunch Catholics and bravely adhered to their faith despite persecution throughout the various Protestant reigns of the sixteenth century. However, when King James I (James VI of Scotland) came to the throne, in 1603, the family feared further pressure on their beliefs and decided to act. Robert Catesby and his co-conspirators were said to have planned the now infamous Gunpowder Plot in the gatehouse of the manor. Ironically, many historians believe that James I was actually fairly tolerant of other faiths but following the failed assassination attempt, significant additional restrictions were imposed on Catholics and, of course, the conspirators were all killed whilst being captured or gruesomely executed.

Several days passed with walks into the village of Watford (small but pretty) and Crick again. On Thursday, our new cratch cover was delivered. It looked beautiful - except for one thing. The cut out to accommodate the chimney had been taken off the wrong side. If we used it as it was, the cover would be touching the chimney with an obvious fire risk. This meant I had to put the old cover back on and wait a few days for the manufacturers to come back with the error corrected. Annoying but not the end of the world. Of possible interest, the new cover cost us £1200. This is a lot of money but the finished product would look great, give us additional insulation and waterproofing and last for many years - making The Frog even more desirable when we finally had to sell her.

That night I ran up to the Crick tunnel and back and was really shocked by the water level in the top pound of the flight. It was extremely low and of particular concern because we were booked to go through the flight the next day. Our passage was ten o'clock, but two CRT volunteers arrived a lot earlier. They walked down to the pumping house, just by the water point ahead of us, and set about turning on the pump to correct the water levels. The top pound was soon full and we were set to go.

The flight went smoothly with the volunteers' help. The turn between lock two and the staircase was a bit tricky but everything else was plain sailing. The locks were built in 1814 and were designed to take narrowboats. Plans to widen them at the time of the major Grand Union refurbishment in the late 1920s came to nothing as it was felt the level of traffic and the high cost would prove uneconomic. Today, the passage through the locks takes about forty five minutes but at the height of the season, boats can wait for two hours or more for their turn. On the day we went through we were told there was just one other boat due that day but the volunteers were really pleased their services were once again being called upon.

The flight completed, we headed off for Crick Tunnel. On the way we met a lady, cruising towards the locks, who did not realise she should have booked the flight. We suggested that she either got a move on (as the volunteers would probably still be there) or call the CRT immediately to ask if they could stay. I am not sure what happened but I hope that she got through ok.

Crick tunnel would be our final challenge of the day. We could not go into the Marina until the 2nd of December - today was Friday 27th November - so we needed to find another mooring for a few days closer to Crick. This tunnel, also completed in 1814, is one thousand five hundred and twenty eight yards long (fourteen hundred metres) and is one of the leakiest I think we have ever traversed. It was built using around two million bricks. It also has the reputation of being haunted by a screaming woman (a bogart) with the name of Kit Crewbucket (not sure how she got that name). Legend has it she will either drive you mad or cook you breakfast. I put in my order for Eggs Benedict and we entered the tunnel with trepidation. In the end, it was dark and wet but quiet and we managed to avoid any calamities. I didn't get my breakfast and I didn't go mad (I can't say the same for Pip who has been acting quite strange ever since!) We left the tunnel, cruised under Bridge 11 and moored just before Crick Wharf. That evening we decided to treat ourselves and I walked to the other end of the village to collect an Indian Takeaway.

The next few days we explored the wider countryside. Yelvertoft is a lovely village a couple of miles from Crick. At that point we did not know that there was a lovely footpath leading from the canal towpath right into the village so we walked the B Road that connects the two settlements. The road is really straight and boring, especially on a misty day in November. Our only diversion was dodging 'boy-racers' who seemed to use the dead straight road for time trials. We completed our walk by creating a large circuit, joining the A428 for the last leg - another ill-advised decision with more traffic dodging necessary for self-preservation.

We needed to stock up, so the next day we caught the bus to the big Tescos in Rugby. The store was very busy and social distancing seemed to be optional! The trip took a total of four hours and we were very relieved to get back to the sanctuary of The Frog. It was now Monday 30th November and we called the marina to confirm our berth and ask if we could come in a day early as we were running low on water. Happily, they agreed.

The next morning we walked the (now found) footpath to Yelvertoft and explored the village in more detail. Toft is a Danish word for settlement so it made sense that at its heart was an Italian deli called Squisito ('Exquisite' in English). It looked fabulous, but unfortunately Covid meant it was not open. On the edge of the village, the lovely Grade 1 listed All Saints Church is worth a peruse. We walked back to The Frog and made our move to get water at the nearby wharf, before heading for the marina. I successfully negotiated the marina entrance and pulled up to the service wharf. We met Mark, the Marina Manager and a few other members of the team. They were all really friendly and we were made to feel very welcome. Our berth was directly opposite the office. This felt close to the action but we soon discovered it was a very long walk around the edge of the expansive basin that lay in between us. Hey Ho - we were only going to be here a month or so…….famous last words.

CHAPTER 22: CRICK: A PAIN IN THE NECK?

Before I explain the title of this chapter I will leap immediately to the defence of the village of Crick. It is lovely. The centre has a charming main street with a mixture of quaint cottages. It has a post office and convenience store within an easy walk of the marina and a Co-op store further down Main Street, opposite The Wheatsheaf public house (then closed because of Covid of course). On a side road, it has a fab Indian takeaway and nearby a deli to die for, called '*Pickle and Pie*'. They did the most amazing themed Friday night takeaways (Italian, Great Pies of the UK, etc..) and we made use of them on more than one occasion. Oh - and my sister Helen lives here with her husband, Graham - who grew up in these parts. If we were passing through, on our continuing Odyssey, we would have reflected on Crick's prettiness, facilities and a lovely visit with my sister - no doubt. However, the ever-continuing restrictions of Covid (which switched from lockdown in November to a 'zonal' system from December onwards) meant we actually ended up being 'guests' of Crick for over two and a half months!

By the time we left in late February let's just say we had 'done' Crick. When you are in a marina, especially through winter, when many boats are left here for safekeeping, there is inevitably a boat on either side of your own. This meant we only had a view from the bow and the already dimpsy light of mid-winter struggled to get in through the side portholes. Thankfully we had three skylights, but nevertheless we still felt very hemmed in. We also did not have any means of transport, and Covid (that word again) meant we could not do anything with our nearby family without breaking the social distancing rules. I must stress that the team in the Marina made the whole thing more bearable. Mark was no Derek. I am sure he did wonder at my boating prowess at times (more about that later) but he never made me feel stupid. We were welcomed with open arms and that feeling never faded in the time we were there. When we needed help - Mark and the team gave it to us. Pip and I look back fondly on them as a group of people.

So, in summary, Crick was not the 'Pain in the neck' and it is very unfair to even suggest that it was the village or the marina team that made us feel this way. It was Covid that bore the burden of blame -

Crick and the marina just happened to be the backdrop of our moored-up misery.

Well, having now really brought you down I guess I should try and pick you back up again. I am sorry for the mini rant but it is always a good thing to contextualise the story. All that follows from now until our departure in February can be read with greater understanding of the monotony and repetition of our 'groundhog' existence (maybe we should have left the marina on February 2nd and not, as we eventually did, on the 21st - note to self: plan better for comic references).

My diary has a note at the bottom of the page dated 2nd December 2020. It reads: '**CRICK MARINA 12 WEEKS!!**'. The next entry is for Monday 22nd February, when we left our mooring (it was a travel log after all). However, for completeness, things happened in Crick that I should record here - some of them were even good. So, as I search my memory banks, here goes.

We were of course in December and our attention turned to where we would spend Christmas and indeed most of this month. Pip's son, Ian, and his family lived in London. We had agreed that we would catch a train from Rugby and spend some of the month leading up to Christmas with them (that being, technically, our 'home' address). Helen kindly drove us to the station (not sure that was allowed really but she worked in a surgery and was one of the first to be double vaccinated). Unfortunately, the train was cancelled and after a long wait at Rugby station we finally managed to get a train to Milton Keynes. There we had another long wait until we eventually made it into Euston. We arrived very late and struggled across London on the sparsely populated, but still unnerving, subway system.

We spent a couple of weeks in London but the time came to leave as other family members were intending to visit there for Christmas (the one that Boris promised would see restrictions lifted for). This relaxation also meant that we could visit Pip's sister for a few days over Christmas. It was all planned: we caught the train to Chippenham to pick up our hire car. We were booked into a pub in Wotton Under Edge for a night - allowing us to explore some of the local villages as possible places to live after our odyssey. I remember the day well. We had a fabulous time and loved Wotton.

It was the 20th December, the 'Strictly' final was on the telly and we were planning a meal in the bar to watch it. Our evening (and much more) was ruined however when Boris made his shock TV announcement - reversing his previous commitment to 'make Christmas happen' by allowing a five day moratorium on restrictions. He introduced a new Tier 4 (covering huge areas of England - including all of the South East) where mixing of households was banned. He also said that in other tiers you could only gather for one day (Christmas day itself).

This decision effectively scuppered our Welsh Christmas plans. Instead, we met Pip's sister at the services just over the Severn estuary and traded presents from the boots of our cars (it looked a bit like a drug deal going down) and headed back towards London (which was our home address when we were cruising and where we were, technically, allowed to be). The other relatives, who were intending to go there for Christmas, could no longer do so, consequently, there was now space for us to stay through the festive season. However, en-route we received a call from our daughter-in-law Brittany. Billy, our eldest grandson, had been in contact with a positive case. At this point, there was still a huge fear/paranoia surrounding positive cases, so we agreed that we would not stay after all. Unfortunately, we still had some of our clothes in the house. This meant we had to drive all the way to Thornton Heath and collect our things before taking the long drive back to the marina - making a sad day even worse. Our festive plans in tatters, we had a fleeting hello/goodbye with Ian and Brittany (the children stayed inside) and we headed north up the M1, facing Christmas alone on The Frog!

Needless to say, we made the most of it. We put up lights - inside and out. Christmas day was cold but bright and after we exchanged presents we walked around the marina seeing who else was in residence. There were a few boaters on site - but not many. We called family to trade season's greetings and I erected one of my presents - a weather station that sat on top of the boat and sent information to a monitor fixed to the inside wall of The Frog. It gave us internal and external temperatures, wind speed and direction, air pressure, rainfall and a forecast of what we could expect in the next twenty four hours. All of this displayed in a 'take your pick' of coloured LED digits. It was made by Bresser (great German technology) and I loved it. The only thing it struggled with was wind direction (or at least it did when we were cruising). I had to reset the orientation to get any sense out of it everytime we re-moored. In the marina, of course, it worked fine.

It was now post Christmas and our plan, now that Billy had not contracted Covid and was a week post 'contact', was to go back down to London and spend New Year at our 'home address'. The day we were packing up to go Mark, the manager, paid us a visit. He saw that we had packed bags and asked us what we were planning. We filled him in - only to be very disappointed by his reply. The South East was in Tier 4 (the highest and 'worst'), whilst the marina was then in Tier 3. Understandably, Mark had a responsibility to protect his team and other boaters and he told us we would not be allowed back into the marina if we made this trip. Whilst we understood, we were very upset by yet another change to our plans. In the end we negotiated with Mark and undertook to self isolate for ten days upon our return if we could get back into the marina. Thankfully, he agreed as he could see how important this trip was to us. We also made the point that whilst in Thornton Heath we would only be in the house with the family - effectively self-isolating there.

We took the trip but in the end we only stayed a couple of days - and returned to the marina on the 30th December - to spend New Year alone and begin our ten days of isolation (only leaving the boat when others were not around). It was a dreadful way to see in 2021. The only upside was that the weather turned really cold and it snowed on a number of occasions, making the forced exile onboard a cosy alternative to the outside. Our fire was burning all day, everyday!

We kept ourselves distracted as best we could. One of my presents to Pip was a customised 1000 piece jigsaw puzzle. It had a picture of me at the tiller of The Frog. After the inevitable, and deserved, narcissistic references from Pip, we took a few days to complete it. I can honestly say that there is nothing more sobering than spending hours scrutinising every imperfection on your face (of which there are many).

Once our lockdown was over we emerged bleary-eyed into a very snowy landscape. We walked - a lot. We got faster and faster as we criss-crossed the village on our many outings. I am sure the neighbourhood watch would have had us on some form of suspect list. There must have been countless CCTV images of 'that couple walking as if they were being chased'. We can honestly say that we now know every footpath, lane, muddy field and dangerous main road that Crick and its environs has to offer. We did at least get fitter, a continuation of the plan we made in Cornwall to 'out-fit' the virus.

In previous chapters I wrote about the boxes on the roof of our boat and explained that they were (expensively) tailor-made. I have already highlighted that they leaked but there was one other major design flaw that only came to light in the harsh winter weather at the marina. When we had them built, the carpenter asked what paint he should use. We took advice from Emma, in Newbury marina, and she recommended a certain marine grade paint that was very hardy and was designed to withstand the harsh weather associated with life at sea (and, on that basis, more than adequate for our cruising on the canal network). They looked great (to start with) but by mid January the outer layer of paint was peeling off in great swathes! Underneath this top layer was what was clearly a primer or undercoat and having researched the fabulous paint the carpenter had used, I read that it should only ever be applied directly to raw wood and NOT onto any other painted surface. With all the best intentions, the carpenter had effectively created a peeling time-bomb by not following the paint instructions fully.

One thing we did have, in bucket loads, was time, so we decided we would re-paint the boxes in a standard external white gloss. The challenge, of course, was where to do this in the depths of winter. We could not paint them in-situ as this risked getting paint on the roof of The Frog as well as the obvious likelihood that they would be rained/snowed on during what we knew would be a long drying period. We approached Mark and he offered us the use of a small 'garden' shed right next to the office - for a nominal monthly rental. This was perfect. We could fit both boxes in (up on their edges) and paint them over the next month - rotating them as we did so. First we needed to get the boxes off the top of the boat and around the marina to the shed (quite a long way). The boxes were heavy but Pip and I managed to get them off the boat and onto the shingle road running around the marina. We balanced the first one on a wheelbarrow and started to walk it around. The boxes were big and the wheelbarrow was tiny and as a result, the box kept tipping and falling off. This was going to be a long and difficult walk!

Mark came to our rescue. It was now about five PM and he was heading 'home' to his own boat at the other end of the marina. He saw us struggling and offered the use of his large van. We opened the back doors and managed to get one box in - but not the second. Creative as ever, Mark grabbed one of the green trolleys that boaters used to carry things from their cars to their boats. This was lower than the wheelbarrow and slightly longer. It also had a hook on the front arm that could be placed over the tow bar of the van. It was still quite unstable, so Pip and I had to walk alongside the trailer holding the box in place. Mark drove off slowly but still fast enough that Pip and I had to jog to keep up. Nevertheless, we made it and we were soon sliding the boxes into the newly rented shed (which was brand new and, as a result, very clean).

Our first job was to get the rest of the outer layer of paint off. This was dirty and hard work. Ironically, whilst in places it was falling off, elsewhere it was stubbornly staying put. We placed each box, in turn, onto a folding picnic table we carried on The Frog and got the sandpaper out. It took hours to get back to a surface I was happy to paint but I would not compromise on the look. They had pride of place on the lovely Frog and, therefore, they had a lot to live up to. I lost count of the number of visits I made to the cold shed to apply the two layers of paint all over the tops and sides of the boxes but the Forth Bridge came to mind. Finally, they were finished and all we had to do then was get them back to the boat. Having learnt our lesson bringing them over, we simply waited until our next pump out. To pump out, we would leave our berth and bring The Frog over to the service quay - right in front of the office and about fifty yards from the shed. I asked Ron, one of the marina team, to help me carry the boxes down to the quay and, with Pip's help, we lifted them up onto the roof a lot more easily than Pip and I had got them off.

The final two steps, having returned to our berth, were to clean out the mold on the inside of the boxes and reconnect the solar panels. The former was not a nice job but at least it was not taxing. The latter was harder than it should have been. Foolishly, I did not label the cables when I took them apart. Not only did the boxes have to be re-connected to the boat but they also had to be connected to each other - in the right order - for the system to start working again. Needless to say, I did not get it right the first time and it was a few days of trial and error before I was happy. My distant reflections are that whilst painting the boxes was a complete pain, the task did at least help January pass with a distraction. That was how boring our existence was by this point.

I mentioned, above, the need to pump out regularly and take The Frog over to the service quay to do this. This seemingly easy task brings me to the next 'highlight' of our stay in Crick. I think it was late January and we were on the service quay having completed our pump out. The usual process to get back into our berth was to pull out and forward and then reverse. As you cannot steer when in reverse the process took several forward and backwards motions - steering as we move forward to help line us up with the narrow gap that was our berth. By this time I must have completed the manouvre four or five times but on this particular day the wind was howling across the exposed marina - coming from the South. The net result was that the Frog would not turn. Every time I started reversing the stern was blown back the other way - effectively straightening us up. Mark spotted my repeated attempts and came out of the office with one of the female marina staff (sorry I have forgotten her name). They suggested that I go down the marina and turn around, through 180 degrees, and come back past the berth. I was then to swing out and reverse back in from the other side. In that way, the wind would be working to push the stern in the right direction to straighten her up for entry (rather than stopping her turning at all). So, I headed off down the marina and tried to turn. At that point the wind was still raging and no matter how I tried I could not get The Frog to turn. I was, it had to be said, very nervous about using full revs in a confined space - as I did not want to hit any of the other moored boats (and, yes, I could hear Derek's voice in my head as I pussyfooted around).

Eventually, realising I was not going to make it on my own, Mark asked me to head back to the quay. The two of them climbed on board and the lady took the controls. It turns out she lives aboard, in the marina, but has a sideline as a boat mover and she clearly knew what she was doing. She put us into high revs and headed across the marina, swinging at the last minute and accelerating even more to ensure the bow swung around. Once she was past a certain point, the wind did the rest and before we knew it we were facing north. She cruised past the berth and started the reversing manoeuvre to get us in. Mark jumped onto the pontoon holding a line and helped pull her in. Job done, I had a brief chat with my saviours. Once again they were so gracious. The helmswoman even went into detail about a similar problem she had had with a boat she was moving - really making me feel a lot better about needing her help.

It's now February and there is really only one more thing to catalogue about our stay in Crick. Covid stopped us spending any intimate time with my sister, Helen, and her family despite them being only about a mile away. One cold and miserable Sunday, Pip received a Facebook message from Helen offering us one of her legendary roast dinners. She said she would plate it up and bring it covered in tin foil - along with a jug of gravy - into the marina. We did cook the odd roast on The Frog but it was not easy with such a small oven, so we rarely went to the trouble. To get a lovely Sunday roast delivered to our door was a thoughtful gesture and we were very grateful for both Helen's generosity and her prowess with a roast potato!

CHAPTER 23: FREEDOM!

Partial lockdown was still in place and there was no indication of when it would be fully lifted. We had booked a passage into Liverpool (through the canal link off the Leeds and Liverpool canal) for the middle of April and we needed to start making our way north at some point (whilst sticking to the rules about only moving for essentials). It could be argued that staying in the marina until lockdown was fully lifted would be the right thing to do. We had food, water, power and a pump out all on hand. So there was no real reason to move - no reason other than our sanity and the fact that we were paying a monthly mooring fee. At this time, we were also seeing an increasing stream of other boaters coming in to use the services. Boaters who were not based in the marina. It was clear that spring was not far away and other boaters were starting to move in greater numbers. We also had to make a decision before we paid mooring fees for the next month. Do we stay or start heading slowly north, obeying restrictions and assuming that they would be ended soon.

We wrestled with the decision but finally left on Sunday 21st February. I remember it so well. The River Soar was in flood which meant we could not take our planned route up the Leicester Line, so we left the marina and turned back south - heading once more for Braunston.

That first afternoon we only cruised two and a half miles - back through Crick tunnel to a mooring near Bridge 8, waiting for our booked slot to descend the Watford Flight. When we stopped, we both commented on how light and bright the boat felt. Our view was once more the canal on one side and the towpath on the other and it felt good to be moving again - albeit at a snail's pace.

So what was the plan? Well, we would retrace our steps back to Braunston but instead of turning onto the South Oxford Canal (the way we had come) we would continue straight onto the North Oxford - heading for the Coventry and the Birmingham and Fazeley canals, before joining the Trent and Mersey. There was clearly lots more after this but that is enough scene-setting for now.

Monday 22nd February saw us wake to pouring rain and a very wet descent of the Watford flight. Once again, we thanked the CRT volunteers and apologised for getting them out on such an inclement day and, as before, they both said how much they loved doing this job and that we were very welcome. Bless them. We moored for lunch in our previous nine day mooring spot. There was one other vessel moored in front of us. We had seen it before - when we had walked down to the flight as one of our 'escape from Crick' rambles. When we saw it the first time it looked a little neglected - today it looked ransacked. It had a message pinned to it that told us the owners were aware and there was no reason to report the damage. A chill went down my spine. We moored here for nine days and at the time we had felt quite isolated. Had vandals checked out our boat too and saw that we were always here overnight and decided against attacking The Frog? The sad sight of the second boat was a reminder of just how vulnerable we were out there and just how careful we had to be - especially as we would now be heading north towards the metropolis of Coventry.

After lunch, we couldn't wait to pull away from the flight and head back towards Norton junction. On the way, Pip was experimenting with her new selfie-stick taking wide shots over the side of The Frog. It was not good for the nerves as her IPhone was dangling precariously above the canal. We pulled into a lovely mooring point on the approach to Norton Junction. The views were great and we were near other boats and felt safe. Today was Monday and we decided we would stay here until Saturday. Our timing was driven by a grocery delivery we had arranged for Sunday in Braunston and the fact that we would almost certainly need to pump out by that point. I also note that in my diary I had started to record the distance we cruised and the number of locks we completed each day. Today's read: *'21/2 miles, 7 locks'*.

Having just rewatched Vlog 13 I am reminded that whilst we were moored here the time came for me to have a haircut. Finding a good barber/hairdresser at any time, when you are on the move, is not easy. During the pandemic they were one of the establishments that had to close so I had no option but to let Pip cut my hair. The clip in the video is quite funny as I berate Pip's cutting skills (a red rag to a very accomplished seamstress) and she defends herself whilst stabbing me in the scalp! In reality, she did a very good job and she was quite right to remind me that in the previous Autumn a hairdresser had commented positively on her efforts when I had my last 'land-based' haircut.

We had reached the stage of the pandemic where vaccinations were available for ever decreasing age groups. Pip already qualified for her first dose and so she booked herself into Asda (yes, Asda) in Watford (the big town, not the little village near Crick) - not somewhere we would have naturally had on our odyssey bucket list. On Wednesday, we walked up to Long Buckby to check out the train station and, happy with what we saw, we went back to the boat to book our trip for the following day. On the walk back, we reunited a man and his card wallet - which had fallen out of his back pocket. He was VERY grateful. My diary tells me that the weather was really warming up (after our depths of winter in Crick, I guess everything is relative).

Next day we walked a total of six miles - to and from the train station at Long Buckby and to and from Asda at the other end. Pip received her vaccination (which felt good in what were still uncertain and troubling times). We asked if I could have mine ahead of schedule (being five years younger than Pip, I didn't yet qualify but we explained how difficult it was to arrange a vaccination when cruising). Unfortunately, they were too busy (with three hundred and seventy six people booked in) and all of their doses for the day had been allocated. We could have hung around until the end of the day and taken any that were then left over but we didn't fancy walking back from Long Buckby in the dark (and, to be honest, by this point we had had enough of Watford for one day).

Unfortunately, Pip had a reaction to the injection and overnight her temperature reached thirty nine degrees (according to our 'in your ear' thermometer). She was not up to doing much the next day and had to rest after a very short walk up the towpath. The sun was shining and it was about thirteen degrees (balmy for February) so I headed off to walk the towpath to Braunston Tunnel to check out the route ahead of our departure the next day. I remember the bridges approaching Norton Junction looked fabulous in the winter sun and I put my camera to good use. The round trip was about six miles and the highlight of the walk was being surprised by a wonderful singing voice coming out of the tunnel exit. I was so entranced that I waited until the boat emerged and I could congratulate, what turned out to be, a lone female boater for her performance. I know the acoustics in the tunnel would have helped but this young lady really did belong on stage. She was clearly embarrassed, having not expected to come across anyone, and told me she hated the darkness of tunnels so much and singing helped her get over her fears. I thought about trying it myself on the next tunnel traverse, but when I suggested it to Pip you can guess at her reaction. There would be only one thing worse: Pip singing. She is a lover of all things seventies (and *Come on Eileen*, by Dexy's Midnight Runners) and seems to know the words to every '70's classic. There is only one problem; she thinks her voice is better than it is (but I wouldn't change her for the world).

On Saturday 27th we made a move down to the waterpoint under the bridge to fill up before our next leg back to Braunston. I took us around the junction (rather less successfully than when I did it in the opposite direction. Ironically, I oversteered and managed to put our nose into the bank of the garden belonging to the little cottage we so admired). Pip took the helm from here until we approached Braunston Tunnel. I took over just in time as we heard a boat coming the other way and I decided, for both our sakes, that we would hover outside the entrance until it had passed. I also had decided to take a new approach to tunnels: increasing our speed. This was partly inspired by the fuel boat we followed through in November but it also made a lot of sense. At higher speeds you had greater control as the rudder was more responsive and, unlike on the canal, there were no banks that would be damaged by a slight wake. Higher speed also meant you spent less time in the tunnel - a real benefit in my view. This method meant dominating the middle of the channel to avoid any risk of hitting the wall and, it followed, that the only time you needed to slow down was if a boat came the other way. Thankfully, on this occasion there were none and we were soon emerging into the daylight above the Braunston flight.

We completed the top three locks. Unfortunately, I forgot to take up our fenders and we lost one in the top lock. Despite our previous concerns at being in a small pound, as we were not staying for very long we moored in exactly the same spot as November - just facing the other way. We shopped and then settled down to watch England lose to Wales in the Six Nations (not sure why I put that in my diary or into this account for that matter. I guess I am feeling generous; as I write, England have just beaten Wales 3 - 0 in the 2022 FIFA World Cup).

The next day we walked the towpath, past the marina, and onto the North Oxford Canal. This was new territory for us and we wanted to check out potential mooring points for after we pump out in a couple of days. The sun was shining but our walk was cut short by the need to get back to the Admiral Nelson Pub car park and our expected Sainsbury's delivery. Chores completed, we walked back to the Stop House and visited the, now open, Gongoozlers' Rest Cafe. We were glad we did. I had an amazing bacon and fried mushroom bap which was big enough to feed a small family. Pip had a cheese scone. She definitely had 'bap envy' and proceeded to eat most of the lovely sauteed potatoes that came with my sandwich. I didn't mind - my 'half a pig' bap was more than enough - even for me.

My diary entry the next day started: *'February 29th - 1st March - idiot'*. Harsh but fair in what was obviously NOT a Leap Year. That was about the most interesting thing that happened that day (I cleaned the boat and bought a paper).

Braunston had an amazing shop for all things a boater may need. It was called West Midlands Chandlery and, on this visit, it was open and we needed a new chimney. The old one was starting to send drips of tar back down the outside of the internal chimney shaft. It also bore the scars of a few tunnel 'incidents' and, aesthetically, it was detracting from the rest of The Frog. We chose one that was a foot long (the previous one was 18 inches). Whilst this would sacrifice a degree of draw on the fire, it would help us going under low bridges and through tunnels. I have to say, looking back now on some of the close scrapes we were to encounter later in our odyssey, this was a very good decision. I drilled a few holes to fit the cap and the job was a good 'un. You can see the chimney in Vlog 13 (when we were still filming every mundane act to help fill our sad pandemic-impacted days).

Wednesday saw the need to pump out. We completed the final three locks and Pip walked ahead, with the radio, to check that the service wharf in Braunston Marina was clear. We turned into the marina, under the grand wrought iron bridge that reminded us that this entrance was where the Oxford Canal used to join the Grand

Union. We pumped out, filled with diesel and bought two bags of coal before reversing out onto the cut. The entrance was wide enough for me to make a 'several point' turn and we then pulled in immediately to fill with water.

Pip walked off to the Post Office to send her latest baby blanket (sold under her *'Narrowboat Knitting'* brand). I really should have highlighted this in my account of the 'Crick' hiatus. Pip knitted every single day whilst we were in the marina (and indeed when we were not in the marina) and was often walking up to the Post Office to send off her latest creation to a lucky Etsy customer.   On this occasion, she returned with pasties for lunch (Pip is half Cornish and, if she had less discipline, I know she would succumb to her 'pasty problem' more frequently).   I wasn't complaining.   My willpower was much worse and I didn't take any persuading to go 'St Piran' native! Our short cruise that day finished just past the South Oxford Canal junction (Bridge 94) where we moored at the very start of the North Oxford Canal: *1 Mile, 3 locks*

We did not move for the next few days and they were filled with domestic activity - the highlight of which was my sister, Helen delivering our inflatable kayak (which she kindly agreed to have sent to her home in Crick). We had long thought about getting a kayak. This one was an Intex K2 Challenger and was designed for two people to use together. Our thinking was sound - we loved walking, but there had to be other ways to exercise and fill the many lockdown hours when on board. We took our new purchase back to The Frog and immediately thought about where we would store it. It was so big (even when deflated) that it would not fit in the overhead boxes. Our only option was to keep it on the platform behind our bed, right in front of the stern door. This was fine, if we were not moving, but it did mean whenever we set off we had to move it onto the bed. That afternoon it was very cold - so we decided not to christen the kayak (which we eventually did on my birthday - three weeks later).

On Saturday 6th March Graham Norton announced, on his programme, that people who were fifty six could now book their vaccinations. We didn't hesitate and went online immediately to book a slot for me on 16th March in Coventry (which was kind of in the right direction for where we were heading) and a second, in June, in Chester.

That afternoon we left our mooring and headed north towards Hillmorton. Pip did most of the steering over the six miles or so until we reached the Hillmorton Locks and we moored before descending. We went for a walk but when we came back we noticed we were actually on a long term mooring and had to move again. We were so close to the locks we had no option but to go through the first (locks 6 and 7 - at Hillmorton the locks are in pairs). We were quite tired by this point so we moored again in the first pound above Locks 4 and 5. About forty minutes and a cup of tea later we heard a tap on the window. A passing boater, who had been moored above the locks for sometime, very kindly pointed out that Locks 4 and 5 were very leaky and it is not uncommon for the pound we were in to be half empty by the morning. This meant we risked at best a disturbed night (as the boat would lean as the water level fell) and, at worse, the ropes snapping and even toppling over (depending on the shape of the canal bed). We did not fancy either, so, despite our fatigue, we upped mooring pins and moved again. We completed the next two locks and finally moored a few hundred yards down from the water point below Locks 2 and 3 (we stopped to top up with water before we did so). Needless to say, having not moved much for some time, the seven miles and three locks had taken it out of us and we were pleased to finally put our feet up. My diary footnote today read: *'WIFI Download 80!'* (meaning our mobile wifi was delivering eighty megabytes per second. My WIFI at home is currently delivering twenty eight).

Hillmorton Locks are interesting. The CRT claimed in 2019 that they were the busiest locks on the entire network with more boats per year passing through here than any other locks on the system. Not sure how they know that but, needless to say, in the partial lockdown of early March 2021 it certainly didn't feel like it! The two-lock system I mentioned above came about when the Oxford Canal was straightened in the 1830s and 1840s. The Oxford was originally built as a contour canal (wherever possible following the lie of the land to avoid expensive cuttings, tunnels and locks). This meant the navigation distance from Napton to Coventry was about forty three miles (compared with only sixteen miles the way the crow flies). This was not an issue as long as the Canal had no competitor but, following the creation of the Grand Junction Canal, the Oxford came under severe commercial threat. The South Oxford lost traffic immediately as it switched to the Grand Junction route at Wigrams

Turn. The new Grand Junction company was forced, by Act Of parliament, to pay compensation to the Oxford Canal company, recognising this commercial impact. They also had to pay for the use of the five mile stretch of the Oxford Canal from Napton to Braunston - a vital 'gap' on the Grand Junction.

In the early nineteenth century, an alternative route to the Grand Junction Canal, from Birmingham to London, was to go north on the Birmingham and Fazeley, join the Coventry Canal at Fazeley Junction and then head South to Hawkesbury Junction to join the North Oxford and so reach Braunston to link up with the Grand Junction. It followed that there was a pressing need to improve this section of the North Oxford Canal to reduce its length and increase its capacity. The 'big guns' were called in: in 1827, Marc Isambard Brunel (father of the more well known Isambard Kingdom) was commissioned to survey the route and recommend amendments. Charles Vignoles carried out a further survey the following year and a new route was agreed upon - reducing the distance from Braunston to Coventry by just under fifteen miles. The remains of the original Newbold tunnel, a 'victim' of the changed route, can still be seen next to the churchyard in the village.

As part of this straightening project, it soon became clear that the single width locks at Hillmorton would become a bottleneck and in the late 1830s and into the 1840s, work was carried out to add the twin locks we now see on the flight. Not only would this allow twice as many boats to use the system at one time but an ingenious extra paddle was added linking the twin locks to each other. This meant that as long as another boater was not going in the same direction in the twin lock, the paddle could be opened to allow water to flow from one lock to the other. This reduced the lock filling time to a remarkable one minute twenty seconds!

Despite all this investment, competition from the Grand Junction and, later, the railways, sounded the commercial death knell for the Oxford Canal and it continued on a slow decline. Thankfully, it has now been preserved as a popular waterway for leisure cruisers and we can all still enjoy it today.

The next morning (Sunday 7th March) we needed groceries, so we walked the two and a half miles to Tescos at Rugby and took the opportunity to check out moorings nearby. When we travel to

Coventry for my vaccination, it would be by train, from Rugby, so we wanted to be moored as close as possible to the station. The moorings looked good, so we decided to go the next day and secure a good spot. Part of the rationale for this early move is in my diary which refers to the *'vaccination trip on Tuesday'*. The observant amongst you would be questioning this when my appointment is not until the sixteenth March (a week on Tuesday). Surely they can't get that wrong - can they? Oh yes we can - more later. We put the final touches to Vlog Number 13 and use the amazing Wifi to get it uploaded before we move.

We woke the next morning at ten to nine - reflecting our travails of the day before. The trip to Rugby was only about two and a half miles and we arrived before lunch - mooring just before Masters Bridge (58). In the PM, Pip is upset by a comment on the newly posted Vlog - criticising us for moving our boat during lockdown. I rationalised it with Pip: the correspondent was almost certainly a pleasure boater who did not live aboard. Consequently, he would not have understood the lockdown rules in detail as they applied to live aboard boaters. In addition, many non-live-aboards could not even access their boats and he was probably feeling the surge of spring sap in his tiller hand and would have been frustrated that he could not join us on the network. At the end of the day, if you post on social media you may well get lots of positive feedback but, along with this, you do put yourself out there to be shot at. I was sanguine about this but Pip took things very personally.

The next day we walked into town to the station and caught a train to Coventry. The journey was only about ten minutes and we arrived well ahead of my appointment time. We walked into the City Centre and took a look around to kill some time. Finally, we took a taxi and headed off towards the vaccination centre - which was out in a suburb - and I looked at my appointment booking to check the time we were expected. This is when I noticed the date of the appointment and realised that we really were there nice and early; seven days and one hour early to be precise. We were, by this time, committed to paying for the taxi so we decided to go to the vaccination centre and try and cadge a slot. The centre was at a local chemist and the staff were very friendly and understanding but gave the same response as we received in Watford (they were fully booked but we were welcome to wait until six o'clock and hope for a cancellation). Coventry was ok but those of you who have been will understand why a whole afternoon in the city, during lockdown, was not high on our to do list. We decided to make our way back to Rugby and return next week. To save booking another taxi we walked back to the station (about three miles) and returned to The Frog, as my diary says, '*empty-armed*'.

CHAPTER 24: RUGBY ANYONE?

We had not planned to move anytime soon, but the fact we still needed to travel to Coventry meant we were now committed to staying in Rugby for a further week.

Our bin was full and our Nicholson told us that there were CRT facilities at Newbold - about one and a half miles along the towpath. We set off, carefully carrying a full and very flimsy plastic bag of rubbish. Not the nicest way to get to know the local area. We arrived at where the bin should be but couldn't find any trace of it. There were a number of moored boats and we asked a fellow boater if he knew where it could be found. He said there had been no bin here for about eighteen months and the CRT had relocated it to……….the park by Bridge 58 (where we were moored)! One forehead slap later we set off to carry the rubbish back to the boat - with the bag getting thinner and flimsier with every pot hole I stepped into. Thankfully, it held out and we finally crossed the bridge to the park opposite our mooring. The bin was actually tucked away in a car park - out of sight of The Frog and some distance from the water point or we may have spotted it. Rubbish dumped, we returned to the boat and Pip searched online for CRT messages relating to Newbold and read a notification telling us the bin had been relocated - a message that we both recognised as one she had read out to me a few days before. We were not covering ourselves in glory this week.

Faced with a week in Rugby we explored the town. The walk into its heart took us over the railway and through the lovely Caldecott park - which was full of unique art installations. The centre of the town is dominated by the famous Rugby School. It's the home of the glorious game and we didn't spare the camera, capturing lots of images of the ancient school buildings that would have provided the backdrop for young Webb-Ellis as he impudently picked up the ball and ran with it. We also found an old black and white version of the film *Tom Brown's School Days* - based on the well known book by Thomas Hughes - and we spent a wet afternoon watching it. Talking of watching television, Vlog 14 includes a clip of me watching rugby in Rugby - as the Six Nations matches continued. Pip was really pleased with her voice over.

Whilst we were very near a waterpoint, it was on the other bank and required us to cruise over and then reverse back into our mooring spot. Sounds easy. On Friday 12th March I found out that it wasn't. We were almost completely out of water so we had no choice but to complete the manouvre that day. This was unfortunate, as the wind was strong and with the now well documented tendency of The Frog to misbehave when in reverse gear I feared the worst! I pulled away from the waterpoint and moved forward enough to give me a run at reversing without hitting the other moored boats. Our mooring was on a slight left hand bend. This meant that, when reversing, I was immediately heading for the hedge on the far bank. When you added in the natural drift of our bow to port and the wind - I stood no chance. No matter how I tried, I could not go back in a straight line and ended up in the hedge a number of times before the boater moored behind us came to our rescue. I threw him my stern line and he pulled as I reversed again - so keeping us out of the hedge. When I was parallel to his boat, I simply had to move forward and pull into our mooring spot. Our rescuer slipped back into his boat without a word. I found this a bit strange but I was very grateful to this good samaritan - whoever he was.

On the Saturday, I noticed a wet patch on the side of the wardrobe behind the door in the bedroom. This is in the middle of the boat, so there was no risk that it was a leak from outside - but it is directly adjacent to the toilet plumbing. Fearing the worst, I got on my hands and knees and examined all the pipework - praying that I did not feel any escaping effluence! Thankfully there was none but the water remained a mystery until Pip took a shower. She noticed that the shower screen was allowing water to escape underneath it. This water was then running down the side of the bath and going under the bulkhead and into the bedroom. I went to a DIY centre and bought a new plastic sheaf to slot onto the bottom of the glass screen. This was a partial success and from then on we always showered with a cloth on the side of the bath - capturing the errant moisture. We put a small dehumidifier in the wardrobe to try and dry out the water that had already been absorbed. Unfortunately, the wood was a composite and the damage was already done. The wardrobe panel had 'blown' and would now show a permanent bulge! [*To complete this anecdote*: *when we finally sold the boat in*

September 2021 it was to a man whose hobby was renovating yachts. He was a master craftsman and he later told us he had replaced the bath with a shower and that most of the wall in this area had been damaged by what had obviously been a long term problem. He was a fantastic carpenter and I am so happy The Frog was in such capable hands - much more capable than mine].

It's now Tuesday 16th March and, a week on from our fruitless trip to Coventry, we repeat the journey and this time I come away with a vaccination. That night the poo tank and the loo both filled up and we concluded we had to move the next day. Thankfully, I did not react at all to the jab, so, after refilling with water, our nine days in Rugby came to an end and we moved off. My mood is brightened by a call from my daughter Charlie, with news of a successful job interview. Well done Charlie!

CHAPTER 25: WELCOME BACK TO BRINKLOW

Our departure from Rugby was really picturesque. Bridges 54 and 55 are both ornate aqueducts and just before Bridge 53 we passed the entrance to the Rugby Arm. This short stretch of canal takes craft down to Rugby wharf which, once upon a time, had a short rail link back to the main line that runs through the town. In Nicholson, the course of this line is now shown as a footpath that crosses the cut on an unnumbered old railway bridge just after Bridge 52. All of these features have wonderful wrought Iron railings adorning them - similar to those in Braunston.

We cruised about two miles to the 'new' Newbold tunnel. This tunnel is only two hundred and fifty yards (two hundred and twenty eight metres) long and was completed in 1834 as part of the canal straightening I have already detailed. It has a more modern appearance than most canal tunnels and, very unusually, it has a tow path running through it on both sides. This would have allowed horse drawn vessels to pass each other whilst still being attached to their 'engine' - speeding up the transit.

Our next stop was about a mile and a half further on at Brinklow marina. This was our first visit but, we soon found out, The Frog had been here before. Immediately we cruised in, the attendant who was going to help with our pump out had a broad grin on his face. The Frog is very distinctive and there was no way he was going to forget the boat that was moored here for three years! He was even a friend of the original owners (the couple who had her built) and he was excited to let them know The Frog had 'come home' - albeit only for a flying visit! We had no idea of this history and thanked him for filling us in. The marina had recently been acquired by Castle Marinas (who also owned Crick Marina) and extensive work was underway to improve the facilities and increase the number of moorings. This at least meant the marina had lots of clear water - which made manoeuvring easier. I popped into the office to pay for the pump out and fuel and was greeted by the new manager who said it was good to see The Frog again. I was confused - if he was the new manager, how could he know The Frog. It turns out he had spent a long time moored just four boats away from us in Crick whilst he prepared to take on his new role. It really is a small boating world!

We cruised on and stopped about a mile from the village of Brinklow - just before the Rose Narrowboats yard at Stretton Stop. We wanted to stay on this side of the yard as there was a water point just beyond it and we were also planning our next pump out. Mooring was not easy however. The bank just before the bridge carrying the B4428 down to the village of Brinklow, was in a really poor state of repair. Large clods of earth were slowly falling into the water and finding a decent pin position proved very hard. In the end I had to use the chains normally reserved for armco to lengthen the mooring lines so that I could reach firmer ground.

It was still only lunchtime, so we walked up the main road to the village of Stretton-Upon-Fosse (the Fosse Way being the old Roman Road that ran from Exeter to Lincoln - about two hundred and thirty miles). Pip and I were both brought up in Devon and towards the end of my career I would often drive along the Fosse Way in Somerset when visiting Frome and Midsomer Norton. Just off the main road was the biggest farm shop I think I have ever seen. That afternoon we didn't have time to fully explore it - but we knew we would be back.

The next morning we walked the other way to the village of Brinklow - and were really pleased that we did. The village is beautiful and we were not surprised to hear that there was a preservation order in place, covering the entire village centre. We chatted with some locals who filled us in on the history. Just outside the village are the remains of a Motte and Bailey, dating back to the late eleventh century, that was originally built to provide protection for the Fosse Way. The village was also once dissected by the Oxford Canal but was left 'isolated' (from the water at least) by the mid-nineteenth century engineering works that straightened its course. At the time, that alteration would probably have dealt a significant blow to the village economy but there are no signs of that today. Now we are left with a main street full of unique and quaint houses and I can see why the locals love it so.

The next day we finally ran out of coal and I walked down to the narrowboat hire firm to buy some more. Whilst they were 'open' and the owner/employee was there, I was told that the chandlery was closed until May. Ouch! This meant two things: in the short term I had to secure an alternative fuel for the fire and then, immediately, find another coal supplier. With unusual forethought (for me) I had packed my bow saw for the odyssey and set about scouring the hedgerows for suitable wood to cut up and burn. Live wood was not an option; not only would it damage the hedge but the wood would be too wet to burn immediately. It would also create some pretty nasty deposits on the inside of the chimney. So I was ideally looking for dead wood - but branches that had got suspended off the ground and had, therefore, at least dried out a little. The alternative was to find 'processed' wood, like old fences, that had fallen over but kept dry. With that very specific wish list I was not surprised I had to walk some way to build my collection. Finally I had enough for a couple of days and I started to put the Bow Saw to good use.

At that point the fire still had the last of the coal embers in it, so placing the wood on top meant there was no risk it would not light - only that it would eventually put the fire out. So I fed it in small pieces, initially, until I was confident it was both lighting and then burning well. Using wood like this was nice in one sense, or should I say FOR one sense: it smelt amazing. The downside was it did not burn as hot as coal and it burned through very quickly. It soon became clear that my two days' supply would only last one night. I also realised it was very unlikely the fire would still be alight in the morning (as it always was when I stoked it up with coal) so we would face a cold start to the next day. We really did need to find some coal tomorrow. We researched fuel boats but a couple of calls revealed that there were none nearby over the next few days - so that was not going to be our solution.

In the morning we revisited the fantastic farm shop we spotted upon our arrival and stocked up with expensive things that we could have bought cheaper at a supermarket, but convinced ourselves they were of much higher quality. As we wandered around our eyes fell on several bags of black gold - they sold coal! Immediate joy from us both was followed by continued joy from Pip but by slight consternation from me. The bags weighed twenty Kilogrammes (or forty four pounds, just over three stone in old money). The shop was over one and a half miles from the boat and we had no trolley/trailer. There was no way we were not going to buy it, however, and in Vlog 14 you can see a clip of me striding determinedly up the driveway out of the farm shop with a bag of coal draped across my shoulders - like a very uncomfortable stole.

That night we were warm but we were kept awake by the mooring lines slackening slightly - allowing the boat to drift on to an underwater ledge. This had the effect of tipping us very slightly. I have explained before that Pip is very sensitive to this disorientation (possibly something to do with her brain tumour) so she was awake several times that night.

Sad news reaches us of the loss of Peter Lorimer - the Leeds Legend - at the age of seventy four. Peter, along with Alan Clark, Billy Bremner et al, were part of the Don Revie team in the early seventies that explains why I still support them today - some fifty years later. He will be forever one of my boyhood heroes. In his honour, Leeds beat Fulham 2-1 and this makes up, somewhat, for England losing to Ireland in the Six Nations.

CHAPTER 26: SENT TO COVENTRY

We needed water - so the next day we moved off through the little swing footbridge outside Rose Narrowboats, filled with water and cruised just three and a half miles to the village of Ansty. We found a lovely mooring and set off for a walk to explore the village. Anstey is sweet but tiny with few amenities. The highlight of my day was finding a large suspended branch which I cut up to supplement our one bag of coal.

The weather the next day was nice so we decided to walk the towpath to Hawkesbury junction - where the North Oxford joined the Coventry Canal. When we reached it we recognised the lovely wrought iron bridges and realised we have actually cruised this section of the network before. We should have remembered that the North Oxford from Braunston to here, is part of the Warwickshire Ring - as is the Coventry Canal all the way to Fazeley Junction (north of Birmingham). Our only excuse was that the last time we cruised here was some seventeen years earlier when we took Charlie, Ali and Sophie (my children) and Mark (my step son), on a week's holiday. I have mentioned this trip before but did not explain that when I first fell in I had panicked until I realised the water only came up to just above my waist!

On the walk, we sussed out possible mooring spots and decided we would try and get right up to the junction just before the Stop Lock (more about the history of the junction later). It would be a good place to stay for a while: the CRT provided bins and a waterpoint and there was even a toilet (albeit the scariest looking toilet on the network). There was a pub right on the wharf (closed of course) but it would at least provide a destination address for a supermarket delivery - It was my birthday in a few days so it was important we could get hold of goodies. The moorings looked quiet, so we decided we would move the next day (earlier than planned) in the hope that we could secure a spot.

The next day is Tuesday 23rd of March and as well as moving we also noted that it was the anniversary of a very dark day: we were now a whole year on from the very first lockdown. We chuckled when we remembered that the original timescale given for the complete lockdown was three weeks. Here we were, fifty two weeks later, still having our lives affected by the dreaded lurgy that is Covid. That said, restrictions were being relaxed slightly on March 29th, which would allow us to move more freely (i.e. not just for essentials). We had also been told they would relax further on the twelfth of April - and that PUBS WOULD BE ALLOWED TO OPEN! So no guessing what we planned into our schedule for that day.

We arrived at Hawkesbury and realised we had now cruised the entire length of the Oxford Canal on our odyssey. Isis Lock in Oxford seemed a long way off as we settled into my 'birthday mooring' at this historic junction, just north of the centre of Coventry. Just after we moored I was working on something outside of the boat when a vessel left the stop lock and cruised past us back towards Rugby. Despite passing a whole line of moored boats, it was doing a ridiculous speed - causing all of us to rock on our moorings. We were attached by chain rings through the armco, but the boat directly behind us was using nappy pins and you might recall me mentioning this incident in Chapter 11 when I was explaining the different methods of mooring. The nappy pin jumped clear of the armco and the boater would have been unaware had I not pointed this out. We chatted and both cursed the selfish attitude of the boater who had just passed. Hirers have a hard time (and I have listed a few incidents already in this account) but if they do something wrong it is often (not always) a mistake. The 'wreck' of a narrowboat that had just passed us no doubt had an experienced boater at its helm and I can only put his behaviour down to bad manners or, at best, a bad day.

Hawkesbury Junction is lovely. It was finally built in 1803 at the point where James Brindley's Coventry Canal met his Oxford equivalent (actually Brindley died before the completion of the Oxford canal and this work passed to Samuel Simcock in 1778). It is not the original site of the junction. Planners wanted a spot much closer to the Coventry Basin and, for reasons relating to the payment of tolls, this was objected to by the Oxford Canal Company. Finally, a compromise was agreed and the junction was built at Longford (about a mile closer to Coventry than the current position). This location meant the Oxford Canal would run parallel to the Coventry Canal for about a mile. Then, when you passed through the junction, you had to turn through one hundred and eighty degrees and cruise a further mile to effectively get back to your starting point! This was clearly driven by politics and commercial considerations, rather than common sense. Initially, the Oxford Canal Company, still unhappy with the toll arrangements, refused to open the junction. There had also been a miscalculation in the water levels and, as things stood, they would lose water to the Coventry Canal every time the stop lock was used! Eventually the Coventry Canal Company took legal action and forced the junction to be opened in 1777. However, it was clear that this location was not sustainable and the junction was moved, in 1803, to Hawkesbury where a new pump house could be installed drawing water from nearby coal mines to feed the canal.

Hawkesbury is also known as Sutton Stop - named after a family who provided a number of Lock Keepers in the nineteenth century. The various generations would have lived in the little cottage situated beside the stop lock. I have explained the concept of a stop lock before, so I will not repeat it here. In this case, the lock had a drop of a few inches and allowed the boater leaving the Oxford to enter a small basin in front of *The Greyhound* public house. Once this basin would have been filled with commercial boats, mooring and loading or unloading their wares on the wharf for onward delivery down the Coventry Canal to the Coventry Basin, down the Oxford to join the Grand Junction (Union) or up the Coventry to Fradley and the busy artery that is the Trent and Mersey Canal. The canal designers clearly recognised the importance of this location and built the infrastructure to reflect it. Over the lock is a lovely crossover bridge with wrought iron rails across the centre span. Even more impressive is the wide wrought iron bridge that crosses the exit where the basin joins the Coventry Canal. It must be forty feet or more in length and its span is a gorgeous curve of engineering elegance.

So, history lesson over, we resume our account. The next day we thought we would walk to the Coventry Basin. We reached The Ricoh Stadium - now the Coventry Building Society Arena and home to both Wasps Rugby and Coventry City football teams, when we finally took a good look at Nicholson. This tells us the round trip to the basin is about ten miles so, understandably, we decided to turn around and head back to the boat and end up walking only about three and a half miles. Unfazed, the following morning we pulled the folding bikes from their home behind our bed, pumped up the tires and headed down the towpath into the heart of Coventry.

We used the mobile phone App 'Strava' on all of our walks and the few rides we did and were surprised when it recorded us having ridden six miles to our destination. On the smooth towpaths the trip was not that challenging but we were doubly pleased we turned around on our walk the day before. There were some nice features on our route and one that stands out were the, presumably, authorised murals on a bridge close to the Basin. The extremely talented artist had represented some of the wildlife that could be found on the waterway. Around the last bend the canal opens up into the Coventry Basin - now empty apart from a few long term moorers. The Basin is surrounded by converted warehouses with outlets including a little coffee shop and a Polish food market. Right at its heart is a life size statue of James Brindley. He is depicted looking over a map of his creations. Brindley was truly an engineering pioneer being asked to assist The Duke of Bridgewater to design and build a canal from his coal pits at Worsley into the middle of Manchester in 1759 - arguably the first 'modern' British canal. Through his life he built nearly four hundred miles of canal, including the Trent and Mersey and the Chester but his vision was much grander. He envisaged a network of waterways that linked the four major rivers of the Mersey, the Trent, the Thames and the Severn. Unfortunately he did not live to see this achievement. He also pioneered the use of clay to make canals waterproof and his lock design, based on longer versions of the narrowboats that carried coal from the mines at Worsley, had implications for the whole future of the canal network and could be claimed to have given birth to the dimensions of the narrowboats we see today.

Such was his importance in our industrial past, there is now an office and leisure complex in the middle of Birmingham called Brindley Place. It occupies the waterside previously full of warehouses and factories that were once the commercial heart of the city. After the decline of the waterways, it is encouraging that a decision was taken to redevelop the area and build the International Convention Centre and Symphony Halls nearby. It is now a real go-to location for business visitors and tourists alike and in our careers, Pip and I both had many occasions to saviour the delights of Broad Street and the Gas Street Basin.

Back in the basin at Coventry, we grabbed a coffee and some Portuguese almond cake before starting the return leg. This part of the canal was littered with rubbish (like a typical city centre canal) and we concluded that whilst it was nice to see the Basin, we were glad we did not take the trouble of bringing The Frog down here.

Saturday 27th March was my birthday. One of the downsides of being on the boat was that no one could send me a card or present but Pip recognised this and had pulled together a video of friends and relatives wishing me happy birthday. It was a lovely way to wake up and it included old friends from Cornwall and even featured Wolgang and Marlene in Germany. Whilst not on the video, it was also lovely to receive a phone call from my sister Patricia. It was a still and reasonably clear day so we decided to christen the kayak (although it was quite cold so we didn't paddle too far). The kayak was great - albeit a bit small with us both in it. We also noticed that one of the inflatable seats leaked and, after a while, the person using it had no back support. We complained to Amazon - for it was they who supplied it - asking for a replacement seat. They didn't quibble and gave us a full refund instead. Pip made Eggs Benedict for lunch and, after a chilled afternoon, she conjured up some gorgeous duck breast with a port reduction while I relaxed watching Pink Floyd in Concert - a perfect end to my day.

On the Sunday we woke late - largely due to the clocks having gone forward the night before. This was a landmark day and it would mean from now on the nights would be lighter for longer. It was also the last day of the current lock down, with the rules relaxing slightly on the 29th March. Recognising this and getting near to needing a pump out we knew we would be moving off the next day, so we took our usual exploratory walk - this time up the Coventry Canal to Marston Junction (where the Ashby Canal joins). This was our planned mooring spot and it was good to see armco and space to moor here. I remember the walk very well and Pip and I listened to *Just a Minute* on the return leg (life in the Radio 4 fast lane). In the afternoon I worked on the next Vlog, which we would only publish after we have moved and the lockdown rules have changed. In this way we would, hopefully, avoid the risk of upsetting anyone who thought we were playing fast and loose with the restrictions. From what you have read so far I am sure you can see that there was nothing fast about our progress. Loose, maybe, but not fast - we had just spent the last nine days at Hawkesbury.

It's Monday 29th March - happy birthday to my (dearly departed) mum and my son, Alasdair! It is also the day when lockdown rules change. We pulled across the canal to the far bank and started filling with water. The water pressure was really low and we had a long wait until the boat was full. The start of our next leg meant negotiating the stop lock at Hawkesbury - a drop of only a few inches - before entering the basin and turning sharp right to start the one hundred and eighty degree manouvre to get us pointing the right way up the Coventry Canal. We waved goodbye to Hawkesbury. Overall, it had been a good place to moor but I would not miss the CRT toilet at all!

CHAPTER 27: LOCKDOWN IS EASED AND FAZELEY BECKONS

Despite the slight relaxation in rules, we did not want to overdo things ahead of the further relaxation on 12th April. So, as planned, we moved only two and a half miles to Marston Junction and the start of the Ashby Canal. This waterway, that lazily winds its way from Marston for about twenty miles to just outside the village of Measham, was not on our list to cruise. Recognising this, we decided to add it to our 'navigated waterways' by getting the kayak back out. I paddled up the canal about a mile and a half and Pip brought her back. The canal had clearly not been cruised much recently and, as a consequence, we had a bit of a battle with weed. I remember the day really well: the sun was shining with a warmth that belied the fact it was still only March and we really enjoyed this alternative way of exploring the network. The high temperatures reminded us of long forgotten summer evenings and the gin and tonics and beers we imbibed just reinforced that sense of summer nostalgia.

A pump out beckoned and the nearest facilities were in Nuneaton. The next morning the weather was just as balmy, so we set off with a spring in our step and, as it turns out, something wrapped around the prop. I pulled over immediately and investigated. Luckily the sacking that had attached itself to us was relatively easy to remove and we were soon underway again. Our next stop was Boot Bridge (29) and the services of Starline Boats. We received a really warm welcome from the owners who, I sensed, were quite pleased to see traffic moving more freely up the narrow cutting in front of their premises. I am sure they were also very happy to hear we needed 'the works': a pump out, diesel and a new gas canister.

We said our farewells and continued through the centre of Nuneaton (stopping briefly for groceries) and out into the lovely countryside towards Atherstone. En-route we passed what is now a CRT yard at Hartshill Wharf. Once upon a time this would have been a hive of activity as it serviced the nearby Hartshill granite quarry - producing much of the stone used to build the nearby towns and canal bridges. The architecture at the wharf is lovely and worth slowing down to view. The main building, abutting the canal, is topped by a clock tower that would have graced the stables of any stately home.

We really did like the Coventry Canal and this stretch was the first time we had noticed how lovely it was. Yes, the weather helped, the fresh green leaves on the weeping willows, the vibrant colours of spring flowers dotting the hedgerows and the abundant birdsong all warmed the heart, but really all of these things just added to what we recognised as the intrinsic beauty of this part of the network. That evening we moored at what we still agree is one of the top three mooring spots on our travels. There were no facilities, no shops and no other boats (unusual for us). After we had passed under Mancetter Bridge (36) and negotiated a slight right hand bend, the hedges on the offside fell away and there was nothing but a majestic green meadow, sweeping up and away from us to the edge of the woods at Purley Park in the distance. As soon as we saw the view we swung our bow into the bank. This was going to be ours - well for that night anyway.

Before we settled down for the evening we walked into Atherstone (about a two mile round trip). The town felt slightly industrial. We explored the centre and learned that it has a fascinating history. The settlement dates back to Roman times and sits astride the A5 - which we already know is the Roman Road of Watling Street. It thrived after being given its own market and developed various industries including clothing, leather and, later, millinery. On Shrove Tuesday each year a large football match takes place through the town - a tradition that dates back to an enormous (and presumably chaotic) mediaeval match that predates the creation of any football league by several hundred years. This original melee is also commemorated by a statue in the town centre. Finally, on the eve of the Battle of Bosworth in 1485 it is believed Henry Tudor (soon to be Henry VII) and his men stayed in the town before travelling to Market Bosworth in neighbouring Leicestershire to defeat Richard III and change the course of English history forever. Not bad for a small town sitting between Nuneaton and Tamworth.

As was our custom, whilst here, we also checked out the waterpoint and the start of the Atherstone Lock Flight (eleven locks dropping a total of eighty feet) - which it would be our pleasure to descend the next day.

April Fool's day came with a 'Mary Poppinesque' change in the wind direction (but this time to the north) and the temperature dropped to below ten degrees. These were not ideal conditions to tackle the Atherstone flight but at least it wasn't raining. We filled with water at the top lock and whilst we were doing so another boat approached. Pip opened the top gates for him and he entered - eventually. The helmsman, on this owner-occupied boat, was clearly either new to boating or having an off day. Despite approaching the lock gate relatively straight, they ended up taking three separate attempts to finally get in (and then with a few more scratches on their bow and flank). The timing was not great as there were another ten single-boat-width locks in the flight and we would be following him down. If he took the same time at each lock we were in for a long day. It was really tempting to offer to take the helm for him (he was elderly and alone on board) but I was not sure how such an offer would be received. He clearly owned the boat and may have considered himself the Chay Bligh of the canal network for all I knew. After two locks he pulled over for a cup of tea and, to use a golfing analogy, he waved for us to play through. As we passed I asked him if he would like any further help with the locks. He said no - he was fine and that he was in no hurry.

We moored for lunch after lock seven (bacon sandwiches, I do believe) and then finished the remaining four locks of the flight by mid-afternoon. By this time the temperature was dropping again and the wind was getting up. I was tired, cold and boat handling was becoming a problem so after about another mile we moored just short of the lovely village of Polesworth - a total journey of only four and a half miles but with eleven locks.

The next morning we walked down to explore the village. It feels more like a town - not sure what the difference is - and, indeed, the parish had a population of over eight thousand people! Village sounds nicer I guess and it certainly felt like a warm and welcoming community. We moved The Frog about a mile so we could moor right next to the park and make use of the tennis courts. We were glad it was still early April and there was no-one around to witness just how abysmal we were. The most exercise we got was walking to the net or the surrounding fence to pick up the ball. Overall, it was just good to be outdoors and doing some exercise that did not involve walking the towpath for a change. We enjoyed it so much we went back again the next day but not before we walked down the canal to Pooley Nature Reserve. This walk took us past Pooley Hall - former home of American soul legend Edwin Starr - who lived there for many years. He had a huge following in the UK and moved here in 1983. He is still a favourite for many people of a certain age. He died in Nottinghamshire in 2003, aged only sixty one.

We loved our walk through this leafy stretch of the canal and looked forward to cruising it the following day when we would head for water at Fazeley Junction - north west of England's second city and where the Birmingham and Fazeley canal meets the Coventry.

Easter Sunday saw us make an early start. The weather was clear and sunny but cold and we wanted to get moored up in Fazeley before a predicted snow storm. We were struck by the contrast with the weather of a few days ago at Marston Junction, when Pip was sunbathing in an attempt to tan her legs. Having passed Pooley Hall, we enjoyed the beautiful woodlands and open countryside that tracked our route to Tamworth. Alvecote Marina looked lovely in the spring sun and it was a hive of activity as the hire company based there was clearly gearing up for the relaxation of rules and the re-commencement of boat hire on April 12th. We were just waiting for the pubs to re-open!

The canal route through Tamworth was a succession of lucky householders' gardens backing onto the canal bank. Most took full advantage of this lovely position with patios and benches close to the water's edge and had no fence or wall to restrict their view of the waterway. Many also had lovely magnolia or willow trees overhanging the water and the scent was intoxicating.

We didn't stop in the town and pressed on to negotiate the two Glascote locks, a drop of about fourteen feet. We were soon passing under bridge (77) and entering the Fazeley Junction basin. The basin is attractive with its walls decorated with fantastic murals of wild birds. The Birmingham and Fazeley canal could be seen heading off to the South West towards Birmingham city centre, where it linked up with the Birmingham Canal Network or BCN. We moored at the water point, filled and then moved on a few hundred yards to a lovely mooring spot opposite Peel's Wharf. Our journey today had been six miles and two locks and we stopped before the expected temperature drop hit us. That afternoon we walked a couple of miles towards Birmingham before hunkering down against the weather.

The temperature dropped that night and was still very cold the next morning. We liked our mooring and as the weather was not encouraging us to up sticks and move on, we decided to stay another day. We walked ahead to check out a large Sainsburys, by Sutton Road Bridge, where we would stop the next day for supplies. On the way we saw a fallen tree just south of Bonehill Road Bridge that was blocking the waterway (and our route tomorrow). I called the blockage into the CRT on the way to the supermarket and by the time we walked back, CRT workers were on site cutting through the heavy trunk to clear the canal. Now that's what I call service!

CHAPTER 28: RETURN OF THE BRASS MONKEYS

The next morning, our path now clear, we moved The Frog down what is, more accurately, the Birmingham and Fazeley Canal (more about this later) to Sutton Road Bridge. We moored so that we could do a big shop at the same large supermarket we visited the day before. We were making our way, slowly, to a boatyard at Streethay Wharf - a distance of about six and a half miles - to pick up some new glass for the front of the woodburner. Some careless individual - me - had broken it when cleaning out the fire. As we set off, we were still not sure if the boatyard even had the right glass, so we planned to stop at the village of Whittington (about four miles) and hopefully hear from the chandlers that they had it in stock. However, the weather was so bitterly cold that we stopped after only two miles, in a little village called Hopwas.

Hopwas is a sweet Staffordshire village with two lovely big pubs (both still closed) straddling the canal and I am sure it would have made a lovely summer stop over. Today, however, it was bitterly cold. We explored the village on foot, visiting the unique Church of St Chad. Designed by architect John Douglas, it was built in 1881 so, for a church, it is a relatively modern building. It is constructed of brick but has a timber frame on its upper half, making it look more like a large Mock Tudor house than a place of worship. As we walked around the grounds it started to snow so we made our way back to the warmth of The Frog.

April seventh should not be as cold as it was. We woke and started our preparations to head off again towards Streethay - with the intention of getting there this time. Just before we left our mooring we heard an enormous bang and felt the boat lurch towards the bank and slightly forwards. I rushed out to see a narrowboat (again privately owned) reversing away from our flank. The helmsman was waving his hands in a gesture that I can only assume constituted an apology. I examined our hull and saw a large new scratch just below the gunwale. The boater passed us and pulled over a few boat lengths down. Pip and I scratched our heads. There was no wind, it was a bright clear day and we were not on a bend. We know accidents happen but it must have been a fairly major lapse in concentration to cause him to plough into the side of our moored boat. We pulled out and passed him - more apologies - this time verbal. I have previously explained that bumps like this are an occupational hazard and there was none of the reaching for insurance details that would have been the case had we been in land-based vehicles. We took it on the chin - or rather The Frog did - and continued on our way. The 'culprit' pulled out behind us but kept his distance as we cruised in the same direction. Only when we finally moored in Whittington did he pass. We braced ourselves for impact as he did so but did not hit us again. He did, however, manage to misjudge bridge 78, just in front of our mooring and took a chunk out of the brickwork.

Safely moored again, we had an afternoon to fill. I am not sure how we knew this but we decided to walk up to Whittington Church to find the grave of Thomas Spencer - the co-founder of the world famous Marks and Spencers. Although he was born in Skipton in Yorkshire, Spencer spent his final years and is now buried in Whittington where he died in 1805 - aged fifty three.

Whittington has another claim to fame - this time in the world of Canal history. In 1769 Brindley and the Coventry Canal company ran out of money before the canal was finished. Over the next few years, the Birmingham and Fazeley (B&F) and Trent and Mersey (T&M) Canal companies were desperate for their two respective waterways to link. The delay in the progress of the Coventry canal was holding this up. Seeking permission from parliament, the two companies won the right to build along the planned route of the Coventry canal. The T&M canal company started building at Fradley and headed South East. The B&F canal company started at Fazeley and headed North West. The canals met at Whittington in 1790 - some twenty one years after Brindley stopped building. There is a plaque here marking the spot. If you choose to watch Vlog 16 you will notice that the waterway from Fazeley to Whittington is not called the Coventry Canal and is actually a continuation of the Birmingham and Fazeley. Along its route the bridges are named and not numbered (a tell-tale sign). At Whittington the bridges start being numbered again and the canal reverts to being called the Coventry (despite it being built by the T&M company). Confused?

Thankfully, temperatures rose to a balmy nine degrees celsius and we left Whittington to complete the Coventry Canal and join the Trent and Mersey at Fradley Junction. En-route we passed through the tiny hamlet of Huddlesford and saw the rather grand entrance to the Wyrley and Essington Canal. Now great sections of this waterway are unnavigable and the small arm, that connects to the Coventry at this point, only extends south about a quarter of a mile or so to Watery Lane Bridge. When built, the canal went all the way to Wolverhampton and allowed the easy movement of coal and limestone along its route. Now it is used for private moorings.

Finally, we passed Streethay Wharf (remember) but we did not stop as we already knew they did not have any suitable glass for the stove. Instead we cruised on, under Streethay Bridge and tried, in vain, to ignore the roar of the traffic on the A38 trunk road that runs right alongside the canal at this point. The waterway swings east and then back to the west, passing under the offending main road before reaching the tranquil tree lined section beyond the village of Fradley.

When we reached the junction, we stopped for lunch and filled with water. I walked down the Trent and Mersey to drop off rubbish at the CRT bins. On the way back I captured the beautiful Junction Lock (17) on video and panned across the front of the Swan Inn (lovingly known as the 'Mucky Duck' to boaters and locals alike). The 12th of April is now only four days away but unfortunately it is still too early for us to sample the hospitality of yet another milestone pub on the network.

CHAPTER 29: SPRING IS IN THE AIR

After lunch we opened the small footbridge at the end of the Coventry Canal and completed the sweeping manouvre to join the Trent and Mersey Canal. This great waterway, designed by Brindley, was built in the late 1770s to link the River Trent with the River Mersey - and so create an inland waterway between the great ports of Hull and Liverpool. The canal is measured as starting in Shardlow in Derbyshire but actually links to the Trent at Derwent Mouth. It covers some ninety three miles over seventy six locks and through the infamous Harecastle tunnel to join the Bridgewater Canal at Preston Brook. En-route it links with the Coventry, Staffs and Worcs, Caldon, Macclesfield and Shropshire Union canals - making it one of the most accessible waterways in the UK. On our Odyssey we would cruise on it twice. On this occasion we were travelling north west as far as Great Haywood junction.

Having made the turn onto the Trent and Mersey, we head west towards our next mooring spot. We had no firm plans and we completed three of the single-width locks before the wind really picked up. The locks were attractive with lovely brickwork adorning the narrow entrances under the footbridges built to make lock usage easier. As the helmsman, I had a great view of these bridges as I approached each lock and Pip liked the fact that it meant she did not have to walk all the way around to operate the double gate entrances to these single locks. At Wood End lock (20) the crossing bridge had been built so close to the lock gates that the metal arms on the gates (usually completely straight) were shaped at a 90 degree angle and two large grooves had been cut into the bridge to allow the gates to swing open. We had never seen this before and we were glad that the gates were light and easy to move as the 'bent' arms did not give as much leverage as other lock gates. The afternoon was drawing to a close and after we exited Wood End the wind had turned to the north west and was pushing us across the canal and onto the bank. The wind was so powerful we struggled to pull The Frog back into the middle of the stream. Pip and I agreed: it was time to stop for the night; however, we were in the middle of nowhere, with no facilities. As there were no more locks, we decided to push on a further two and a half miles to the town of Handsacre, where we moored just before bridge 58.

The forecast for Friday 9th was not great so we decided to stay put and explore on foot. Whilst cruising the previous day we had noticed an awful lot of development work along the canal side. On our walk we saw a lot more - including a compulsory-purchased cottage that was slowly falling into disrepair and looking very forlorn behind the tall, temporary wire barriers keeping us off the land under development. Security was high and we soon realised why. The land was part of the planned route for HS2 and I am guessing not everyone was in favour of this huge engineering work carving a new, industrial scar across the beautiful countryside. We would see further evidence of the HS2 development over the coming months. I can only hope that the benefits it will eventually bring are worth the disruption and destruction we were witnessing back in April 2021. We got back to the boat and the news was full of the death of Prince Philip. We are not huge royalists but on a human level we reflected how difficult today would be for the Queen and her family.

Finally, for anyone passing through Handsacre in the future, that night we bought Fish and Chips from Michael's Fish Bar - not far from Bridge 58. I commented in my diary and in Vlog 17 that there was enough food for six people - and I am a big eater. Not only was there loads of it, but it was also delicious and I would highly recommend trying it for yourselves.

The cruise the next day past Rugeley was a joy. Pip was almost decapitated by a duck flying under a bridge and just missing her head (that wasn't the joyful bit). The weather was warm and the canal was beautiful. I particularly remember the cascade of birdsong that surrounded our cruise. The ducks and swans were really active as the wind had died down and the temperature had risen. Spring was definitely in the air. En-route we cruised past the *Plum Pudding Brasserie* (multi-award-winning, apparently) and cursed that it was still not the 12th April. Shortly after, we entered the narrow gorge of the Armitage 'tunnel'. Until 1971 there had indeed been a tunnel on this spot - cut through the sandstone that now formed the walls on either side of the narrow passage. In that year, a new road was built over the canal and the tunnel was removed, for safety reasons, leaving an attractive cutting - not much wider than the boat itself. The canal widened out and we approached Spode House. Built in 1760 this grand, listed property was extended in 1840 to become the home of the widow of Josiah Spode, the pottery magnate.

When we reached Rugeley the view changed somewhat. The town was dominated by four enormous cooling chimneys. At one time there were two coal fired power stations: A and B. Rugeley A was opened in 1965 and closed in 1995. Rugeley B was opened in 1970 and finally closed in 2016. Its four unsightly chimneys were demolished in June 2021 (about two months after we passed through). They can still be seen in Vlog 17, however. Speaking of Vlog 17, I have just rewatched the Rugeley section and noticed two glaring errors - both relating to Bridge 67A. Firstly, I have tagged it as a 'Brtidge' (blame my poor spell checking whilst editing) and secondly it is not Bridge 67A. It is actually Bridge 65B - where a branch line crosses the canal and not where the main railway line crosses later at 67A. Sorry to be anal but I really liked Bridge 65B. It was built at an angle across the canal and the arch is high and magnificent in its dimensions. The arch brickwork was laid at an angle that created a series of appealing spirals across the span of the bridge. It is a wonderful example of skillful engineering and construction in the nineteenth century (when the railway and not the canal was built).

Just on the edge of Rugeley the canal takes a sharp turn to the right and crosses Brindley Bank Aqueduct. Here Brindley designed a series of attractive brick arches that carry the canal over the River Trent. The aqueduct is famous for much more gruesome reasons, however. On the 15th of June 1839 a thirty seven year old lady by the name of Christine Collins hitched a lift on a narrowboat heading to London to be reunited with her husband. Unfortunately she never made it. Her badly mutilated body was found in the canal by Brindley Bank. She had been brutally slain. The subsequent trial led to the execution of two of the narrowboat crew and the transportation of a third. Interestingly, this true story was the inspiration for a Colin Dexter, Inspector Morse mystery. 'The Wench is Dead' was later made into a TV episode of Inspector Morse and released in 1998. There is actually much debate about how safe the convictions of the crew members were but what counted against them was Mrs Collins claims, prior to her death, that she suspected they were going to 'interfere' with her and that she hated their rough ways and foul language. The full truth will never be known but, as Pip says in the Vlog, as we cruised along that lovely stretch of canal it was very hard to imagine such a tragedy had occurred there. As the rain returned late in the afternoon, our eight mile cruise came to an end and we moored near the beautiful stately home of Shugborough Hall and settled in for the night.

Sunday 11th April started with bright sunshine and finished with snow - such are the delights and uncertainties of British springtime weather. We rose early and walked up to Great Haywood Junction where the Staffordshire and Worcestershire (Staffs and Worcs) joined the Trent and Mersey. We needed to drop off some bins and get the water bottles filled, but I also wanted to eyeball the junction - which I was planning to tackle later that day. On our walk back we diverted onto a footpath over the River Trent via a lovely narrow stone bridge that was clearly designed for earlier times when horse riders would need to pass pedestrians. Small triangular 'bays', large enough for one or two people, were built into the walls on either side adding to the bridge's appeal. To the right the confluence of the River Sows and Trent added further interest.

Our path finished in the grounds of Shugborough. Adorned with a splendid ionic colonnade, the front aspect must make this property one of the most attractive of all the National Trust sites. Previously owned by the Anson family as far back as the early seventeenth century, it was passed to the nation in the 1960s in lieu of death duties. William IV made the second Viscount Anson Lord Lichfield and the last direct descendant who lived in the house was the famous photographer, also Lord Lichfield, who rented an apartment until his death in 2005. Unfortunately, lockdown meant we could not even enter the gardens in April 2021 and it remains a 'must do' now we are in different times.

We return to The Frog and 'up pins' before heading off through Haywood Lock (22) and starting our approach to Great Haywood Junction. The canal is really wide at this point, making the turn nice and straightforward - in theory anyway. What actually happened of course was a boat was coming up the Staffs and Worcs just as we approached, so I had to slow down and hover until it had made the turn onto the Trent and Mersey. Thankfully, he made it in one and headed north (away from us) giving me plenty of space to complete my turn. We took the junction with no problems. There was even a comical moment as runners on a fun run were being applauded by onlookers on the bridge over the junction and it sounded like my boat handling skills were being appreciated by the gongoozlers! We were now on the Staffs. and Worcs.

CHAPTER 30: IS THIS THE WAY TO AUTHERLEY?

The Staffs and Worcs canal is forty six miles long and links the mighty River Severn at Stourport with the Trent and Mersey at Great Haywood - the junction we had just negotiated. It was designed by, yes you guessed it, James Brindley. It was completed in 1771 and has forty three locks. We cruised different parts of the Staffs and Worcs on two separate occasions. This time we were aiming to link up with the Shropshire Union at Autherley Junction before turning back north. I liked this canal. It has a classic Brindley contour route (hence the minimal number of locks) and I remember enjoying the slow meander south very much. Maybe it was because the weather was getting better and better - I distinctly remember an azure sky over the tower at Gailey Top Lock as being typical of this part of our odyssey.

We were immediately struck by the quaint, low brick bridges that all carry both a name and a number. Shortly after Swivel Bridge (108) the canal opens into the magnificent Tixall Wide. This looks like a natural lake but was actually built in 1771 as part of the canal construction. Hugh Clifford, 3rd Baron Clifford of Chudleigh, owned nearby Tixall Hall and the land the canal now cuts through. The landscaping in front of his house was designed by Lancelot 'Capability' Brown and the Baron was determined it would not be compromised by this modern construction project. Consequently, he only gave permission for the navigation to pass through his estate if the waterway was widened to resemble a lake. He got his wish and today we all benefit from his self-interest. The 'Wide' is a haven for all forms of wildlife and is beautiful to cruise through. Thank you Hugh.

We cruised for a couple of miles past lovely properties with lush grass lawns bordering the offside of the canal. We stopped for lunch at Sow Aqueduct and then pressed on. Just before Tixall lock we saw *NB Spookie*. So far I have not called out many individual narrowboats but we were tickled by this one. Many owners not only name their boats but also add their names to the boat signage. Examples may include: 'The Parsons family' or 'Barry and Jayne'. On *NB Spookie* the sign simply read: *'Mark and Vacancy'*. I am only surprised that there was no phone number underneath for applicants to use! Our next mooring was near Radford Bridge (98) in the area of Baswich on the South Eastern side of Stafford. As we approached, we passed a canal junction signpost on the towpath, pointing to Stafford. This is the only remaining evidence that an arm used to leave the Staffs and Worcs at this point via Baswich long. The waterway once joined with the River Sow and linked Stafford with the wider canal network.

It's the 12th of April (our Glorious 12th!) and today pubs would be allowed to open to serve customers outside - so where we positioned ourselves tonight was going to be important. We had one simple criteria: be near a pub with a garden. Early that morning we walked the five mile round trip into the centre of Stafford. It is a lovely town with lots of historic buildings at its heart. We explored, bought version 4 of the Nicholson Guide (which would be needed for our Shropshire Union leg) and took shelter from a surprise snow shower in a local coffee shop. Late in the morning we left our mooring and stopped after about a mile at Stafford Boat club. Here we pumped out, got water, coal and diesel and had bacon sandwiches for lunch. The boat club is lovely and the members are very lucky to have such a delightful setting and fantastic facilities. They were also very welcoming.

After lunch we had a landmark sighting of a brood of ducklings. This would be the first of many but, on the 12th April, it was reassuring evidence that spring was definitely here - despite the morning snow. The afternoon was spent travelling a further four miles through some of the loveliest locks on the network and under the M6. We finished in the village of Penkridge and moored just above Penkridge lock (38). We immediately called around the local pubs and the second one we contacted said they were expecting a large crowd but we were welcome if we didn't mind queuing. The weather was cold but we really didn't care! We had not been anywhere near a pub since before the temporary lock down in November - so this was well overdue! The pub was nice and we only queued a few minutes to secure a table in the 'garden'. It was bonkers and it felt like half the village was there. We had a couple of drinks and ordered scotch eggs, pork pies and chips (there was a limited menu). You may recall that when we were planning our travels, we intended to do two things en-route: the first was to ring bells at as many churches as we could. The second was to visit as many lovely pubs as possible. The attraction today was not the alcohol - we had plenty of that on board. Rather, it was the amazing sense of liberation that we and, judging by the excited, happy conversations around us, everyone else, was feeling. A priceless moment after so much isolation.

Our southerly course the next day started with a real contrast of experiences. Just outside of the village the canal took on a very natural feel and, ignoring the lack of a significant current, the lovely tree lined banks made us feel like we were on a river. The contrast came from the M6 which runs directly alongside the canal for about half a mile just after Otherton lock (36). The water course pulls away from the M6 at Rodbaston Lock and after a couple more inclines and some gentle meandering, we approached the wonderful Gailey Tower. The sun was shining and the sky was a bright blue making the tower even more attractive than the obvious appeal of its architecture. It was built to allow the toll keeper to have a good view of the approach to the lock to ensure no payments were missed. The wharf is still busy with moored boats but now they are all leisure rather than commercial vessels.

Two miles on we looked left and saw the entrance to the old Hatherton branch - once a link into the BCN but now a short stretch with a couple of locks and a marina. There is a campaign to try and reopen this line and reconnect to Birmingham. As the helmsman, it was easy to be confused here; the Hatherton arm felt like the natural course to follow and the continuing mainline canal went around a sharp right turn and under the low Calf Heath Marina bridge. Some helpful person had painted a sign on the bottom of the bridge reading: 'THIS WAY AUTHERLEY'. Their intention was clearly better than their grammar, but it worked and I made the turn and cruised onto the very short stone aqueduct just after.

Two more bends and we saw a sight we have enjoyed a few times on our travels. Herons are beautiful birds. Their long legs and sweeping necks make them well equipped for the stealth fishing technique they are famous for. They are used to narrowboats and quite often will not fly away when one passes and this was our experience this time. Every now and then, however, it was obvious that they were feeling playful and wanted to 'race'. It must have happened four or five times that a heron, not so much spooked by us passing, but, seemingly challenged, would rise majestically into the air and fly ahead of the boat for a short distance before landing again and waiting for us to catch up. The process would then be repeated, sometimes three or four more times. When it happened it was a joy to see. In Vlog 18 there are a couple of slow-motion clips of a heron in action.

That night we moored just before Moat House Bridge (74). We had cruised six and a half miles of some of the most attractive water in the UK and had completed six of the nicest locks. Until I was researching for this book, I had not watched Vlog 18 for some time and had forgotten just how special this section of canal is.

Planning ahead is the key to happy boating. We moored where we did that night because we were still out in the countryside. The huge sprawling conurbation of Wolverhampton was only about four miles to our south and we wanted to stay away from any built up area. However, we still wanted to be close enough so that the next day we could complete the trip to Autherley, make the sharp turn at the junction and cruise a few miles north up the Shropshire Union and moor again back in the peace of the countryside. The next day started well with lovely weather and the joy of the meandering Staffs and Worcs canal continuing for about three and a half miles. After passing under the M54 the canal straightened and we noticed more buildings on either bank. We were entering Wolverhampton. Our Nicholson guide referred to a 'Very Narrow Cutting' between Forster Bridge (68) and Marsh Lane Bridge (67). We soon realised what they meant. The cutting, known as Pendeford Rockin, is over half a mile in length and it would have been interesting if we had met a boat coming the other way. Despite the mental anguish placed on me as helmsman, we both appreciated the beauty of this stretch with its hewn sandstone walls - especially as it was positioned on the edge of Wolverhampton.

Less than a mile ahead we approached Autherley Junction. The canal was wide at this point which, as it turned out, was just as well. The Shropshire Union heads north west from here and we were travelling South West on the Staffs and Worcs. This meant the turn we had to make was about 135 degrees. The stop lock, just beyond the junction, was hidden from my view as we approached and even

Pip, standing at the bow, could not see around the tight bend. I began my turn but after a few moments Pip shouted: 'STOP!' As we turned, her angle of view had changed and she could now see that there was a boat coming through the stop lock to leave the Shropshire Union. There was no way we could pass them under the bridge that took the towpath over the junction, so I had no option but to abort my turn. I went into reverse and then forward again but with an even tighter lock. My intention was to effectively wind and be facing back up the canal and be perfectly placed to make the junction - this time heading North East. Thankfully the emerging vessel was heading north - or staying out of his way would have been tricky. Unfortunately, I think the helmsman was new to the boat and struggled to make the turn. I could see from my position that he was 'over-tillering' - I should know all about that - and consequently his boat just kept heading for the far bank. Eventually he made the turn. I was quite proud of my ability to hold The Frog midstream and hover until he had finished his manoeuvre - something that would have panicked me a few months before.

CHAPTER 31: CANAL SUPER HIGHWAY

Excitement over, we waved goodbye to the lovely Staffs and Worcs and joined the slightly more prosaic Shropshire Union. I will immediately contradict myself here. It is fair to say that our first impressions of the canal super highway that is the Shropshire Union, was not favourable. We could not moor easily (we ran aground on our first attempt to stop for lunch) and the canal was wide and boring for a large part of the early passage. I guess we had got used to the meandering beauty of the Staffs and Worcs and this new waterway came as a bit of a shock to us. That said, when I think about the Shropshire Union (or Shroppie as it is known) in its entirety, I must admit I have come away with not a small amount of affection for it. There are some lovely stretches of varying interest, challenge and beauty. It also has some of the most appealing lock flights on the network, numerous stunning bridges and some of the sweetest villages in the Uk - Gnosall and Audlem standing out.

The Shropshire Union was largely designed by Thomas Telford and was completed in 1835. It runs some sixty six miles from Autherley Junction near Wolverhampton to Ellesmere Port near Chester. Thus it links the canal system of the West Midlands with the River Mersey and The Manchester Ship Canal - making it a very important waterway in its day. It incorporates a number of still navigable arms and branches (such as the Middlewich) and some no longer in use (like the Shrewsbury Canal which used to join at Norbury Junction). It connects to the Llangollen at Hurleston and its history is entangled with that of former canals, like the Ellesmere, which ended up being incorporated into what we now call the Shropshire Union. Its width and long straight sections, whilst challenging to leisure cruisers seeking interest, made it ideal for commercial traffic and it competed successfully against the well-established Trent and Mersey - which runs parallel to it. The most demanding commercial challenge was caused by the waterway being built so late and competition from the railways was evident from the outset. Indeed, consideration was even given to building a railway from Autherley to Nantwich (which is a large section of the mainline) rather than a canal. I have to say, I am very glad they did not.

So back to our adventure; we had made the turn at Autherley and after stopping for water, we pushed on north and looked for a mooring spot for lunch. This proved harder than we expected. Used to the many mooring places on the Staffs and Worcs and seeing the wide open spaces on either side of the Shroppie we assumed we could pull in anywhere. Not so. In many places there were large obstructions under the water and we ran aground twice before finally finding a spot at Pendeford Bridge (4). Lunch finished, we passed under Pendeford and saw for the first time what is typical of the Shroppie: a long, wide and uninterrupted waterway stretched ahead of us into the distance. If I had cruise control I would have set it and gone below for a cup of tea. Unfortunately I didn't, so I stood patiently on the tiller hoping that a bend or something else interesting would appear soon. The bridges of Upper and Lower Hattons (5 and 6) provided slight distractions but the canal failed to entertain. We made good time - that is the upside - and after about three miles we were approaching the outskirts of Brewood (pronounced *'Brood'*). The canal was now passing through a short stretch of beautiful woodland and it was here that we saw the first of the wonderful bridges that the Shroppie is famous for. Avenue Bridge (10) is Grade II listed and made of pink stone, with a beautiful balustrade running across it. It carries a bridleway to nearby Chillington Hall and it swept majestically over our heads.

Brewood gets its name from the old Celtic word 'Bre' - meaning Hill - and is literally a wood on a hill. Consequently, the canal builders had to create a deep cutting to bypass the town and avoid the need for locks - that would slow boaters down. We moored near Brewood Bridge (14) and walked up the steep embankment to explore the town. That day we had covered ten miles with one small stop lock and achieved our desire to be mooring away from the conurbation of Wolverhampton. Contrast this with the slow progress we made on the Staffs and Worcs.

Morning dawned with an azure sky, dotted with fluffy white clouds. We left Brewood and travelled two miles in a straight line towards Wheaton Aston. The highlight of this stretch is the Stretton Aqueduct, carrying the canal over the ever-present Watling St (A5). Crossing a river on an aqueduct is a joy but crossing a busy 'A' road, whilst less bucolic in nature, is more exhilarating. The sound and sight of cars and lorries hurtling underneath you at high speed was such a contrast to our sedate cruising that it really made us appreciate life at four miles per hour. We must have made quite a sight for those drivers lucky enough to pass under us just at that moment; twenty tons of blue steel floating graciously over an ornate stone arch, bordered by tall, classic columns.

The good weather tempted us into stopping early. The washing machine was on and this was a great drying day - what a rock and roll lifestyle we had. Wheaton Aston was just three miles and one lock up from Brewood but *The Hartley Arms*, dominating the aptly named Tavern Bridge (19) was calling our name. It was only Thursday but we decided to pretend it was Friday and we booked a takeaway meal for later. That afternoon we walked into the village to explore (it is quite small so this did not take long). In the evening we sat in the pub car park, high above the canal and imbibed our second 'pub drink' in six days (I know) before carrying our take-away back to The Frog. Pip had salmon fish cakes and I had some sublime braised beef. Take note, assuming it has not changed hands or chef, The Hartley Arms at Wheaton Aston is definitely worth a visit.

The next day we wanted to get as close to Market Drayton as possible and were pleased to wake to another bright sunny morning - albeit with an external temperature of only ten degrees. The canal, as ever, was straight and for the first few miles, at least, had no locks. We made great progress. Although straight, the canal was anything but boring. We passed through a series of beautiful wooded cuttings and then over long engineered embankments - with views to die for. Rye Hill cutting was the first and I clearly remember the not yet fully green arc of trees that leaned protectively over the waterway, casting pretty shadows on the water. It felt a bit like passing under a military guard of honour.

The embankment, near Church Eaton, that followed, was home to another heron and shortly after this sighting we approached Cowley Tunnel. The tunnel was designed to be some seven hundred yards long, however faults in the sandstone cliff here meant it was not safe to leave it all standing. Now only eighty one metres are covered but the fact that its walls and roof are bare sandstone gives it a majesty beyond its length. Designed by Telford, it took five years to build and was recognised as a massive feat of engineering at the time (1835). We emerged from the tunnel into a cutting that took us on to the wonderful village of Gnosall. I am not going to say anything else about the village now, as we cruised right through it heading for Market Drayton. In August we will cruise in the opposite direction and moor for the night so I will expand on its delights then.

It's still only about eleven thirty but we have already covered seven and a half miles and are now cruising past Shelmore Wood on the Shelmore embankment. All of a sudden the tone of the engine changed and I was really concerned we had a problem. We were not far from Norbury Junction, so we cruised on and moored there for lunch and called the RCR to come and check the engine over. Whilst we were waiting, Pip and I explored the junction. Here a link, to connect the then Birmingham and Liverpool Junction Canal (this section of the Shropshire Union) to the Shrewsbury and Newport Canal, was built in 1835. Today only a short arm remains and it is used for mooring.

Anyway, back to the engine issue. The RCR mechanic arrived and asked us to turn her on. We did this and then turned the ignition key back to '0' and removed it. We had done this ever since we owned the boat, as we discovered early on that if we left the key in and on the 'I' setting, an alarm would sound. The mechanic was really surprised. He explained that by removing the key we were completing disengaging the instrument panel. The rev-counter (which we thought was broken) would not work and nor would any warning lights should they be needed. Further, he suspected that we were also disengaging at least one of the alternators and he was amazed our batteries were charging. We explained that they did take a rather long time to do so. He asked that we leave the key in and see if the alarm sounded. We did and it didn't and we concluded that the original alarm problem was probably linked to our old alternator and battery issues. Ever since we had both of those replaced, we could have kept the key in place! Oh - and now we also had a working rev-counter. So here we were, about twenty one months into our ownership of The Frog and we were still learning something new. I was just glad that Derek was nowhere near - I could only imagine the eye rolling this revelation would have drawn. As for the engine problem: it seemed the noise was probably an alternator belt working loose. The mechanic tightened a few nuts and we were ready to continue our journey.

About a quarter of a mile from Norbury we approached High Bridge (39). There are actually lots of high bridges on this stretch, carrying lanes and footpaths from one side of the deep cuttings to the other. This bridge is special. Not only is it a beautiful Grade II listed construction, designed by Thomas Telford, but about half way up its height there is a strengthening span that reaches from one upright to the other. On top of this strainer sits a short telegraph pole dating from about 1861 when electricity cables were installed along the length of the canal. Today the wires have been removed but the telegraph pole has, quite rightly, been left in place as a marvellous curiosity.

We reached the end of Grub Street Cutting and drifted onto Shebdon Embankment. When it was built, this stretch presented a severe engineering challenge as it lifted the canal many feet above natural ground level. It has often been subject to water egress and has failed on more than one occasion. The latest major breach was in 2009, when a football-sized hole appeared in the bed and caused the closure of the canal for some weeks. Thankfully, it remained intact for our crossing. At the end of the embankment is Knighton Wharf where, early in the twentieth century, Cadbury would have unloaded gallons of milk from barges every day, turned it into chocolate crumb and then floated it via the Shroppie and the Worcester and Birmingham canals to their factory at Bournville to be made into some of the nation's favourite nibbles. Remarkably this practice continued until 1961.

Our long day finally came to an end at Black Flat Bridge (47). We had covered twelve and a half miles, not bad considering we had a long delay at lunch time, but we were ready to put our feet up.

Market Drayton is now only six miles away and we would definitely reach there in one cruise. Our journey started with more of the same - wide and straight water with bridges being the only reason to adjust our speed. It was a beautiful day, which made the cruising enjoyable - despite the unchanging landscape. I observed how isolated this stretch was; there were very few houses and about half the bridges were for farmers/footpaths only, so there wasn't even any traffic noise to blight the tranquillity of the canal. The only slight irritation was another boater pulling out into the canal from a private mooring. The helmswoman didn't even look behind her and I had to slow down to avoid a collision. She then proceeded to cruise at what felt like below tick over speed and I had to keep going into neutral to avoid catching her up. Maybe the difference in hull shape and engine size/performance explained why my tick over was faster than hers. The Frog did move really easily through the water and we occasionally attracted negative shouts from moored boaters of 'slow down' even when we were passing at tick over. Anyway, we stayed behind our new 'guide' for about a mile before she finally looked behind her and pulled over to let us past. She then winded at the next turning point (presumably to fill with water before returning to her mooring).

The terrain changed dramatically after Cheswardine Bridge as we entered the Woodseaves Cutting. Stretching about a mile and a half in length, the cutting is not as narrow as Pendeford Rockin but is longer and passing other boats is very tricky and, in places, simply not possible. The cutting was made through sandstone, which now lines the waterway, and is topped by woodland. This makes the banks really imposing and High Bridge (57) is as tall and impressive as the nave of a Norman church. A few days earlier we had read that the cutting was closed due to a landslip and in two separate places we saw evidence of significant landslides. There were the remains of decapitated trees that had obviously once been the reason for the waterway closure. The sight of these obstacles made me touch the throttle slightly to speed up and get through the cutting as quickly as possible, without causing a wake that would have added to the erosion problems the area obviously suffered from.

At Holling's Bridge (58) the canal bends to the right and the cutting ends. One more left hand turn and we were passing under Tyrley Farm Bridge (59) and the Tyrley Lock flight came into sight. The Tyrley flight has five locks, dropping about thirty three feet and is really attractive, whilst having some hidden dangers to spice things up. At the top lock is Tyrley Wharf and a lovely lock keeper's cottage with various 'official' signs on it. There is one very 'unofficial' sign that reads: '*ON THIS SITE, SEPT.5.1782, NOTHING HAPPENED'.* Cleverly, it was painted in the same blue colour as the historical plaques we see on buildings of significance and, as a result, it reels you in to reading it. I would not be surprised if there was not a hidden camera somewhere, with a live online feed capturing the many and varied reactions of gullible passers-by. It certainly made us smile!

Each of the locks here have a wicked bywash and I was only glad I was descending - where the 'kick' given by the water re-entering the canal had only a minimal effect on the boat as we left the lock. I would learn in August, on our return trip, that negotiating the stream when trying to enter the lock was a lot harder. This was my first experience of a gushing bywash but there would be many more - particularly on the Llangollen later the same month. At lock four there is a sign telling you to stay in the lock until lock five is ready to enter. This is necessary as the bywash on four is particularly strong and there was also an underwater obstacle just before the entrance to lock five making it impossible to moor and wait to enter. So when the last lock was ready, I left four, using slightly higher revs to counter the cross current and went straight into lock five. Pip was helmsman on locks two and three but I did locks one, four and five in view of their vagaries.

Less than a mile later we moored on the edge of Market Drayton. We walked the half mile or so into the town for lunch at a pub called *The Vaults*. We ate on a very strange roof terrace but the food was nice. After refuelling we then explored the rest of the town, the centre of which has a very strange layout. It didn't really feel like it had a 'heart' - physical not emotional. The church was fabulous and, like they often are, sat perched on the highest point in the town. A lone bellringer was tolling a solitary bell for what we think was ninety nine times in memory of Prince Philip, whose funeral was taking place in Windsor. It was only early afternoon but we had cruised six and a half miles and completed five locks and we decided we were 'done' for the day.

The good weather continued and the next morning we walked the seven mile round trip to the Adderley Flight - both to check it out and because it was just such a lovely day for a walk. I remember the walk well; Pip was emboldened by the straight canal and wanted to be on the helm the whole time the following day - including the flight - which would continue our descent towards Nantwich, about thirteen miles and twenty two locks away. This was where we planned to moor the following weekend whilst taking a trip to London.

In the morning Pip took us out of Market Drayton and we cruised the three and a half miles to Adderley, retracing our steps of the previous day, and negotiating a large fallen tree between Victoria and Bretton Wood Bridges (65 and 66). The sun was shining and I was wearing shorts and a T-shirt for the first time since the previous summer - a landmark moment. As we approached Bretton Coppice Bridge (67) I was standing at the bow of the boat, giving a filmed commentary on the use of 'stop planks'. We had been struck by the many little shelters we saw along the side of the canal - usually at bridges and locks - that contained long planks of wood arranged on racks. These pieces of wood are called stop planks and are positioned, strategically, in these locations, so that they can be deployed easily. In Vlog 19 I talk the viewer right through Bretton Coppice Bridge and point out the groves that had been cut in the canal bank under the bridge, into which the planks could be dropped - effectively sealing off a section of the waterway. This would be done in two circumstances: firstly, when there is a breach (this section of the canal was built on an embankment, and we learned at Shelmore how devastating a breach in an embankment could be). If the canal wall ruptured, the CRT (or indeed anyone who knew what they were doing) could drop the planks in place, one on top of each other, and protect the rest of the canal from losing any more water. The other occasion they would be used would be for when repairs were needed and a particular section of canal, or lock, needed to be drained in a controlled way. I have just rewatched the Vlog and the thing that strikes me the most, apart from how informative it is on the use of stop planks, is just how loudly the birds are singing. They too are clearly enjoying the warm weather and it was a delight to hear them.

Adderley has five locks that take the canal down some thirty one feet. At that time, Pip had limited experience of single width locks and at locks one and two she caught the bow slightly as she entered. By locks four and five she was entering as straight as an arrow. She really was a quick learner and I know that her boat-handling confidence took a huge boost that sunny morning at Adderley.

We cruised on and stopped for lunch above the top lock of the Audlem flight, before walking down the flight and into the village. The locks were lovely and were trumped only by the village itself. We explored for a while, taking in the lovely village shops, the canal themed artefacts in the historic Audlem Mill and the church. Outside the lovely *Shroppie Fly* pub is an old wooden hand crane - once used to unload cargo at the wharfside. Nearby is a plaque on the subject of the village's 'Bear Stone'. The Stone is what is known as a glacial erratic (a rock that does not match the other rocks in the area because it was deposited by a moving ice sheet during the ice age). It now has a ring attached to it and was once used for bear baiting (hence the name) - a practice that, thankfully, was stopped many years ago. Whilst walking back up the flight, we noticed a lovely mooring spot between locks two and three, in what was quite a large pound. It had fabulous views and was in full sun. So we upped our pins and Pip took us down the first two locks before mooring up for a well-earned rest. We would tackle the remaining thirteen locks the following day. We had cruised four and a half miles and completed seven locks.

The Audlem flight has a lovely variety of locks and, unlike Tyrley, the bywash is controlled on most with a barrier protecting the passing boat from the full onslaught of the current. This can be seen very clearly in Vlog 19. There are exceptions, but I will write about those when we ascend the flight later in the year (as that was when they caused me the most problems!). As with all locks on the Shroppie, the lock gate arms are painted grey (most are black) and this quaint variation dates back to the existence of the Shropshire Union Canal Company - being the colour of their livery. The flight has fifteen locks and takes the canal down a total of ninety feet. Pip and I share the driving and lock work and I note in my diary that Pip did not hit a single gate on the descent. Finally, we completed all fifteen locks and, being tired, headed off in search of a spot to moor early. We found it just before Mickley Bridge (84) where the onside bank is really flat and wide and picnic tables have been installed, alongside the odd bench. We caught our breath and then researched how to spend the afternoon. Google came up trumps and told us we were very near a 'secret' nuclear bunker at Hack Green. We walked the three quarters of a mile to find the compound - which is usually open to the public. Officially called RAF Hack Green, the bunker is one of seventeen regional sites adopted by the government in case of nuclear attack. It would have been where those important enough would be taken to help run whatever was left of the country after an attack and it's now a museum. We walked back to the canal at Burrow's Bridge (85) and popped down to check out the two Hack Green locks (the last before Nantwich) that we will tackle tomorrow. They drop twelve feet in total and will be our last locks on the Shroppie mainline before we leave and join the Llangollen. Today we have only covered about three miles but have completed thirteen locks.

April 21st saw us completing the final two locks and pulling into Nantwich - under Pip's expert helmsmanship. We moored just after Marsh Lane Bridge (91) and as we were staying here until the weekend, we made sure the mooring was sound and near other boats. We walked into the town. Nantwich is lovely with lots of historic buildings. We popped into a curiosity shop and bought a large frog to add to the many already adorning our boat (you can't have too many). Our route back took us down to Telford's magnificent aqueduct - which we will cross when we leave the town. When we arrived at Nantwich our next move was unclear as the Middlewich Arm (linking to the Trent and Mersey at Wardle Lock) was closed and the Llangollen had suffered a major breach and was also unnavigable. We had already planned to put The Frog into a marina for a few days over the weekend whilst we popped down to London (where we could still visit as it was, technically, our home address) so we did not need to make a decision which route we would take just yet. So, instead, we decided to just let fate decide; we would simply take the waterway that opened first.

CHAPTER 32: DON'T LOOK DOWN - THE LLANGOLLEN CANAL

After our weekend away we left our mooring - still unsure which direction we would finally take! We stopped at the marina near the Nantwich Basin for a pump out, diesel and more coal. This small arm marks where the historic Birmingham and Liverpool canal met the older Chester Canal. The only clue to this is the change in the size of the bridge holes (The Chester is bigger). Now, of course, both historic waterways are part of the Shropshire Union main line. Whilst we were waiting at the service point Pip read that The Middlewich would not re-open for another four days, as a minimum, BUT The Llangollen had reopened that very day. So it was decided and I immediately contacted the CRT and deferred our booking in Salthouse Dock in Liverpool so we could make this detour. We headed for Hurleston Junction and the wonderful Llangollen Canal.

We had fully intended to navigate this waterway at some point and, in a way, the fate-led decision to do so at the end of April, following a breach, was a good one. With the famous Pontcysyllte and Chirk Aqueducts along its route and some of the most scenic stretches of water in the country, the Llangollen was very popular - especially with hire boaters. So the closer to summer you got, the more traffic you would encounter and the less enjoyable the experience would be.

We left Nantwich and completed the final two and a bit miles to Hurleston junction - where we bumped into our old friends on NB *That's Amore*. It was nice to see them again and they lent a hand with the tricky Hurleston Locks (where we also had some CRT volunteer help). The junction was wide and easy to negotiate - even though it sat directly after Hurleston Roving Bridge (97) and required an immediate sharp left hand turn. We started the ascent of the four locks that carry the canal up some thirty four feet in very quick order.

The Llangollen Canal is actually a combination of the historic Ellesmere canal and the Llangollen navigable feeder and was only given its current name in the 1980s. The Ellesmere canal was planned in stages and the first of these was built from Ellesmere Port on the Dee estuary to Chester, where it joined the Chester Canal, in 1795. Deep in Wales the southern sections were built - emanating from Frankton Junction south and, later, west to Trevor (over the two, now famous, aqueducts). The original plan was to then build a very challenging route directly north from Trevor, past Wrexham and join the Dee at Chester. This proved unviable, however, and in the end, the current, more circuitous, route was built from Frankton to Hurleston. The canal is fed directly from the higher ends of the River Dee via a specially constructed weir (the Horseshoe Falls) bringing water into the feeder waterway near Llangollen.

The canal thrived until the end of the first world war, but over the next thirty years the traffic using it fell away dramatically. Unlike many other waterways, however, it was never likely to close entirely as it provided a really important supply of fresh water to the burgeoning population of North West England (the impressive Hurleston Reservoir sits proudly above the junction with the Shropshire Union main line and is evidence of this important role for the canal. As are the demanding bywashes at each of the many locks on its route (it seemed the more water that could be pulled out of Wales the better and the handling impact on novice boaters was not a major consideration in the early nineteenth century)). We loved the Llangollen and I am really looking forward to reliving our time on it by sharing it with you.

On our first day we made great progress and finally moored outside of the little village of Wrenbury. We covered eight and a half miles and completed nine locks: the Hurleston, Swanley and Baddiley flights - a total climb of about sixty eight feet. Between bridge 3 and 4 we saw evidence of the significant, newly repaired breach. The surrounding field had a large area of sodden/flattened grass and the pump, used to reunite the errant water with the canal, was still in place. There was brand new Armco along the offside bank and it was clear that this had been a significant repair and clean up operation.

Our first task the next day was to negotiate the two lift bridges that sandwich the Wrenbury Mill Marina. The left hand bend into the second at the mill itself was sharper than Nicholson suggested it would be but we made it through unscathed. What followed was a long, almost straight, stretch of water until Marbury Lock loomed into sight just after Church Bridge (23). There are four well-spaced locks in the next section of canal: Marbury, Quoisley, Willeymoor and Povey's. Each takes the canal up about six feet. Willeymoor is particularly charming and, being positioned adjacent to Willeymoor Lock Tavern, has a ready-made audience of gongoozlers on the tables outside. All of these locks have the now familiar strong bywash and Pip did a great job of capturing this on Vlog 20. There is a clip of the weir at Baddiley Lock No. 2 (completed the day before) where she shows my struggles keeping the boat straight as I enter the lock. On today's cruise, I remembered being thrown sideways into the bank at Marbury Lock and struggling to get The Frog moving again against the strong current in shallow water.

If I thought the locks so far had been a challenge then I had not yet encountered the combination of six locks at Grindley Brook - which included a three lock staircase. The approach to Lock 6 (the first of the flight heading south west) was under a wide railway bridge (27) and it was recommended you only entered the bridge entrance if you knew you could go into the lock or the lock pins were clear. Pip walked ahead and prepared the way. The first three locks were as challenging as all the others so far. We emerged from Lock 4 and saw another boat moored on the onside with a crew member holding the centre line. We guessed they were waiting for the staircase - which was hidden around a bend and under a wide road bridge (29). It seemed that there was a bit of a wait as another boat was coming down. We pulled in and moored up properly so that we could walk ahead and take a look at the staircase. The three locks rose nearly twenty feet and looked narrow and intimidating as we walked out from under the bridge. Volunteers were on duty so we stood and watched the action. When the descending boat had passed under the bridge the waiting boater (who was on a hire boat) came through and entered the first lock with no problems. Unfortunately they then had an issue as they tried to enter lock 2 (the second in the staircase). The water level was too low for them to get over the cill of lock 3 and their keel grounded. They backed up and tried again - with the same result. The volunteers opened the top paddles on lock 1 and let a bit of the water in and scraped the bottom of the lock with a fork. Thankfully, these interventions had the desired effect and our hirers were on the move. Now it was our turn. We made it with no issues but there is a wonderful shot, in

Vlog 20, of the grimace on my face as I took The Frog over that troublesome cill.

We finally moored up, unusually on the off-side, at the town of Whitchurch. I remember pulling in as a boat came in the other direction - at speed. Their wake and the 'natural' current on the Llangollen combined and pulled our bow out across the canal so I was almost sideways. I jumped off the stern, centre-line in hand, and managed to pull her back to the bank. It was an event that had not happened before and demonstrated the 'drag' of a passing boat when consideration is not being given to moored craft (or, in our case, mooring craft).

Whitchurch is historically significant - and very sweet. A settlement dates back to Roman times (it is the oldest continuously inhabited town in Shropshire) but the modern town is named after a Norman white church that was one of several built on the site where the magnificent St Alkmund's now stands. The church is almost 'too big' for the town and reflects the former status of this conurbation. Its interior and large stained glass windows mean it is definitely worth a visit. The town developed as a market town and was well connected with road and later canal and rail links. Despite being in Shropshire, Cheshire cheese production became an important industry in the town and the Whitchurch Arm of the Llangollen (now significantly truncated) used to extend well into the town, making it easy to bring in raw materials and take the cheese onto markets elsewhere. The town also boasted a good hairdresser, so I took the opportunity to get a professional correction to Pip's handiwork (she will kill me for that).

As we cruised down the Llangollen, we were planning to meet up with Pip's sister Trish and her husband, Dave, for a weekend cruise over the Pontcysyllte aqueduct - so the next morning we needed to cover as many miles as possible to ensure we were well-placed when they arrived. The canal 'helped' us as there were now no locks for some considerable distance. The weather was sunny and bright and our only hindrance were the few lift bridges we had to manage. Most were not motorised and were lifted by windlass - typically taking many many turns to raise! At Hassells No 1 Lift bridge (33) I filmed from the tiller as I took us through the narrow opening. This footage in Vlog 20 gives a real feel for just how tight the passage was.

At some point that day we cruised in and out of Wales, crossing the border a couple of times. We also passed the stunning entrance to the Prees Branch - which breaks south near Whixall Moss Roving Bridge (46). A whole book could be written on Whixall Moss - which, along with Bettisfield, Fenn and Cadney Mosses form part of a Site of Special Scientific Interest. The area, which straddles the England Wales border, is the third largest raised peat bog in the UK and is now a nature reserve. Pip and I took a lunchtime walk along one of its many paths and agreed it was a strangely beautiful environment with big skies and lots of open pools of peaty water.

Following some long and straight sections we were soon passing what must be one of the most beautiful canal landscapes in the world. The Meres (Cole Mere, Blake Mere and The Mere neighbouring the town of Ellesmere itself) were framed by tall trees and on the sunny day we passed them the successive wide expanses of water looked stunning. It really was magical and felt even more so when we entered Ellesmere tunnel. It's only eighty seven yards long but boy was it tight. The brick lining felt very close as I worked hard to keep The Frog straight and avoid contact (some nice footage can be seen in Vlog 20).

The bridges were also a challenge on this section. The current seemed to get stronger the closer we got to Llangollen and the narrow openings of the bridges made them run even faster as we passed underneath. They were also set at strange angles, which meant emerging with our bow heading straight for the bank on a few occasions. We passed Ellesmere, our target for that night, by mid-afternoon, so after a brief stop for a cup of tea (it started snowing!) we pressed on and finally moored just short of Frankton Junction and the start of the Montgomery Canal. The 'Monty' is over thirty miles long and terminates at Newtown. There was a major breach in the 1930s and now only the first seven miles are navigable with boaters having to wind just after Crickheath Bridge 85. What is significant is this bridge numbering system - which points to the antecedents of what we now call the Llangollen Canal. The bridges down the Montgomery canal are a continuation of the numbering sequence seen on the Llangollen mainline. This means that as we continue our route west past Frankton junction, the next bridge we come to is Bridge 1W - the letter being added to distinguish it from the other Bridge 1 near Hurleston Junction. By the time we stopped, we had broken our cruising record, covering fourteen and a half miles in a day and we were now well on track for our weekend rendezvous. More about Ellesmere on our trip back.

Friday 30th of April saw us cruise a further six and a half miles and complete the two final locks on the canal. We moored at the Poachers Pub by Bridge 19. This location was deliberately chosen, as it gave both a 'googleable' meeting place for our visitors and a delivery spot for Tesco's. My diary for the next morning has us cleaning the boat - inside and out - '*so we looked our best for the aqueduct*' (not because we were having visitors). Midday came and with our extra crew on board we set off towards Llangollen. The canal was busy and seemed to take a more meandering course as well as becoming perceptibly narrower as we moved further 'upstream'. It felt like cruising was going to be a challenge.

Between us and the Pontcysyllte crossing lay the Chirk aqueduct and two tunnels: Chirk and Whitehouse. The Chirk aqueduct was a revelation. It is hardly talked about as its much bigger neighbour takes all the limelight, but I thought it was delightful. Like the Pontcysllte, it was designed by Telford and also has a cast iron trough. But: it is shorter and the trough is encased entirely in masonry - so it is not as obvious as that on its bigger 'cousin'. To the left there is also a wide plinth which makes the sensation of crossing it less dramatic than the crossing of the Pontcysyllte - but, having not yet enjoyed the latter, I was still impressed by its scale. It stands seventy feet high and is seven hundred and ten feet long and the fact that it was dwarfed by a much taller train viaduct, crossing the same valley, only added to its interest. To me, it meant we were able to appreciate the architectural arches of the railway and apply this awe to those that we knew were holding up the waterway we were cruising on. This crossing was also the last time we would leave England and enter Wales on our 'out' leg.

At the end of the aqueduct we immediately entered the Chirk Tunnel. We followed a hire boat through and as the tunnel was not wide enough to pass oncoming craft, it was great to have a pathfinder ahead of us. As the current got stronger at bridges, you can imagine what it did in a four hundred and fifty nine yard tunnel. We were on very high revs but were still moving very slowly. We were relieved, finally, to emerge onto a pretty wooded stretch - only to see a moored hire boat blocking the canal ahead. The boaters had obviously gone off for a walk and had underestimated the strength of the current and the impact of passing traffic. Their bow mooring pin had been pulled out of the ground and the front of the boat had drifted out and was now across and blocking the canal. Trish and a passer-by took a mallet and pulled the offending vessel back to the bank before ensuring the mooring pins were driven in at the right angle to stop them being pulled loose again.

The Whitehouse Tunnel may be only one hundred and ninety one yards long but as it is very narrow it was still a bit tricky. We got through without incident and after a sharp turn at Irish Bridge we were on the final approach to Froncysyllte and the two small lift bridges that would be our last challenge that day. We pulled in and moored about two hundred yards short of the Pontcysyllte - intending to complete the crossing the following morning, when we were fresh.

That evening we took the opportunity to walk across to Trevor and examine the aqueduct close up - including dropping down to the River Dee and filming the view from below. It really is an amazing feat of engineering. Our Nicholson describes it as: *'Easily the most famous and most spectacular feature on the whole canal system'* : they are right. It crosses the Dee valley at a glorious height of one hundred and twenty six feet and is over a thousand feet in length. Originally there were plans to build a series of locks on either slope which would have been joined by a much smaller aqueduct. The canal company recognised that this would have been an expensive, as well as time and water consuming, option. However, they also recognised that because of the height and span needed to cross the valley in 'one go', a traditional aqueduct was not a viable option. Thomas Telford, came up with an innovative solution: he proposed a new construction technique of 'simply' joining a series of cast iron troughs together on top of a number of very high pillars. Greeted with derision initially, the project went ahead and was completed in 1805 after only ten years' work. It cost £47,018 (very precise) at the time (about £3 million today) - which is incredible. Yes, no doubt there would not have been the health and safety measures in place that we would see today (and labour would have been a lot cheaper). Nevertheless, to create such a beautiful structure, which still stands today, with very few leaks and little masonry decay, for such a low cost, was a remarkable achievement. The construction secrets are also fascinating: the blocks in the pillars are joined by very thin layers of mortar made from a mixture of lime and ox blood.

Whilst the troughs are dovetailed, for a tight fit and were made even more secure by being sealed with a mixture of welsh flannel and boiled sugar. Bravo Mr Telford!

The next morning we were preparing to start our crossing when we were passed by a young lady on a paddle board. She was working her way towards the aqueduct: 'You are not planning to cross on that thing are you?' I shouted (genuinely concerned). She said she was. I asked if she knew how tall the aqueduct was and how low the trough edge was on the off side? She said she had walked across it many times and that she would be 'fine'. I was incredulous. If you have ever crossed the aqueduct on a boat, you know that the experience is very different to walking across. On the on side there is not only a wide path but also a set of high railings between you and the 'drop'. On the off side there is nothing more than the side of the trough (measuring about twelve to eighteen inches above the water level). When you look in that direction you really do get the sensation of flying as you cross. The Nicholson guide strongly recommends that small children are kept inside on the trip over - such is the risk to them falling over the edge. This was clearly a very brave paddle boarder.

Finally we began our own crossing. The trough is wider than the channel itself and extends under the pedestrian path. This clever design feature means that, as boats cross, the water is dispersed sideways as well as forwards and this avoids creating a 'wave' ahead of the bow - keeping the crossing nice and smooth. As I am at the helm Pip is filming from the bow and gets some amazing footage of the drop to the River Dee below. Finally we were across and, whilst the canal continued under a low bridge out of the Trevor Basin and onto Llangollen itself, we were not going any further. Not only did we need to get back to drop our guests off at their car but we had also researched the route and had learned that only boats with a draft of twenty one inches or lower should attempt the route. The Frog drew twenty three inches and as the canal was very narrow in places we did not fancy becoming an obstacle for any other boaters. Having turned in the basin we began our journey back over the aqueduct and I was really grateful to Dave for taking the helm. When you are concentrating on steering, as I was, coming in the opposite direction, it is hard to appreciate the spectacle around you. On the way back I sat at the bow and took in what was truly a fabulous experience. Oh - and the paddle boarder survived!

For our journey back I will simply highlight a few of the key events that happened to us - rather than recalling the same section of canal again. That said I did promise you some comment on Ellesmere - which I will honour. Following a couple of wet days moored near Rhoswiel we set off for Ellesmere. In our path were the two New Marton locks. The day was windy and as we approached the first of the locks I moored to allow Pip to set the mechanisms and then open the gate, only to find that I could not get off with normal throttle - the wind was so strong I was forced back onto the mooring pins. I reversed to give me a longer run at the lock and more time to gain speed and pull away from the bank. After three attempts it worked.

At the second Marton lock we met a hire boat coming the other way. It was just entering an empty lock and we waited for it to fill and leave. We were moored above the lock and I was holding The Frog with my centre line wrapped once around a mooring pin. I was glad I had taken this extra step. When the hire boat left the lock they must have been at full throttle - I had honestly never seen anything like it. The wake they caused was enormous (by canal standards) and it was all that I could do to stop our boat going along with them, such was the drag. The mooring pin made all the difference. After a few metres they throttled back to normal speed and went on their way. Pip and I were left scratching our heads when a man who had helped them through the locks came up the path towards us: "Sorry about that - I think that may have been my fault". We asked him what he meant. He explained that he was a boater who was moored down the canal some distance away. He came across the holidaymakers at the lock, clearly having no idea what they were doing and had stopped to help. It seems the couple had hired from a boatyard a couple of miles away and this was their first experience on the canals and, consequently, their first ever lock. He helped them with the mechanism but they remained very nervous about the bywash (at the top of the lock near to where we were waiting) which fell away with quite a current following a couple of days of heavy rain. They thought they could be dragged sideways by the force. In reality, the bywash is only really a challenge at the bottom of the lock when you enter (as I have described previously) but, to put their minds at rest, the good samaritan boater told them that if they were worried they should give the boat a little bit of throttle as they left the lock. As the Germans would say: 'Alles Klar!"

We did not make it to Ellesmere until the next day as the weather was really windy and cold (five degrees on the 5th May) and I decided to moor part way there. When we finally made it we stopped directly opposite the CRT yard near the Ellesmere Arm and we began to explore. The town is named after the beautiful Mere beside it and is definitely worth a visit - especially if you are on the canal. The arm protrudes right into the heart of the town and the warehouses and crane, that still stand, are testament to its busy canal trading past. There has been a settlement here since before Norman times and there are the groundworks of a motte and bailey castle near the mere. Now there is an attractive mix of architectural styles in the town and it was once so important that it gave its name to the original canal cutting that terminates at Netherpool on the River Mersey (renamed Ellesmere Port in the early 19th century). Incidentally, Ellesmere Port (as opposed to Ellesmere) is the home of the National Waterways Museum.

Our next stop is back at Whixall Moss and we moor just beyond bridge 44. I am recording it as I remember going out in the evening to see one of the most beautiful sunsets I saw on our travels. I still have one of the images as the 'wallpaper' on my laptop to this day! We reach Whitchurch the next day and moor again next to the Arm. A couple of hours later we were hit from behind by a boat which then reversed, rapidly, across the canal. The helmsman seemed to be struggling so I asked if I could help. He explained that he had just caught the overhanging trees on the other bank and had lost his chimney in the canal - hence the loss of control and the collision with us. Now he was trying to reverse over and use his sea magnet to recover it. I stayed out on the bank and helped keep his bow in the middle of the canal whilst he searched. He had travelled all the way from Rhoswiel that day and was absolutely on his last legs when he finally gave up the search. I helped him moor and then spotted a hire boat trying, in vain, to wind at the entrance to the Arm. I ran across the bridge and gave some advice as well as pulling on the stern line to help them around. There's always something happening on the cut.

Our passage through Grindley Brook saw us being the victim of grounding between locks two and three - on the same cill that the hire boat had found on the way up. The CRT volunteer reopened the paddles on the top lock to bring water down to us and eventually we were able to move into the next lock. There was a queue of three boats in either direction, so the sole volunteer was facing a busy day.

Our next 'experience' was at Willeymoor Lock. The descent went fine but as I exited through the lock gates it was clear that something was wrong. The Frog was sluggish and there was a terrible banging noise coming from under my feet - where the engine was. I feared the worst. It sounded like something major had 'gone' in the engine - possibly a piston. Having pulled in, I asked Pip to engage the engine again whilst I stood on the bank. To my great relief, the banging sound was clearly external. My thinking then went to the prop, accessible through the weed hatch. However, I was still concerned at the level of the noise and vibration I had felt and still thought something awful must have happened. The shaft did indeed have a foreign body wrapped around it. At first I thought it was just a rope and it was only when I cut it free that I learned the full truth. A previous lock user had obviously lost a fender and we were unfortunate enough to catch the trailing rope around our propeller. When the engine was engaged, the fender was flying around the prop and hitting the underside of the boat - making the awful noise I had heard. In Vlog 20 I look quite relaxed removing the offending item, but I can tell you the relief I felt that we did not have a major engine failure was immense!

The next morning we reached Hurleston Locks and began the descent. I was leaving the top lock when I saw a hire boat coming out of the lock below. They were clearly 'new out' and gestured frantically that they wanted me to move to my left and allow them to go straight into my now vacated lock. I was not happy but as they looked terrified I complied. This was a big mistake. The top of the Hurleston flight is very exposed and today there was a strong wind coming from my right. By moving out to the left I was heading straight for the top of the lock bywash and I quickly started to feel its drag. I tried to pull the nose around but, as this manoeuvre was against the wind, I failed miserably. Faced with the prospect of grounding on top of the weir I had no choice but to put The Frog hard into reverse and head for the bank. Another boater was waiting, having seen the challenge I was facing. I threw him the stern line and, when I could, I threw Pip the centre line. Together they pulled The Frog back straight with me helping with the engine. So what should have happened? Ideally, any boat coming up the flight should move to their right. They would not have been at the mercy of the weir as they would have been moving in the opposite direction. Adrenaline is a powerful thing and I eventually stopped shaking as we negotiated the final three locks.

We exited the last lock and said our goodbyes to the Llangollen and turned north back on the Shropshire Union Canal to start the next stage of our adventure.

CHAPTER 33: MIDDLEWICH - BREACHES AND STEAM TRAINS

We were now heading north on The Shropshire Union canal and closing in on the Middlewich Branch and its link to the Trent and Mersey. The wind that had made the second Hurleston Lock so tricky was getting even stronger and, whilst we were planning to go a few more miles and possibly turn at Barbridge Junction before nightfall, it was not to be. As we approached Stoke Hall Bridge (99), we saw a hire boat approaching from the other direction. It was some distance from the bridge so we had right of way. I did not realise how fast he was cruising, however, and I had only just cleared the bridge when he was upon us. The helmsman was trying hard to slow down and steer away from us but the wind (and possibly his inexperience) was making that impossible and I could see he was probably going to hit us. I steered The Frog hard right towards the towpath and jumped off with the centre line to try and get out of his way. Unfortunately, he slewed even further to his left and hit the bank and our front fender at the same time. After many apologies, he was trying desperately to get his boat off the bank but the wind was so strong he could not move. I grabbed our barge pole and pushed against his front fender until his bow was facing out into the canal. With hard throttle he managed to get clear and carry on his journey. We realised, however, that without the same help we could not. We were both tired and the wind was clearly going to make the Barbridge Junction turn tricky - so we took a line each and pulled The Frog away from the bridge and moored up using our pins. So ended a challenging day on the cut.

The next morning we changed our plans and headed past Barbridge and on towards Chester. Pip was due to have her second Covid vaccination there and we would have liked to have completed the journey by boat. Luckily for us we had to stop for water at the Calveley slipway. We got chatting to a fellow boater who expressed surprise we were heading in the direction we were. Apparently, the route to Chester had been closed for sometime and had no end date for the repairs to a lock to be completed. There was only one winding hole before the stoppage and it was about half a mile after Calveley. We thanked our informant profusely and headed for the turning point and started our trip back to Barbridge. It seemed that the Middlewich and the Trent and Mersey would provide our next adventure after all. We reflected on what a close call this had been; had we not met the lady at the services we would have definitely missed the winding hole and been 'stuck' en-route to Chester for who knows how long.

At Barbridge the turn onto the Middlewich went well and for the first (and I think last) time we included some 'Go-Pro' footage in our next Vlog. The benefit is you can capture long passages of canal and then speed them up for the viewer to enjoy. The downside is the picture quality - which was not as good as that taken on the Iphone.

We took our time traversing the Middlewich arm. As we could not get to Chester by boat, we were now planning to head for the famous Anderton Boat Lift so that we could drop down onto the River Weaver and cruise to Northwich - from where we could get a train and still make Pip's appointment. The Middlewich was designed by Thomas Telford and was built as a shorter route from the Trent and Mersey to the Shropshire Union than that offered by the Staffs and Worcestershire. It is only about ten miles long and has just four locks along its route (albeit each has a drop of between nine and twelve feet with intimidating Cills - see Vlog 21). This new canal link was a vital commercial artery when it was built, bringing coal for the many saltworks in this part of the world (the suffix 'wich' means salt) and taking away the finished product. The canal has an interesting history. In places it is very straight and in 1888 the canal owners experimented with installing a small steam train on the towpath between Bridges 5 and 6. The locomotive could pull up to eight barges at once at a speed of seven miles per hour. The idea did not take off however and horses remained the preferred power source. The canal has also seen some significant breaches. The most recent being the Church Minshull breach in 1958 and the Wheelock breach in 2018. In the former incident, over twenty million gallons of water were lost to surrounding fields and the River Weaver. The latter event drained three quarters of a mile of canal (effectively the contents of the pound between Stanthorne and Wardle Locks) - a huge loss. Repairs for the Wheelock breach took over six months to complete; they used four thousand tonnes of stone and cost over three million pounds! An investigation by the CRT found that paddle gates on the Stanthorne lock had been left open and this extra water flow caused the weir at the Wheelock

Aqueduct to fail. Never has the importance of good housekeeping on the canals hit home more strongly.

We had time to kill, so we stayed for a day near Cholmondeston Lock and enjoyed a long walk - circling away from the canal and then back to the towpath near Minshull Lock. Our next cruise was over eight miles and we almost completed the branch. We reached Middlewich at about three in the afternoon and found a great mooring - quite near the town centre and the junction with the Trent and Mersey (between Bridges 29 and 30). We would stay here for two days and then join the Trent and Mersey. The end of the Middlewich Canal is interesting. As you enter Wardle Lock, which is positioned a few yards from the junction, you technically leave the Shropshire Union and enter the shortest canal in the UK. The Wardle Canal is one hundred and fifty four feet long, which includes the lock itself. It was built by the Trent and Mersey Canal Company to ensure they maintained control of the junction (and, therefore, both the water and tolls payable). Until it was built, the company had refused permission for the Middlewich branch to join their canal.

CHAPTER 34: DROPPING IN ON THE WEAVER!

When we moved off I remember very well that it was raining and it was not going to stop! We had delayed our move in order to reach the boat lift on the day we had booked our descent, but now we regretted not travelling when it was dry. The turn out of the Wardle (under the relatively low bridge) was tight. A tourist cruise boat was tied up opposite the exit and I could not turn too tightly as I risked hitting the low bridge with the tiller and my head if I did. Reverse gear was needed but we were soon back on the Trent and Mersey and heading north west. We immediately faced three locks (the Middlewich 3) which had a drop of over thirty two feet. The second of these was positioned around a ninety degree turn and was just after the first. Very strange. The artwork adorning the towpath was really impressive, however.

Lock 75 (about a quarter of a mile after the first three) is aptly named Middlewich Big Lock and was the first double lock we had encountered since we left Braunston. The size of the lock and the width of the canal here reflected its role in transporting salt in large barges. Not far from the Big Lock is Croxton Aqueduct. Once fourteen feet in width, it collapsed in the 1930s and was replaced with an eight foot wide alternative - to save money. This decision reflected the waning importance of the canal for trade - with roads and rail taking up the slack. Today it just makes an interesting way for leisure cruisers like us to cross the River Dane.

Between Croxton and Northwich there are a number of 'flashes' alongside the main waterway. These flashes look a bit like Tixall Wide (mentioned previously). The difference is whilst Tixall was created on purpose, to appease a local landowner, those near Croxton have been caused by landslips - probably the result of mining. Big warning signs tell boaters to steer clear or risk grounding on already sunken vessels lurking under the water.

Bridge 177, on the approach to Whatcroft, is known as 'Murder Bridge'. In October 1967 the body of Bertie Wilkinson, a local solicitor, was found in a shallow grave by the side of the canal. He had been strangled and had taken a blow to the head - possibly from a windlass. Why he was killed, and by whom, has never been worked out and to this day his death remains a mystery.

As we continued on our way the canal took us right through the middle of a Tata Chemical works. Not the most scenic of locations but fascinating nevertheless. You can see why the plant was based here originally, straddling what was once its prime source of transport bringing raw materials. After eight and a half miles of non-stop rain we decided to moor near the Salt Museum at Wincham - all set to reach the lift the next day.

Sunday 16th May was a red letter day for us. If the Pontcysyllte Aqueduct is the most famous piece of engineering on the canal network, the Anderton Boat Lift can't be far behind. In this area, both the River Weaver and the canal were key to the burgeoning salt industry. However, at Anderton the canal sits about fifty feet above the river and, once upon a time, the only link between the two waterways was a series of chutes down the hillside. Salt was dropped down these chutes to waiting vessels below. The lift was built in 1875 to allow boats carrying the precious cargo to continue their journey along both waterways, without the need to unload and reload onto another vessel. The metal structure of the lift looks impressive but in reality most of the weight of the water and boats is carried by two huge pistons that drop into underground cylinders. Today the lift is operated electronically.

My first job in the morning was to recover the anchor we had used on the Thames from its storage place in the bow and re-attach it at the stern. I won't repeat here why anchors are needed on rivers but not on canals, but needless to say, with the rain we had experienced the day before, I predicted a strong flow on the River Weaver. We cruised the final few miles to the services at Old Check Office Bridge (199), pumped out and filled with water. We edged our way towards the Lift and moored again, before taking a walk down to have a look at the lift up close. I would classify this impressive structure as part of a working museum, with exhibits in the gardens that surround it as well as in the building that has been erected next to it. Unfortunately, Covid meant the inside museum was closed that day but we still enjoyed walking in the grounds, down to the banks of the weaver and looking back up at the engineering brilliance of the lift itself. As we walked we bumped into Paddy and Gail, two boaters whom we first met on the Llangollen.

We also approached the owners of the boat at the front of the queue. They explained that the lift was actually out of action and they were now running late as a result. We feared the worst and grabbed a passing CRT employee to get the full lowdown. It seemed, remarkably, that the River Weaver water levels were too low (despite the rain) and that a sensor was preventing its use until the water level came back up to allow a safe exit from the lift onto the river.

A couple of hours later we got the nod and we moved off towards the lift. The entrance is a bit tight and it meant brushing The Frog along the right hand hedge as we swung hard left to enter the aqueduct leading to the lift. In doing so we passed under a walkway, full of 'picture hungry' gongoozlers who had clearly been waiting for the lift to start working again. We made the turn with no problems and were soon drifting out about fifty feet above the ground, onto the aqueduct that leads to the caissons (the 'tanks' in which you travel down to the river). Each of the two caissons holds two hundred and fifty tonnes of water! The view from up here is amazing and you have a weird sense of flying, not dissimilar to the famous welsh aqueduct, but with a few extra gongoozlers. We enter the caisson and two gates close behind us, creating a watertight tub in which we will descend to the river. The drop, which takes about five minutes, went smoothly and we were soon at the bottom, waiting for the front gate to open. We waited and we waited some more. The gates were not working, as the many attempts to open them were clear to see. Finally, after about thirty minutes, the gates lifted and we were 'free' to leave and join the River Weaver.

First impressions of the Weaver were good. Like the Thames, it felt wide and deep compared to the canals we had just left. We motored south, against the flow, and moored in the middle of Northwich, right opposite the marina (and a very handy Waitrose). Exploration of the town centre did not take long that evening and we were ready the next morning to explore further upstream, traversing two river locks, before lunching and returning to our mooring.

The locks on the Weaver only operate at certain times so it is important that boaters check before heading off on a cruise. We could not complete Hunts Lock until ten o'clock so we delayed our start. Immediately after leaving our mooring we passed under Hayhurst Swing Bridge. Its size reminded us of the scale of the other vessels that used this stretch of river. For the bridge to have to swing, the passing craft would have had to be well over twenty feet high (at current river levels). Two other boats joined us in the cavernous bowels of Hunt's Lock, our first river lock since leaving the Thames. Vale Royal Lock was just as big but both of the locks we used sat next to even bigger chambers designed for the enormous craft that work the river up to Runcorn and the Manchester Ship Canal. After leaving, we cruised about another half a mile and moored for lunch. I have to say that the lock keepers here were really friendly - despite having to close the large gates by hand using a wheel mechanism - and we were waved on our way at every crossing.

The next morning we walked to the station and caught the train to Chester for Pip's second vaccination. We sat on the platform and watched the rats coming out of the drains and climbing into the bins on the opposite side of the tracks. Little did we know the drama that was going to unfold about thirty minutes after our departure. When we tried to get a train back to Northwich we were told they were all cancelled. We learned that the roof above the platform and ticket office at Northwich Station had collapsed shortly after we left. Remarkably and luckily, nobody was injured. The replacement bus journey was long and tedious but I guess our day could have been a lot worse. Images of our visit can be found in Vlog 22. It is a beautiful city and I recommend it to anyone as a place to visit. Its history shines through, from the majestic city walls to the remains of a Roman amphitheatre. All of this architectural splendour is framed by the impressive River Dee - the original lowest crossing point of which led to the development of a settlement in the first place. Whilst there was probably a settlement here before the Roman occupation, it was the building of a Roman Fort in the first century CE that accelerated its growth. Its proximity to Wales and the Wirral peninsula, with its two estuaries, also made it strategically important. For us the priority was that Pip was now fully vaccinated!

We left the Weaver the next day, ascending on the boat lift with Paddy and Gail. As we left the lift enclosure, it was impossible to turn left, so we had to turn right and immediately wind and head back west towards the Preston Brook Tunnel and the terminus of the Trent and Mersey Canal. Soon after turning, we passed under Soote Hill Bridge (200) and moved into single file at very low speed. The canal was closed here for three months following a significant landslip in January. The evidence was plain to see (Vlog 23 has these images) and I did not want to be responsible for starting another collapse.

A little further down the canal we entered Barnton Tunnel. It's only five hundred and seventy two yards long but it has such a kink in the middle that you cannot see the other end until you have passed it. It is also wide enough for only one boat but strangely has no timed entries (unlike the Saltersford - which is the next, shorter, tunnel less than half a mile further on). In September 2020 two forty foot narrowboats met each other in the middle and got royally stuck - having to be rescued by three fire crews. Luckily we did not meet anyone on our transit. The Saltersford Tunnel can only be entered at certain times. Its kink is even worse than Barnton, so these timed entries are essential to avoid a potential collision.

It felt like it had been a long morning and we were struck by the panoramic views of the Weaver valley as we turned onto a short straight near Dutton. So we decided to stop at what was a fabulous mooring. To our left we could see for miles over the expanse of the Weaver valley - including the impressive Dutton Rail Viaduct. Behind the boat was one of the iconic mile markers that can be found along the entire length of the Trent and Mersey. This one told us we were just two miles from Preston Brook tunnel and the end of the canal (and the start of the Bridgewater). In front of the boat was another sign, screwed onto the concrete blocks which made up the bank of the canal. The plaque commemorated the Dutton Breach that had happened on this very spot on September 2nd 2012. We looked over the hedge and realised just how high the navigation was above the surrounding land and it became clear why any breach would have been devastating. A hole the size of twelve double decker buses was caused by twenty nine million litres of water flooding onto farmland and down to the river below. We reassured ourselves that, following the extensive rebuilding work in 2012, another breach in the same spot was extremely unlikely. This reassurance was needed as the forecast for the next two days was constant rain and we were not planning on going anywhere.

That afternoon we walked the two miles to the other end of the Preston Brook tunnel to get a feel for what lay ahead on the next phase of our odyssey. Preston Brook looked magnificent. Built in 1777, it is one thousand two hundred and thirty nine yards long and, as it is quite narrow, can only be entered between the hour and ten past the hour. Above it sits a lovely cottage, the gardens of which sweep down to the canal side in front of Dutton Stop Lock (a small lock with a drop of only five inches - the typical barrier marking the meeting point of two canals). We returned to The Frog, looking forward to our final cruise on the Trent and Mersey and the chance to say hello to, arguably, the most historic canal in the UK - the Bridgewater.

CHAPTER 35: THE BRIDGEWATER CANAL

We cruised down to the stop lock the next day - arriving at 10.01 - perfect timing to enter the tunnel. As I am writing this I have just read a post on social media, made by another boater about to enter Preston Brook, bemoaning meeting another boat coming the other way - despite entering at the right time. I am glad I had not seen that just before we started our traverse. I hate tunnels - in case you did not realise - and on this occasion I was glad that it was at least very straight. As we started our passage, it became clear that I was not standing in the centre of the stern. I found this out because despite using the television aerial as my guide (keeping it in the 'window' of light created by the distant tunnel exit) we kept cruising towards the wall on one side. Poor old Pip was getting very stressed at the front and shouting back to me to adjust my line. I only thought about moving my body when I was writing up my diary that evening - not very helpful. However, we did manage to avoid the wall and soon emerged into the light and onto the famous Bridgewater Canal.

This canal is steeped in history. To be fair, most are, but this one holds a special distinction: it claims to be the first 'modern' canal built in the UK. I add the qualifier 'modern' as I believe the Romans built a few waterways during their time here - 'what did the Romans ever do for us?' - well they built canals, amongst many other things. In reality, the small Sankey canal (connecting St Helens to the River Mersey) was opened four years earlier than the Bridgewater. Maybe it is the scale, the engineering brilliance and the involvement of James Brindley that gives the Bridgewater its dubious 'first' claim to fame. Either way, it can definitely claim to be the first canal that did not follow the natural route of a pre-existing river and it is still recognised as the inspiration behind the tremendous 'explosion' of canal building that followed its construction.

The Bridgewater is not named after the town in Somerset but rather Francis Egerton, the third Duke of Bridgewater who once owned a great deal of land in the north west (and, more importantly for our tale, the mines beneath this land). In the mid-eighteenth century, he needed a cheaper and more efficient way of transporting his coal from Worsley into the burgeoning industrial city of Manchester. Inspired by waterways he had seen in France, the solution he devised was a canal, which was completed in 1761. Initially it ran just from the mines to Manchester but was later extended from Worsley to Leigh (connecting with the Leeds and Liverpool Canal) and from Manchester to Runcorn to meet the River Mersey. It also links up with the Rochdale Canal in the middle of Manchester (more on this infamous waterway later). The barges that first used the canal actually cruised right into the mine entrances (as can be seen in Worsley Delph basin) and this meant mined coal did not have to be carried up to the surface but was 'simply' taken out by water to join the canal proper. As a result, the price of coal from the Duke's mines was cut in half - further fuelling the nascent industrial revolution.

Today the canal is not under the jurisdiction of the CRT but is privately owned by the Peel Group (who own lots of land and infrastructure in the North West - including the Trafford Centre). Because of this we had to book our passage. The first seven days are free but a fee is payable thereafter. Our goal was still Liverpool, via the Leeds and Liverpool canal, so we knew we would cover the thirty five miles to Leigh well within that time frame. It helped that the canal was wide and had no locks, which meant we could cruise at a good speed and did not have to slow too much for narrow bridges.

We covered the first twelve miles to Lymm by two thirty and decided to stay in this beautiful little village. It was built around the canal and a natural stream that gives the village its celtic name (Lymm means 'place of running water'), which cascades over a lovely weir near the village shops. The centre of the village is a designated conservation area - with many lovely old buildings. At its heart is Lymm Cross - a Grade I listed structure that dates back to the early seventeenth century - which stands on a natural sandstone outcrop.

We started our next day, cruising under Lymm Bridge (23) and past the bulging windows of the historic toll house, behind a hire boat that was clearly under less time constraint than us. The first few miles were painfully slow. That said, the countryside here was beautiful, including the grounds of the National Trust property, Dunham Massey, which we had visited a few years ago with my daughters Charlie and Sophie. We passed our hire boat 'companions' here and headed towards the more urban areas of Sale and Stretford. At this point, the canal has a three and a half mile perfectly straight section and, not surprisingly, it is the home to many rowing clubs and small boat hire companies. This meant I had to keep my wits about me to avoid a collision with other water-users less visible than our fifty seven foot narrowboat.

Safely through this section, we headed for Waters Meeting junction, where the canal branches off into Manchester city centre to the right and where we would turn left onto the Leigh Branch (which is actually the original route of the canal through Eccles and the mining village of Worsley). Just after the junction we enter Trafford Park and pass the sweet smelling Kellogs factory - which sits right next to the canal. The factory still has its own small canal arm - which was used to carry raw materials in and finished products out as late as the 1970s. Our journey continued past the huge Trafford shopping centre and onto the historic Barton Swing Aqueduct - which carries the canal over the much larger Manchester Ship Canal. The original aqueduct, constructed in 1761, was masonry and solid and carried the canal over the River Irwell. It was fit for purpose (and indeed was seen as an example of great engineering at the time) but when, in the late nineteenth century, The Manchester Ship Canal was built along the route of the river, much larger vessels needed to pass under the aqueduct. The engineering solution chosen was to build a new 'swinging' aqueduct that could be rotated and then swung back into place after a ship's passage. The iron trough of the aqueduct is three hundred and thirty feet long and weighs one thousand four hundred and fifty tonnes. It sits alongside a similar road bridge and they were both controlled from a tall brick tower set on an island in the middle of the ship canal. Two ships could pass either side of the island at any one opening.

A couple of miles on and we arrived in Worsley for our overnight mooring. I won't repeat here the importance of this small village in the history of the industrial revolution. What I will say is that its modern day appearance belies this; it is so pretty. The canal is a deep reddy brown colour (caused by dissolved iron oxide found in the ground here) and the half timbered houses adjacent to Worsley Delph (the entrance to the old mines) cast beautiful reflections on its surface. Margaret, Pip's step-mother, grew up in the village and her father used to work in the mine offices, long demolished, that stood on what is now the village green. Here you can now find a lonely brick monument (built from the bricks of the demolished buildings it replaced) that commemorates the village's bustling past. We loved Worsley and were sorry to move on the next day - but move on we had to.

The canal winds out into open countryside between Worsley and Leigh and, as the sun was shining first thing, it made really pleasant cruising. We passed Bridgewater Marina at Boothstown and turned the left hand bend to head for Leigh. It started to rain and boy did it rain! We moored for a coffee under a wide road bridge for a while but the downpour only got worse. In the end we just braved it and I got saturated heading into Leigh. We stopped for shopping and then pushed on as quickly as we could. After the quaintness of Lymm and Worsley, Leigh felt very urban and a little depressing. The rain didn't help. Two miles on, the canal passes high above Pennington Flash. We found a great mooring and decided that, as the weather was going to improve, we would stay here for a couple of days and walk. Incidentally, I should point out that in the middle of Leigh (at Bridge 66/11) the canal morphs to become the Leeds and Liverpool. This meant our 'rush' to complete the privately owned section was now over and we could relax back on CRT water.

I didn't really know what to expect when we headed for the Bridgewater Canal but I pictured mostly industrial and urban backdrops. In places this was true, but overall I was pleasantly surprised at how picturesque this major waterway was and would not hesitate to go back again

CHAPTER 36: LIVERPOOL BECKONS

It's May 25th but the promised sun has not arrived. Instead, it's an overcast day with showers which meant we restricted our walking to exploring Plank Lane lift bridge (8) and popping to a post office on the outskirts of Leigh. We love cryptic crosswords - with the Daily Telegraph being our favourite. I asked the shop owner if they had any Telegraphs in. He sneered and in an agitated voice told me they only EVER got one in each day as: 'It doesn't go down very well around here!' I bought a Guardian - of which there were plenty.

The next day we left our mooring and headed for Wigan. We first had to tackle the Plank Lane bridge - which sits on a very busy road called Slag Lane - not a reflection of local inhabitants but the fact that there used to be a colliery nearby. The road is so busy that there are certain times of the day when you cannot use the bridge and Pip was under even more pressure than normal to get us through and avoid any long delays.

As we emerged into the countryside, the canal was wide with lovely views on both sides and we had some great cruising. We passed through the Wigan Flashes Nature Reserve, with Ince Moss and Scotsman's Flash, among others, giving a home to many wild birds and a striking backdrop to our journey. We reached the outskirts of Wigan and the Poolstock 2 Locks. This was the very first time we had needed to use our handcuff key. A handcuff key unlocks the vandal-proofing mechanisms added to locks in certain locations that are prone to misuse. The key is about five inches long and has a bar going through one end to make it easy to turn. The other end is square-shaped and can be placed over a matching protrusion on the vandal-proofing mechanism. The key is turned and 'unlocks' the lock mechanism so the boater can then proceed as normal.

We reached Wigan Junction and turned towards Liverpool on the Leeds and Liverpool Canal 'proper'. After a quick stop for a bite to eat we set off towards Pottery Changeline Bridge (51) and the sharp turn left to run past the famous Wigan Pier. I am sure I was not alone in having heard of the pier whilst not being able to picture it. For me, the word 'pier' conjures up the image of a pleasure beach as I now live near Weston Super Mare. Wigan, however, is a landlocked industrial town so this was unlikely to be accurate. Rather boringly, the original 'pier' was believed to be a tall gantry between two industrial buildings that spanned the Douglas Valley. Why did this innocuous piece of industrial architecture become so famous? One version is that a train, leaving Wigan, was delayed near this spot and a passenger asked: 'Where are we'?, the reply that the train was just passing Wigan Pier started the legend. George Formby perpetuated the 'joke' in his music hall act when he regularly claimed the tide was in at the Pier when he last passed it. As a result, people started going to Wigan to look for it. The gantry was destroyed in the early twentieth century so the sightseers' focus landed on a small, unassuming, landing stage at the end of a rail track that had a tipping 'curl' (or tippler) at its end. This allowed carts of coal to be tipped into barges on the canal below. Let's not forget that George Orwell also wrote a book, commenting on the hardships found in a northern industrial town, and called it *'The Road to Wigan Pier'*. There have been further references to the mythical pier since and locals would have to agree, without this bizarre tale, Wigan would be less well-known than it is today. When we cruised by, the entire area had been redeveloped. The new mix of commercial and residential properties, many converted from the original canalside buildings, are really attractive and I really hope the area continues to be a draw for the town.

After a couple more locks we moored at Crooke - just after Bridge 47. The next morning we tackled Deans Lock (90) and found it very hard work. I remember it well. It sits under a flyover, carrying the M6 motorway. Next to the 'working' lock, is a disused 'twin' - covered in weeds and with its gates crumbling into the water. The lock we were using felt like it wasn't far from joining its sibling. The gates and the paddles were both really tough to move and Pip had a hard time getting me through. I also remember the landing pins were in a strange place and Pip had to climb down beside the lock to get onto our stern.

My face reddens at the memory of the next incident. There are a couple of open swing bridges on this stretch but also one that was closed (and required us to moor to open it). Pip was walking the towpath and went ahead to open the bridge. I pulled into the bank and jumped off to hold the centre line. As I left the boat, however, my coat must have caught on the throttle and flicked the engine into reverse - and not just slightly. I still had hold of the centre line but naturally could not stop her from going backwards. The Frog was heading, at some speed, across the canal. My efforts to hold her may have failed, but they did mean that the bow had swung into the bank in front of me. I dropped the rope I was holding and jumped for the bow. I just made it. I sprinted through the boat, grabbed the tiller and put the throttle into forward gear - just in time to avoid a collision with the far bank. What made the whole sorry tale much worse were the two dog walkers who had stopped to watch the excitement. They walked off, shaking their heads - probably a bit disappointed that the outcome was not as bad as it could have been. Pip had no idea what had happened and was puzzled why I was still on board and panting heavily when she opened the bridge.

Apsley Locks (91) lay around a slight bend and as we approached we saw a *'Bickerstaffe'* narrowboat hovering near the entrance (Bickerstaffe are boat manufacturers who build to a very distinctive style and are immediately recognisable). It had two people on the cruiser deck and both had life jackets on. They finally entered the lock (the delay being caused by CRT volunteers painting) and I pulled in alongside. It turned out they were about to buy one of these iconic boats and were having helmsman lessons on this example. It belonged to the Managing Director of the company and he was busy helping to open the lock. We had a chat and wished them good luck with their new enterprise. We parted ways just before the sharp left hand bend at Parbold. Pip and I ate lunch at a fantastic cafe on the canalside called Yours is the Earth *(*I think this is a quote from The Poem *'If'* by Rudyard Kipling*)*. Their food reflected the positive, adventurous spirit espoused in their name and we both happily munched on tasty meals. They were so good I even made mention in my diary of my aubergine sandwich with dill coleslaw. The cafe is overlooked by Parbold windmill - now a gallery and tanning studio.

We only cruised a few more miles before we started looking for moorings. We passed the entrance to the Rufford Branch (that links to the River Ribble and the Lancaster Canal - not for us this trip) and we finally came to rest in Burscough Bridge - between bridges 32A and B. This was a fab location for us. It was busy with lots of other boaters, it was near shops, bars and facilities and had a fourteen day mooring limit. We needed to stay a while as we were not due into Liverpool, on our timed passage, for another six days. Burscough felt safe and had all we needed close to hand.

The next few days were spent doing chores and walking. We took the Rufford Canal towpath and walked to Rufford Lock before turning for home. On our way back we came across a professional boat mover who had run aground in the shallow waters of the branch. I asked him to throw me a rope and after a lot of pulling he was finally free to go on his way. The experience made me glad we had decided not to head up that stretch before going down to Liverpool. The following day we walked to Heatons Bridge (28) to recce the route ahead. I remember it was a bright, sunny day and the six mile walk was fabulous. That evening I failed to get a barbecue alight and we resorted to the oven and while we were sitting outside, beer and G&T in hand (one each - I am not a lush), Paul, an ex-marine walked up the towpath and said hello. He was heading back to his boat and fancied a chat. This encounter typified what we hoped our boating experience would be. He had an interesting past and we had a connection (Pip grew up a few miles from the infamous Lympstone Camp (near Exmouth in Devon) where all marines are selected and go through basic training). We worked out they had probably visited the same nightclubs together all those years ago. Oh and later that evening Pip beat me at Cribbage - again.

The next day we set off on our final approach to Liverpool. The canal really is lovely here. Whilst we have a few swing bridges to deal with, there are no locks, and we cover over seven miles by early afternoon. En-route, we passed under Halsall Warehouse Bridge (25) and discovered a piece of fascinating history about the Leeds and Liverpool Canal. The business case for a canal that, via other waterways, linked the ports of Hull and Liverpool and ran through some of the major industrial areas of northern England, was an obvious one. Even today, at one hundred and twenty seven miles, the canal is the longest built as a single waterway in the UK. It was a significant engineering feat and was originally led by James Brindley and completed by John Longbotham, following the former's death. Work on building the canal started on November 5th 1770 and the first sod of earth was cut at Halsall and today a statue marks the spot. I will write in more detail about the many interesting features of the Leeds and Liverpool when we traverse the Pennines to Leeds.

We planned to moor near *The Ship* at Haskayne but the CRT had converted the moorings here to 'long term' only so we pressed on. Just past Bridge 21A we were astounded to see five metal frogs, about six feet in height, standing on top of a house next to the canal. They were all 'playing' various instruments. Where else could we moor? We pulled in just past the house and I rigged up a bizarre mooring system by pushing a mooring pin sideways into a crack in a wall and using plastic zip-ties to secure the rope to it. I also put in a centre line as the wind was getting up. It was unconventional, but it worked and we settled in for the night.

The next day turned out to be a very significant one for us. It was the day we first met Mark and Katherine - a boating couple who we now know will be lifelong friends. The original meeting was not ideal. We left Haskayne before nine as the weather was lovely and we wanted to get a long way down towards Liverpool before mooring. On the approach to the city there are only certain places where you are recommended to moor. Our route took us through Coxshead's Swing Bridge (20). Pip jumped off and used our CRT key to open the electric bridge. Whilst she was waiting for the mechanism to fully open and for me to go through, she got chatting with a cyclist who was part way through a charity ride. Pip made a donation and said goodbye. Maybe it was the distraction of all that lycra (I couldn't possibly comment), but after she had closed the bridge Pip forgot to pick up the keys (which included an ignition and a set of our back and front door keys). We did not realise this until we reached Methodist Swing Bridge (15), on the edge of Maghull. The swing bridge before this (Bell's) was being used when we approached, so we could just cruise right through it. Normally this was a godsend but that day it simply meant we were further away from the missing keys before we realised the problem. We obviously could not just leave them but cruising back was not an option so I donned my running gear and set off jogging back along the towpath. About half a mile on I was stopped by a lady walking two beautiful Kelpie-Collie crosses; Stan and Dexter (who I would later get to know very well). The lady was Katherine and her instincts told her that the red faced, out of breath man running on the towpath was not doing so for fun. She later said I looked very purposeful and she had put two and two together and asked me if I had mislaid some keys. I rather defensively replied: 'No - my wife has'! She reassured me that they had found them, having reached the bridge not long after us on their narrowboat '*Double O*' and had hidden them under some grass just beside the bridge control panel. They did not pick them up as they obviously did not know which way we were cruising and may have missed us had they done so. I thanked her profusely and set off once more on my trek. Pip, meanwhile, was having a cup of coffee and recording herself giggling about the whole thing for the benefit of Vlog 25. Five miles or so later I am back at the boat, keys in hand, welcomed by a not very repentant Pip.

Emergency over we headed off and, after a couple of miles, we passed through Holmes Swing Bridge (10) near to Melling - which was one of the 'safe' places we were advised to moor. We were expecting to see other boats here, however not only were there none but we also could not find a place where it was easy to moor. We pushed on a few hundred yards and, as both the weed in the canal and the number of houses started to get denser, we decided we had gone far enough. Navigation notes told us that we had to pass through Hancock's Swing Bridge (9) before 7.30 the next morning. After this time, because it's on such a busy commuter road, the bridge is closed to all craft until 9.30. If we missed the window, we would struggle to pump out, get supplies and complete the ten miles to reach the Stanley Locks (which mark the entrance to the Liverpool Canal Link) by the 1 o'clock deadline. We were only a mile from the bridge so we set our alarms for six thirty the next day - just to make sure we got through. I also removed a huge clump of weed from the prop and guessed that this would not be the last time I did this on the final approach to Liverpool.

The next morning we woke excited and a little trepidatious. The 'Liverpool Canal Link' is a must do for all boaters. You leave the Leeds and Liverpool canal, descend the four Stanley Locks and then cruise through Liverpool's historic docklands, finishing in Salthouse dock. That night we watched *Foxes Afloat* make the same trip, in one of their Vlogs, just so we felt a little better prepared for the next day. They followed another boat through and I was hoping we would be able to do the same. My greatest fear was that we would take a wrong turn and, somehow, end up on the mighty River Mersey heading out to sea. But I am getting ahead of myself….

We made Bridge 9 in good time the next morning and were safely through before we stopped on the mooring pins for breakfast. Our cruise continued around a sharp right hand bend and we looked to our left to see the familiar sight of the aptly named Canal Turn on Aintree Racecourse (where the Grand National is run). The canal runs alongside the course for another mile and you get a really good idea of the scale of the course and the challenge that faces the horses that take on the thirty odd fences. A couple more swing bridges and we were soon circling around Litherland and entering Bootle. Just past Litherland Bridges (2J and 2I) we stop by the services to pump out and visit Tescos. As I hook up a familiar voice reaches me. Mark and Katherine had cruised all the way down the night before and had moored here. The site is protected by high fences and security gates and the facilities are located on the 'off side' away from the towpath (where you are ill-advised to moor). We could have done the same but I think we would have struggled to find a spot - arriving as late as we would have. We chatted and agreed that we would both leave together and tackle the Stanley Locks in tandem. All agreed, we made our final preparations and then set off slowly towards the locks. They were about another four miles away - but we were not allowed through them until one o'clock (thus avoiding any clash with boats leaving the Canal Link in the morning). As a result we crawled at tick over (and even went into neutral at times) to ensure we did not arrive too early.

As we cruised further and further into the city of Liverpool the condition of the canal worsened. At one point we saw a wide beam moored with a whole mattress wrapped around its prop shaft. Finally, and thankfully, we made a sharp right turn under the pipe bridge that crossed the basin above the Stanley Locks. Space was tight with four boats all waiting to descend. Mark signalled that I should come alongside *Double 0* and attach a couple of lines to him. We were greatly appreciative and started chatting again. We soon discovered we had a lot in common including the fact that they lived in South Devon - not many miles from where Pip and I used to live before our move to Cornwall. We clicked immediately and were delighted when it turned out their berth in Salthouse was right next to ours. The friendship was obviously meant to be.

Stanley Locks are manned by three or four CRT volunteers - for several reasons. Firstly, it is not possible for just anyone to enter the Canal Link. Rather you have to book both a mooring slot in

Salthouse and a passage through to it. The volunteers 'gate keep' to ensure only boats that have booked and who can moor safely, are allowed through. Secondly, the locks drop about forty four feet in very short order and help getting through safely is key. Finally, the locks are often targets for vandalism and the boaters using them can also be at risk. On our descent we had first hand experience of what can happen. We were the second pair of boats to descend and everything was fine through the first three locks. As we were moving through the third lock, we could see the first two boats ahead of us. On the bank next to the final lock a group of maybe ten or twelve youths were 'enjoying the sunshine' and possibly other less natural substances. They were drawn like bees to honey to the poor people dropping slowly in the lock. Three or four of the males, possibly trying to impress the few girls present or their mates, decided to 'board' the narrowboats in the lock. Eventually they jumped off and we headed down towards what we knew would be our turn. In preparation, Pip went to the bow to keep an eye on the Go-Pro camera attached to the TV aerial. As soon as we entered the locks we too were 'invaded' by topless (and, it must be said, brainless) individuals who proceeded to run up and down our roofs and gunwales. Mark is an ex-policeman who specialised in cases involving young people. He is also an ex-soldier and Falkland veteran. As a result he was not only not fazed by the intrusion, but he also knew exactly how to handle it. He neither engaged with nor tackled the participants. He just climbed onto the roof himself and walked up and down with his hands behind his back (presumably so that there could be no suggestion that any youth who went into the water was helped there by Mark). The CRT volunteers were powerless to stop the incident and had learned to ignore the many jibes and questions directed at them and simply carried on with their job. Locks are extremely dangerous places and Pip and I read just a few days ago of a youth who died when he jumped into the canal for a prank and the current created as the lock refilled prevented him from climbing out. The CRT volunteers told us that a year before the same had happened here, so they had to be really careful how they handled things. Ultimately, they needed to get us through the lock but they also did not want to endanger the boys any more than their stupid antics were already doing. Slyly they slowly turned the paddles to let the water out of the lock. Eventually, the boats were so low that the 'invaders' realised they would need to leave now or end up in the docklands 'proper' when the gates opened. They all jumped off - but not before one did indeed try to unhook the camera on our boat. Pip intervened and he scurried away. Welcome to Liverpool!

Let me immediately come to Liverpool's defence. Before I describe the wonderful canal link I will also say how much we loved our time here and how we both fell in love with the city. We came back again in September 2021, that time by car, and took great delight in sharing the sights and sounds of this fabulous place with two Canadian friends (more on this later).

We quickly put this inauspicious start behind us and cruised excitedly out into the magnificent Stanley Dock - flanked by two huge tobacco warehouses (one of which is the biggest brick warehouse in the world, with nearly 149,000 square metres of floor space). The building opposite has already been renovated and is now the *Titanic Hotel*. The Grade II listed main warehouse is being turned into over five hundred apartments, with a lovely courtyard at its heart, and its first residents would have been moving in about the time of our visit.

Our course took us out through Collingwood Dock and into the smaller Salisbury Dock - all the time being guided by the impressive Grade II listed Victoria Tower - built in 1847. The tower, known colloquially as the '*Docker's Clock*', has six faces, ensuring that no matter where you were in the dock or out on the river, running alongside, you could always tell what the time was. Just before colliding with the tower we turned sharp left and headed for a narrow entrance onto the Central Docks Channel. This new link, lovingly known as '*Sid's Ditch*' (after the man who still led the CRT team that looked after the link and the docks in Liverpool - we would meet him at Mann Island Lock) connects the Salisbury Dock to the West Waterloo Dock. It is a very narrow channel and it is vital you keep to the left to avoid grounding. As we progress closer and closer to our target the buildings all around us get more and more modern - reflecting the significant investment there has been in this part of the city. As we crossed West Waterloo Dock we caught our first sight of the *Liver Building* - the iconic landmark of Liverpool's waterfront. We would soon pass right under its impressive facade and clock faces.

We entered Princes Dock under a modern footbridge and left it via Princes Dock Lock (5). The sun was shining and reflecting off both the water and the modern architecture that surrounds this section of the Link. The exit from the lock is a few yards from the entrance to the first of three tunnels that took us under the wide esplanade that has been built between the Royal Liver Building and the Mersey. The tunnels are all modern and we were impressed by how clean and graffiti-free they were. To our right, we saw the Ferry Terminal, where the famous Mersey Ferry left for Birkenhead and, in less infectious times, the Isle of Man. The final tunnel took us under the corner of the new(ish) Museum of Liverpool - built in the same style as the Ferry Terminal - giving a hint of symmetry to the riverside. As we left this tunnel the channel turned to the left past a set of concrete steps, designed for office workers and tourists to sit and enjoy their lunch by the water side. Today, the weather being so warm, the area was swarming with young people in swimming costumes - jumping in and out of the water. We passed with care and joined Mark and Katherine in the final lock of the passage, Mann Island Lock (6). It was manned by Sid, after whom the Central Docks Channel had been named. He welcomed us to Liverpool and gave us useful instructions on how to tackle Cannings Dock and to watch out for the buoy in the middle of Albert Dock. Emerging from the lock we headed straight out into Cannings Dock and towards the Liverpool One Shopping Centre. We swung in a wide loop to the right towards the narrow entrance to the outer part of Cannings Dock before swinging out wide to the right and turning left to pass under the impressive, once movable, wrought iron bridge that marks the entrance to Albert Dock. The Maritime Museum loomed large on our left.

Cruising into Albert Dock was a dream come true. The iconic red pillars, supporting the old warehouses and offices of this once thriving commercial dock, looked so familiar. The whole area is now full of restaurants and shops catering for the many locals and tourists who love to visit this impressive example of our industrial heritage. Visiting boats only pass through here twice a day, so we were the object of much fascination as we headed out into the middle of the dock to circle the buoy Sid warned us about, to ensure we were properly lined up to enter Salthouse. I don't think I had ever cruised in front of so many gongoozlers. Finally we passed under the road bridge that separates the two docks and started looking for our mooring point in Salthouse.

Mark was ahead of us and soon found his berth. We knew we were right next to him - however, 'our' pontoon was already occupied, so I could not moor. The wind was starting to get up and we felt a bit vulnerable hovering in the middle of the dock. Just to my left was a floating band stand so I pulled over alongside it and attached the centre line, waiting until we knew what the problem was. To cut a long story short, the boat occupying our spot had arrived the day before and had found their allocated spot was already taken by none other than *The Silver Fox* - home to Shaun and Colin, more well known as *'Foxes Afloat'* (the couple we had watched on Youtube both when planning our odyssey and the previous evening when moored near Mellings). On the one hand we were quite excited to see them here but were also feeling slightly irked that we still had nowhere to moor. To their credit, the boaters in our slot moved out and let us take their place. Meanwhile, I had already phoned the CRT and, after a bit of a wait, Sid came along to find out what was happening. He quickly allocated a new space to the poor boaters who were now *'sans berth'* and had a brief chat with us all to pour oil on troubled waters. He explained that *The Foxes* had not booked their passage in the normal way as they had actually entered the dock from the Mersey itself (having, bravely in my opinion, hired a pilot and cruised up the busy and fast moving waterway). All credit to them for their adventurous spirit. So, here we were: moored in one of the most iconic settings on the UK waterways, Albert Docks brick warehouses to our left and the wonderful City of Liverpool a stone's throw away. The sun was shining and the water was clear. We were going to enjoy our week here - especially as a couple of days later we were to be joined by my son, Alasdair.

I am not going to detail all that we got up to in Liverpool. I have already said how much I love the city and we spent our time visiting all the tourist attractions you would expect in this vibrant centre of culture and history. I strongly recommend a visit if you have not been here before. We even came back again three months later, principally to see Genesis in concert, but also to share the city with our visiting Canadian friends, Julie and Dave - who were with us on our final Frog voyage.

CHAPTER 37: HOW FAR?

After a week, we said our goodbyes to Salthouse and reversed our trip through the canal link on Wednesday 9th of June. The sun was still shining brightly - which was great as Ali was still on board and I really wanted him to experience the link in all its glory. He helped with the tiller and a pump out on the twelve miles we covered that day and he stayed with us for the night in Maghull, where we had a lovely farewell pub meal. The next morning we said our goodbyes and he caught a train back into Liverpool to hook up with the west coast mainline to his home in Bristol. In my diary I wrote how great it had been having him with us (Covid having kept us apart for so long) and how much I was going to miss him.

We had already agreed to meet up with Mark and Katherine (for convenience from now on I will simply refer to them as M&K - I'm sure they won't mind.) in Wigan - just above the pier. We cruised there in three days - largely because we decided to stay in Burscough for two nights to catch up on chores and 'rest'. Nothing significant happened en-route and as we were simply retracing our steps over water we had already travelled, I am skipping ahead to our reunion with *Double 0* and the challenge of the Wigan flight.

When we passed through Wigan a couple of weeks earlier, the flight was closed after some wag thought it would be funny to park a stolen car in the pound near lock 69. Luckily for us it had now reopened and on the morning of the 13th of June we left our moorings above Bottom Lock (87) and set off with M&K to complete the remaining twenty two and climb the two hundred and fourteen feet to the summit near Monks Hall Bridge (59). Thankfully the locks were manned by CRT volunteers and we four boaters alternated roles on our respective craft - helping the lockies with the mechanisms for a few locks and then taking the helm for a few. This variety helped break up the day and made the climb feel a bit easier. It took us about three hours and we had lunch by the waterpoint just around the sharp left hand bend that greeted us as we completed the flight. In my opinion, the locks here are more demanding than those on the Caen Hill and Hatton flights and we were feeling quite weary by the time we reached the top. Pip took the helm for the final couple of miles as I was watching England play Croatia in the Euros (we won 1-0, Raheem Sterling scoring after a brilliant assist from Kalvin Phillips, who was still playing for Leeds at the time). We spent the night near Haigh Hall Country Park (between bridges 60 and 61). I distinctly remember the wonderful sunset that evening which was the perfect end to a demanding but satisfying day.

The next day I wanted to capture some footage of Pip at the helm so I walked the first three miles. The canal was beautiful and the mid-June bird song just added to the bucolic charm of the day. I really enjoyed my walk and Pip loved being at the helm - doing a great job of taking the Frog through the alternating woodland and pasture that typified this part of the Leeds and Liverpool. We needed to refuel and I remember the tricky manoeuvre I had to perform to achieve this. We passed under Rawlinson Bridge (71) and pulled into the on side - opposite the boatyard we were looking for. Another boater was filling with water, and would clearly be taking some time to do so. The boatyard owner pointed to the small space in front of the other boat and suggested that I pull in to fill up from there. The space was probably a couple of feet longer than the Frog. The move also meant abutting a solid stone wall and tying the bow to a hook that was sticking out of the wall - about six feet above water level. The wind was up and I was nervous about: 1. Hitting the other boat, 2. Hitting the wall, 3. Pip falling in whilst tying the bow and getting crushed between The Frog and the wall and 4. Having a gang of boatyard employees watching the whole thing and judging my boatmanship (the last concern, or possibly all of them, can be put down to my natural paranoia). Remarkably we squeezed into the space; missed the moored boat and got close enough for Pip to tie us off without incident. I was very relieved.

We were making great progress and I was astounded when I looked back at the Vlog how far we had cruised that day. My diary then jumps ahead to the Johnson's Hill Locks (64-58). We ate lunch at their base (the canal was still climbing at that point) and as we finished, a descending boat left the lock and the CRT volunteers ushered us in. The first lock was completed and Mark and I noticed that the gates were already open on the next lock (63). The approach was dead straight so Mark suggested that we leave and enter the second lock in tandem. This added an additional element of challenge to the locks but was great fun. The seven locks, with a rise of over sixty five feet, completed, we cruised the final three miles to Riley Green - having travelled twelve miles and completed seven locks on what felt like a busy day. Riley Green is only four miles from Blackburn - whose locks we would face the next day. The placement of our mooring was deliberate as we had heard bad reports about the locks in Blackburn. Not only were they supposed to be challenging to operate but, being right in the city, they were also potentially the target for the 'wrong' kind of gongoozler. We wanted to ensure we passed through them in the morning, when, hopefully, most potential troublemakers would still be sleeping off the previous evening's excesses (a plan we would repeat on the approach to both Leeds and Manchester).

The next morning we decided that Pip would take the helm through the Blackburn Locks (57-52). That way I could tackle the tough mechanisms we were expecting and also be the person walking the towpath with Katherine (so she could protect me if anything untoward happened!) Pip did a great job at the helm and even tandemed a few of the locks with Mark. Her confidence had really grown since her early lock work on the Shropshire Union and it was lovely to see. The flight (a climb of over fifty four feet) passed with only one minor incident - I had to cut a coat from the prop (the canal here has the usual debris you find in any city centre waterway) and we pressed on to the edge of the city. The Vlog captures us passing under two close set bridges at Whitebirk (104AA and B) - the first a traditional brick design and the latter a more modern stone and concrete creation. After a short aqueduct we cruised under Bridge 104C which carried the main arterial road leaving the city and joining the M65. Just after this, we were greeted by the sad sight of the Imperial Mill. The enormous building, now minus its iconic chimney, was a poignant reminder of the city's historic importance as a centre of weaving in a once thriving textile industry. It was built in 1901 and, remarkably, production continued until 1980, despite the industry starting a slow decline as early as the end of the first world war.

That night we were planning to moor at Rishton but we did not like the look of the surrounding area so we pushed on - and we were glad we did. The prevailing countryside changed and as the canal was cut into a hill on our right hand side, to the left we had impressive views of the Pennines, rising majestically above the houses sitting down in the valley. We turned a sharp right under

Tottleworth Bridge (108) and crossed the impressive M65 Aqueduct (108AA) before coming to a stop just after New Barn Bridge (109) - primarily because it was such a lovely location. We moored and walked the footpath to the village of Church, which we would be passing through the next day. Interestingly, the village is exactly halfway along the course of the Leeds and Liverpool Canal and is also the previous home of Robert Peel's ancestors. As an aside, Pip's first job after qualifying as a Nanny was to look after the several times great granddaughter of that former Prime Minister. Sadly, the local church was boarded up and the rundown houses spoke of a degree of deprivation in the village.

'It's not quite the international date line is it?'

Pip was right, but, nevertheless, the next day we still recorded the ceremonial crossing of the halfway point of the Leeds and Liverpool Canal - marked by a line on the towpath and some ornate wrought iron work, designed by local school children. Katherine and I were walking this leg, along with the energetic Stan and the long suffering Dexter. We carried our windlasses, ready to open the four swing bridges between us and the town of Burnley. At this point, the canal weaves it way back and forth over the ever-present M65, past the village of Hapton and, via the Gannow Tunnel (128), into the suburbs of Burnley. I had retaken the helm by this point and I remember the tunnel very well. It is only five hundred and fifty nine yards long but you enter it on a bend and it also has a couple of kinks along its length making its navigation more of a challenge than I expected. The sharp bend approach took me by surprise and I was probably going a little too fast. Pip was at the bow acting as lookout and as I turned the corner she shouted that the tunnel was immediately ahead and, what was worse, another boat was coming in the other direction. I threw The Frog into reverse to avoid a collision only for Pip to apologise and tell me that the other boat was actually Mark and Katherine going in the same direction as us! Panic over.

After the tunnel the landscape changed and we started passing the many industrial buildings that line the canal bank and pointed to a previous time when it was clearly a major trading link through a once thriving mill town. At its peak, Burnley was one of the world's largest producers of cotton cloth and a major centre of engineering - much of this success could be linked to the building of the canal and the connection it created to the major cities and ports in the North of England. Today, Burnley still has a thriving manufacturing base but its communication links are rail and the M65. We were really pleased that the canal still benefited from the remains of the wonderful Burnley Wharf, the striking roof of which hangs low across the edge of the canal. The Wharf is part of the iconic Weaver's Triangle (an area along the canal where many mills had been based) and can be found just before the lovely Manchester Road Bridge (130B). Today there is a museum nearby that celebrates the town's glory days.

A few bridges further on, the canal turned sharp left and as we passed under Finsley Gate Bridge (130E) we cruised onto what must have been one of the most challenging feats of engineering any canal builder had faced: the Burnley Embankment. The structure is almost a mile long and became a necessity when a fourth Act of Parliament, in 1794, authorised the redirection of the canal through the town. It is sixty feet high and carries the canal over a broad valley where the Rivers Calder and Brun meet (two aqueducts at either end of the embankment cross the two waterways). Its construction avoided the need for locks on either side of the wide depression. It is colloquially known as the Straight Mile (I can vouch for its directness) and it is an original member of the illustrious group known as *The Seven Wonders of the Waterways*. It is truly an engineering masterpiece and required the moving of over three hundred cubic yards (about two hundred and sixty cubic metres) of soil in its construction (much of which came from the Gannow Tunnel). It took five years to build and now carries the canal, at rooftop height, straight through the town.

We cruised out of the centre of Burnley and moored near Oliver Ings Bridge (135) for the night. The next morning Pip walked the three miles, or so, from our mooring to the locks at Barrowford. When we arrived she took over the helm to complete the locks with Mark. These seven locks saw us climb a further sixty nine feet up to the enormous Barrowford reservoir (which, along with Foulridge, feed the canal system). It was a bit concerning that the reservoir was no more than a third full. The locks here were also significant as they are the last ascending locks on the canal; we were nearing the peak of the system and from here on, the remaining locks would be part of our descent into Leeds.

At one thousand six hundred and forty yards Foulridge tunnel is one of the longest on the system. It was built at the end of the eighteenth century and was a major engineering innovation. The ground here was too unstable for the usual tunnel building method (dropping shafts into the ground and then digging laterally to join them up). Instead, a very deep cutting was carved right through the hill, a brick channel was then built at its base and soil dropped back in on top. The tunnel sprang to fame in 1912 when a cow, having fallen into the canal near its mouth, decided to swim its entire length! Locals at the Foulridge village end of the tunnel, revived the poor beast with alcohol! As it is perfectly straight and controlled by lights, our passage through was swift. I had The Frog on fairly high throttle, knowing there was nothing coming the other way and having concluded that the boat is easier to manouvre at slightly higher speeds. At the far end of the tunnel we found a lovely cafe and sat outside for a coffee before heading off for our mooring near Salterforth Bridge (151). On the way we re-crossed the Lancashire/Yorkshire border and that night I was introduced to Timothy Taylor's Ale at the nearby pub (*The Anchor*) and, to this day, I still drink the same beer at our local pub in Somerset.

The next morning we immediately passed under Bridge 151 with its historic vertical rollers. These are now a very rare sight and date back to when horses pulled barges along these waterways. Just after the bridge is a very sharp bend and when the horse would have turned the corner, it naturally pulled the boat it was towing in towards the bank. The rollers avoided that happening by ensuring that the rope, and, therefore, the barge behind, was pulled around, rather than across, the corner. Ingenious.

Our route continued past the town of Barnoldswick and on towards the three locks at Greenberfield - our first descent since arriving in Liverpool. Pip handles The Frog through the locks that drop us just over twenty nine feet. As we were on the brow of a hill, the scenery was fabulous. The canal follows the contours of the many hills around here, but whilst the tiller work is constant, the views make it all worthwhile. At lunch time we stopped at East Marton to moor for the night. Whilst we had not travelled far, we knew that a lock was under repair in the Bank Newton flight and we wanted to moor where we knew we were safe. Pip and I walked the couple of miles up to Bank Newton and had a chat with the CRT engineers working on the broken gate. It was a Friday and they predicted it would be open on Monday but advised us to watch out for CRT messages over the weekend as it may be finished sooner.

Faced with staying where we were, the next morning we busied ourselves with domestic chores and then had the well-earned treat of lunching at yet another *Anchor Inn* in the village. We sat outside on a gloriously sunny day and read that the South of England was in the grip of a torrential rain storm. Hey Ho! We met a couple of walkers who were part way through a fifteen day transit of the Pennine Way. The iconic footpath is over two hundred and sixty miles long and runs over some pretty tough terrain. To finish it in this timescale would have meant walking about eighteen miles a day - every day. Not surprisingly, they were taking on the carbs at lunch!

Sunday is Father's day and it was great to get a call from one of my daughters, Charlie and my son Alasdair. I remember the calls well as we were filling with water before heading out to find a country mooring to wait out the lock repair. When I came off the phone two boats cruised by and I asked one of the helmsmen whether they had heard anything about the lock. They confirmed it was now open. This was great news and we agreed with Mark that we would head for an overnight mooring at Gargrave - the most northerly village on the Leeds and Liverpool - after which our course would take us South past Skipton and Bingley and into Leeds itself. Before we get there however, we have to tackle the Bank Newton locks.

Bank Newton has six locks, taking the canal down fifty six feet. They were manned by a single CRT volunteer who was sitting on the beam of the Top Lock (40) when we arrived to start our descent. I asked him his thoughts on the approach to Leeds and where to moor. He immediately understood what I was getting at (where was it safe to moor) but instead of giving me any useful direction he suggested that I should moor wherever I liked and 'to hell' with any would be trouble-makers: 'I find sitting on the welldeck chopping at a large log with a sharp hatchet sends a very clear message!' I thanked him for his 'guidance'. He then noticed our Vlog advert on the side of our cabin: 'Every bloody boater seems to be at it now!' (an exaggeration that felt par for the course). He then told us a story about a very well known boating vlogger (one that we followed but has not yet been mentioned in this account) and how offensive they had been when they had come up the lock flight. Not only was the helmsman very rude to him when he offered advice (which was clearly not wanted/needed) but he was also verbally abusive to his female partner. I have deliberately avoided names here as this account was clearly partial and I could easily see how this particular volunteer may not have brought out the best in anyone.

Anyway, back to the locks. We had not seen locks like this before (and have not since). Rather than the sluice gates being covered by a paddle that you raise using a winding mechanism, here the paddles are a bit like a large oar - bent at right angles and sticking out of the water next to the bank. To open them you have to pull very hard on the projecting pole and so pivot the paddle on the other end away from the sluice opening. We included a picture in Vlog 26 and an explanation of how the mechanism worked. The most important observation is that they were very hard to move and I am glad they are not common across the network. We finally reached our mooring between locks 33 and 32 at Gargrave.

The next morning we completed the final three locks on this stretch. At Holme Bridge Lock (30) the canal noticeably turned to the south and we began our descent into Skipton. We cruised for just the morning, negotiating four swing bridges before finding a great mooring, on pins, just before Brewery Swing Bridge (177). I could write a whole book on Skipton alone; it really is a lovely place. Sturdy buildings, all constructed of the same local stone, line the canal side. The beautiful Craven Court shopping Centre has a magnificent wrought iron roof and reminded me of something you might have seen at the Great Exhibition. At the top of the town sits Skipton Castle. The Norman French word *'DESORMAIS'* ('Henceforth'), espousing great optimism in the future, sits boldly in stone letters across the top of the main gate. Our immediate future entailed lunch from an award winning pork pie 'Shoppe' and then back to exploring the rest of the town. After a long day walking the streets of the 'Gateway to the Dales' we couldn't wait to put our feet up and share a few drinks, on the towpath, with M&K. My diary says we had Frittata for tea: *'Pip a bit tiddly so not one of her best - and she forgot to put the gammon in!'* I'm in trouble when Pip reads that.

The next morning, M&K started their day by cruising up the very short Springs Branch in the middle of Skipton. It is literally a few hundred yards long and has nowhere to turn around. When we cruised by, they were just reversing out. Why go to all this trouble? - you may ask. The waterways in this country only survive because they are used. Remember my earlier reference to Tom Rolt and the pioneers who navigated tricky waterways, in the early days of the IWA, just to keep them open? In this spirit, the CRT launched the Silver Propeller Challenge which encourages boaters to 'boldly go' (sic) onto weird and wonderful stretches of water that might otherwise be forgotten about. The CRT publishes a list of such places and M&K were working through it (they have since received their Silver Propeller award. Well done both!)

Skipton was hard to leave - not just because it was so lovely, but also because the nine and a half miles to Keighley involved opening and closing fifteen swing bridges. It took us all day and we arrived just before five pm. We didn't particularly like our mooring (just after bridge 197) but we needed to stay there as, the next day, we were catching a bus to Haworth - famous home of the Bronte family. I will not go into lots of details but suffice to say, if you have not visited Haworth, even if you are not a Bronte fan, you should take the time to seek out this beautiful village. It is centred on a steep main street that leads to the vicarage that was the home to what must be one of the most talented literary families in history. When we returned to The Frog, despite it being early evening, we decided to 'up pins' and cruise the three miles or so to the top of the BIngley Five - one of the most iconic lock flights on our waterways.

Bingley actually has eight locks - The Bingley Five Rise and the Bingley Three Rise. The Five were built in 1774 and take the canal down fifty nine feet over a distance of only 320 feet. They are awe-inspiring when viewed from beneath and, that evening, we took many photographs in an attempt to capture the grandeur of the locks. It is the steepest flight in the country as they are all staircase locks - meaning they empty into each other - and, not surprisingly, they are always manned by CRT volunteers when they are open. On our descent, Mark and I enjoyed 'tandeming' from one lock to the next and watching the girls do all the hard work helping the volunteers. The Vlog shows the interesting paddle controls on these locks. A windlass is not needed; a metal bar, sitting atop a rectangular box, is attached to the top of a large screwing mechanism - which is attached to the paddle. The metal bar is turned manually - a bit like winding a clockwork motor, only very much harder to do. The locks are Grade 1 listed, which means no matter how hard this method of operation, it cannot and should not be changed (other than when wear and tear dictates that parts need to be replaced).

The Bingley Three take the canal down a further thirty feet in very short order. Both flights were completed without incident and we cruised on - being delayed only by Dowley Gap 2 Locks (21-20) - a staircase that we managed ourselves. We immediately crossed an aqueduct that carries the canal over the River Aire, passed through Hirst Mill Swing Bridge (207) and negotiated the last lock before the stunning estate village of Saltaire. We couldn't wait to moor and explore this almost unique location. The village was conceived and built by Titus Salt, a wealthy mill owner who was appalled at the living conditions of his workers in nearby Bradford. He resolved to build what he thought was the ideal industrial settlement on this new site - right next to the canal and the River Aire. Building took place between 1851 and 1871 and not only were a mill and various other industrial buildings erected but also houses, shops, a chapel and even a community hall - in short, everything his workers might need - except a pub. He was a strict teetotaller and insisted that his workers were too. The mill continued to produce as late as 1986 and today the village is a Unesco World Heritage Site and, at the risk of sounding more and more like the Yorkshire Tourist board, I really do recommend a visit. Oh and by the way, there is now a pub/restaurant - in case that might make a difference. It is called "Don't Tell Titus!"

Our cruise continued into the afternoon and we completed two more sets of staircase locks at Fields (18-16) and Dobson (15-14) before finding a nice mooring at the disused Claverley Lodge Swing Bridge (215) - ideally placed, about eight miles out, to descend into Leeds the next day. We had been warned against venturing further towards the city and mooring overnight. A couple we had met a few days earlier moored their wide beam at Kirkstall. In the middle of the night they were awoken because their lines had been cut and they had started drifting down the canal. They had even moored on an official mooring site. Where we were moored we were still firmly out in the Yorkshire countryside and the old landing pins for the bridge made tying up really easy. That day we had completed sixteen locks (including both Bingley flights) and had cruised nine miles. The hatches were firmly battened down quite early - tomorrow was going to be a big day.

The descent to Leeds started early and we were met at Rodley by a relative of Katherine's who lives at Hebden Bridge but knows Leeds (and this stretch of the canal) really well. The trip down would include another twelve locks - eight of which are in staircases (in two sets of three, and a pair). Newlay 3 Locks (13-11) dropped us twenty six feet and passed without incident. On exiting the last lock, Pip and I swapped places and she took the helm - and soon wished she had not. Forge 3 Locks (10-8) took us down a further twenty three feet - but proved to be a lot more difficult. We had now been joined by Katherine's nephew, so the issue was clearly not a lack of manpower. What happened to us was clear proof that all staircase locks should be respected. The set up when descending a three lock staircase should be as follows: Lock 10 (the top lock) should be full - whilst locks 9 and 8 should be empty (ready to receive the water that will descend with the boats). The set up at Forge was right (on the face of it) and the move from lock 10 to lock 9 went without a hitch. The problem was that when the locks had been prepared, someone had failed to shut the paddle on the bottom lock. This meant that when the sluices linking lock 9 and 8 were opened, instead of lock 8 filling with water (ready to receive the boats) the water was seeping straight out through the bottom paddle. This became apparent when the water in lock 9 almost entirely disappeared and the two boats grounded! The water level was so low that the sluice exits were clearly visible on the side walls. Having spotted this, I reopened the paddle from lock 10 to lock 9 to try and bring some water through. I quickly realised that first I had to open the very top paddles to bring some new water into the flight. The only problem was that the sluice exits in lock 9 were now spurting water directly onto the stern decks of both boats, making Mark and Pip very wet. I had to close them off. Katherine spotted the bottom paddle issue and closed it. We then let water through from above - but at a gentle pace - and slowly the boats refloated. The whole thing took over twenty minutes to correct and Pip was quite traumatised and I have to thank the ever-calm and collected Mark for reassuring her through this frightening incident.

I retook the helm and we completed Oddy Locks (5-4) without issue and we were soon entering Granary Wharf, in the heart of Leeds - our home for the next few nights. We moored facing the River Lock

(1) which would take us onto the River Aire. Its number tells you that we had finally reached the end of the wonderful Leeds and Liverpool Canal - having traversed every one of its one hundred and twenty seven miles. It was a great experience and we now treasure our IWA Trans-Pennine Award, which can be claimed by any boater completing this feat. M&K were our constant companions and we cemented our friendship with every lock, swing bridge and pub visit!

Leeds was not as gripping as Liverpool, I have to say. We met an old friend for lunch and explored the city centre - including a mandatory visit to the Leeds United Club shop. I bought a cap, which I wore for the next couple of stages of our cruise - only removing it when we got too close to Manchester for comfort - but much more on that later. I recommend the Armouries museum and a brilliant Italian restaurant called *LIVIN' Italy* . It was very near the wharf and both the service and food were exceptional. If you seek it out, I hope it's still there for you.

CHAPTER 38: LEEDS TO SOWERBY BRIDGE

The River Aire thunders under Leeds Railway Station near to Granary wharf and turns a gentle corner just below River Lock. We negotiated this final lock on the Leeds and Liverpool and joined the wide expanse of the Aire and Calder Navigation. The two rivers were improved in 1704, with sixteen locks and canalisation in places between Leeds and Wakefield, a stretch of about eighteen miles. This navigation, the River Calder and the Calder and Hebble would provide us with a very interesting journey as we made our way to Sowerby Bridge.

Our first task was to get out of the city. Initially the river is edged on both sides by post industrial buildings - many of which are now residential. A slight left hand bend revealed the glorious, if unimaginatively named, Leeds Bridge. It is Grade II listed and screams Victoriana. It was built in 1870-71, of steel and has a very ornate cast iron balustrade, centred by a crest of the City. It really is a splendid sight and one of those bridges you just love to cruise under. The Victorian theme continued with the colourful Crown Point Bridge spanning the River just before the sharp right turn we took to avoid the weir and enter Leeds Lock. This was the first River Lock we had entered for some time and we had forgotten their scale. Thankfully, it was manned by lock keepers and the huge gates were operated electronically. As soon as we left the lock the Navigation widened and the surrounding buildings fell away to become a mix of the occasional industrial building and rough countryside. The disused Leeds Oil Terminal was like a desolate symbol of this tired landscape and we were glad to pass through Knostrop Fall Lock and move further out into the countryside proper.

This leg, to Castelford, was a poignant one. When we reached the junction at Castleford Flood Lock we would turn right and head west towards Wakefield. Mark and Katherine would turn left and head east en-route to the River Trent. We had been with them for about four weeks and this was a sad parting. Mark even offered to pay us to explore the Trent with them and keep the partnership going but, alas, our sights were set elsewhere.

Our plans included the Rochdale Canal. It has an interesting reputation - which I will explore in much more detail when we reach it. The canal's reputation was reinforced by a boater we met at the wonderfully named Lemonroyd Lock on the River Aire. He was heading north having attempted the Rochdale and turned back at Lock 9 due to water shortages. This was a common problem on the canal that boasts the highest wide lock on the network. We immediately checked our CRT updates and noted that the problem was known and they were taking steps to fix it. We agreed we would stick to our plan and risk the notorious route from Sowerby Bridge to the heart of Manchester.

After waving a sad farewell to M&K, we completed two more miles and then spotted a pontoon on the river bank at Fairies Hill (where Nicholson indicates that the nearby lock is 'disused'). A pontoon like this is unusual and mooring on rivers can be a challenge. Unlike the canals, it is difficult to just pull into the bank and moor - not least because the stronger current can pull pins clean out of the ground. So we grabbed the chance to tie up and settle down for the night - especially as it had just started raining. Our plans soon changed however. It turns out the lock is not disused at all and is actually the eastern entrance to a private marina that sits in a bow shaped arm that leaves the main river here and rejoins it on the other side of Woodnook Lock. The pontoon was placed by the marina owner (who had just knocked on our roof) and it is a landing place for arriving boats - two of which were due shortly. Pip was already preparing tea, it was about six pm and it was still raining, but we had no option but to move off. There was nowhere to moor before Woodnook Lock, which was unmanned. Luckily a passing widebeam owner stopped and gave us some help. We finally moored just before Fox Bridge, near the village of Altofts, and, for the first time, I used a spring mooring technique. I don't think I have explained this process before so here goes: a spring line is attached to either the stern or bow or both. A bow spring line is directed towards the stern at least half the length of the boat and is then secured on the bank (in this case with a pin). The stern spring line is placed in the opposite direction. Their purpose is simply to prevent the forward and backward movement of the boat when in strong currents or when expecting lots of high speed passing traffic. Hope that makes sense. That day we had covered thirteen miles and completed seven locks - no wonder we were tired when we finally settled in for the night.

Fully refreshed, the next morning we tackled two more large river locks. After the second of these (Birkwood), the navigation turned quite sharply to the south west and a long straight section took us over the Stanley Ferry Aqueducts and on towards Broadreach Locks. The Aqueducts carry the canalised section we were on over the meandering River Calder. A couple of miles after Broadreach lock, we would join the river proper just before entering Wakefield. Stanley Ferry plays a key role in the maintenance of our waterways. Every year its workshops build about a hundred new lock gates, meeting part of the constant demands of an ageing system. Every gate is different and is built, to exact specifications, by highly skilled craftsmen (and women no doubt), to ensure they are fit for purpose. They have to be very strong and a great deal of each of them will be below water for most of their working 'lives'. To ensure they will last the expected twenty five years or so until they are replaced, they are made from green sustainably grown oak.

The section after Stanley Ferry is still very canalised and we ploughed a dead straight course all the way to the outskirts of Wakefield. En-route we passed through Broadreach Lock. The lock was open as, unlike most locks, it does not take the water up or down a change in level. Broadreach is a 'flood lock' which is normally open but can be closed at times of bad weather to avoid the risk of the River Calder flooding into the canalised sections of the navigation.

The 'gateway' to Wakefield was another lock at Fall Ing (not a typo). It marked the end of the Aire and Calder Navigation and the start of the Calder and Hebble. We found it hard to keep The Frog straight in this lock - despite using a line. When we left we took a slow, meandering, course through the town and, after passing through a further flood lock, my diary says we '...*burst out onto the broad and impressive expanse of the Calder and Hebble Navigation'.* I remember the sensation really well. After the flood lock and our cruise through the constraints of the town, the river felt really wide. The far bank was an impressive stone wall with the branches of weeping willows crowning it (and in some places reaching as far down as the water surface).

If you are a boater who has cruised the Calder and Hebble you will probably guess what I am going to write about next: the infamous 'Handspike'. When we first bought the Frog we found a piece of wood in the forward storage hatch that was about three feet long. It was tapered and made of some very hard wood (not sure what). Handwritten on it was a message: *'Handspike for use on the Calder and Hebble'*. We had no idea what it was but were very glad that we did not throw it away! This waterway is probably unique in the UK in that some of the locks still need a handspike to be operated. Thornes Lock (our next challenge) is one of them. Pip and I both struggled at first to insert the handspike and get it working effectively. I even had it upside down at one point. Compared with a windlass it really is an archaic and inefficient way of opening and closing a paddle and we were not impressed.

This was not the only peculiarity we noticed with the Calder and Hebble locks. They were originally designed for a particular commercial vessel called a Yorkshire Canal Keel - which were typically up to sixty feet long. As a result, any boat over fifty seven feet finds them hard going. The Frog was that very length and whilst we fitted in, there was an additional challenge of a walkway that was always attached to the inside of the bottom gates. This walkway was quite wide (as it was designed for someone to stand on and use the paddle) and, as such, it further 'shortened' the usable space in the lock. This was most vividly demonstrated at Broad Cut Low Lock. We were rising through this lock and I had, for some strange reason, decided to jump off and hold the boat in place on a line. My diary says that only the gate paddles on the top gate were working (not the ground paddles) and as such the lock could only be filled slowly. This may be the reason I was happy to be off the boat as she was less likely to be buffeted about by the incoming water. As it turned out, this slow rise was more of a blessing than I could have known. I was holding The Frog on a line but had not noticed that she had drifted backwards slightly and that her tiller was now sitting directly under the bottom gate walkway. Pip saw it first and shouted to me to move her forward. It was almost too late, the tiller was already starting to press up into the walkway. Had this continued, it could have been snapped clean off, been severely bent whilst completely wrecking the walkway or, at worse, the stern of the boat could have been forced under water. None of these outcomes were desirable. I reacted quickly and jumped onto the stern deck. I threw her into high speed forward throttle and, with a sickening crunch, the tiller dragged a gouge on the underside of the walkway and came clear (I was on such high throttle that I rammed the front gates in the process). My heart was racing and I was shaking from a huge adrenaline rush. The relief was palpable. Unfortunately, from then on the thick steel tiller on The Frog had a very slight upwards tilt - a reminder of that almost disastrous incident. It would be a very long time before I left the boat again in a rising lock!

The next day we passed through Broad Cut Top lock with no issues but I had read that the next few locks were very short indeed. When we tackled the Figure of Three Locks (bizarrely a set of two), I stayed firmly on board and used the engine and a line to keep the nose pressed up against the front gates and the tiller well clear of the offending walkways. I remember that Mill Bank Lock was particularly challenging - having a very wide walkway. We stopped for lunch before tackling the Thornhill Double and I got out the spanner set for the umbrella spike that sits on top of the tiller. I loosened it and let it swing down underneath the tiller arm. That gave me about another five inches of clearance before the tiller would strike any walkway. Thankfully the Thornhill locks were a little longer and we were soon cruising down towards Greenwood. Here the river felt very much like the Thames - so I immediately sharpened my wits and was pleased that I did. The river took a slight left turn and the lock entrance was obscured down a passage heading off to the right. If I had not been paying attention I could easily have missed the very small opening and the very small sign telling me it was there. The landing point for Greenwood lock was about ten feet long, above a nasty wall and set at about ninety degrees to the lock itself. I was caught unawares that I had to pull in here and, as I reacted late, I hit the wall before stopping. No major damage and I was more annoyed with the lock configuration than my poor boating skills - which is unusual for me. This lock was very short and we spent a long time letting the water in very slowly to avoid pushing The Frog under the walkway. Our last lock of the day was Shepley Bridge. Again, the approach was at ninety degrees and I had to leave the Boat tied up to help with the paddles - which Pip found impossible to move. It had felt like a hard day so, as we had just left the main river and joined a canalised cutting with moorings, we decided to stop and reward ourselves with a cup of tea. The spot we chose felt like a real oasis away from the trials of the Calder so we decided to stay a couple of nights before tackling Cooper Bridge and Brighouse. That afternoon we walked down to Ledgard Bridge Lock and into the Calder Valley town of Mirfield. It had every shop we needed to stock up - including a chemist where we collected two more boxes of Covid testing kits having received notification on the NHS App that we had had a 'close contact' in Leeds - a reminder that we were not yet fully out of the pandemic 'woods'.

Friday 2nd July saw us up pins and move off. We cruised through Mirfield and after Ledgard Flood Lock rejoined the Calder proper. The course took a sharp right hand turn and as we emerged from the shelter of the canalised cutting we looked left and saw the river weir - a few feet away - with the arches of a viaduct, carrying the railway over the Calder, sitting just behind it. As we turned we were greeted by two large metal stanchions sitting in the middle of the waterway - the remains of an old horse crossing bridge that would have spanned the river here. After a couple of miles, we left the river again and entered a cutting at Battyeford before passing Cooper Bridge, where the Huddersfield Broad could be seen heading off to our left. This canal cuts right through the City of the same name and then becomes the infamous Huddersfield Narrow Canal - which boasts the legendary Standedge Tunnel (the longest in the UK and one that I knew we would never be able to navigate with the Frog and its roof boxes). I have spoken to many boaters who see this traverse as a right of passage and, whilst I can understand why, as I was never a fan of any tunnel, the 3.2 miles of Standedge, with its notorious rocky outcrops, was not even on my 'to do' list - let alone high up. So, turning The Frog to the right and heading for Sowerby and the slightly less (but still) notorious Rochdale Canal was a no-brainer.

We were soon approaching Brighouse, famous for its Brass Band. Two locks gave entrance to the basin, where we had lunch and filled with water. We left Brighouse and cruised along a very attractive canalised section, with the Calder meandering to our left and flooded gravel pits sitting to our right. Two more locks were enough for one day and we brought our six and a half mile cruise (with nine locks, all set against us) to a close by Bridge 6 on good mooring pins.

The next day, a Saturday, we would have loved to have stayed put as the heavens had opened and it was raining the proverbial cats and dogs. However, we needed diesel and the marina at Sowerby Bridge was due to close at one o'clock, so we had no choice but to brave the weather and the very short lock at Elland, to continue our journey. The navigation traced a loop south through the town of Elland and then headed back north towards Salterhebble - a suburb of Halifax. Here we were surprised, having not read our Nicholson closely enough, that the first of the Salterhebble locks was a guillotine. In the 1930s, the road crossing the waterway was widened significantly and this meant two tunnels had to be built; one to carry the towpath and the other the canal. As a result of this development, there was also no longer enough room for the long beams on 'normal' lock gates. The solution was to install a single metal gate that used an electric motor to rise vertically. Not aware of this development, I walked through the tunnel and then immediately walked back through it again to get the CRT key we would need to open the lock. This was our first guillotine lock and it was very slow - just what we didn't need on a wet Saturday when we were on a schedule. The entrance to the second and third locks were around tricky angles and at one point I was pinned to the basin wall and had to work hard to get the stern to swing out so we could enter the next lock. The third lock opened onto what is effectively a 'T' junction. We turned the ninety degrees to the left and onto the final approach to Sowerby. Behind us sat the now truncated Salterhebble or Halifax branch that used to carry the navigation all the way into the centre of the once thriving mill town. More on Halifax later.

We finally reached Sowerby, having phoned ahead and warned the marina we were going to get there after one o'clock. They were really good about it and as we turned into the marina basin we could see some of the narrowboat hire company employees still working, filling their charges with diesel and skilfully manoeuvring them around the confined space of the basin. We hovered with one of their team holding a line for us and then we moved forward and filled with diesel. We could not moor alongside the hire boats and had to turn in the basin to moor under some trees at its mouth. This meant me winding The Frog, using a small gap between two hire boats and missing a private mooring on my right. I was amazed at how well this went, especially under the critical gaze of the hire team, and I was soon mooring up on the opposite bank, facing out of the basin. What a shame Derek wasn't there to witness it!

We were, at last, at the end of the Calder and Hebble navigation and I was very relieved to be off what had felt like a very demanding waterway. Little did I know what lay ahead on our journey to Manchester, over the Pennines, via the Rochdale. In the meantime, we had another more pressing issue to resolve. A few days earlier we had experienced a near disaster when Pip almost lost her eyebrows and a lot of her hair. Our gas oven had developed a fault. It had always had the habit of going out when it was still cold. That was annoying enough but unfortunately it had, unbeknownst to us, also developed a problem with the automatic gas shut off, which should engage when the burner goes out. On this occasion when it once again went out, gas had filled the oven. Unfortunately, Pip did not realise and when she opened the oven door slightly and pressed the ignition button to relight it, the result was dramatic and very scary. A fireball blew the door wide open and surrounded Pip's head in flame. The sound was like a mini explosion. Luckily it was very fast and whilst Pip lost some of her hair and was very shaken, no major damage was caused. Alongside this, we had also noticed that the Carbon Monoxide alarm was starting to sound very regularly and put two and two together. The oven was clearly not very well and needed fixing. We were very grateful to the owner of Shires Cruises who allocated one of his team to take a look and let us move our boat back into their moorings whilst he did. The exploration involved removing the oven entirely, servicing it, and then reconnecting it - testing the gas pressure, after doing so, to ensure the whole system had not been compromised. This whole process took thirteen man hours to correct - most of which was the post-installation testing. Dave, the engineer who sorted our oven, was a really nice guy and we enjoyed having him on The Frog (not sure he would say the same). When he finally finished we gave him a bottle of wine and our heartfelt thanks.

Whilst all of this work was going on, Pip and I took the opportunity to walk to Halifax. It was only about three miles away but the walk involved climbing out of the Calder Valley and was a steep uphill for a good part of the trek. Halifax was a complete revelation. The name had always conjured up an image of a grimy northern town filled with Blakeian 'satanic mills'. That may have been true once, but post-industrial Halifax is a very different place. To be clear, I am not saying it is not a thriving town, but rather that it no longer relies on the polluting factories and mills that once dominated. The architecture reminded me of Bath and the best example of this Georgian splendour is the amazing Piece Hall. Once a purpose built market for the cloth industry, this gem is now full of bespoke boutiques and cafes and is a must visit if you are ever in the area.

Our walk back took us right past the impressive Wainhouse Tower which is visible for miles around. It is two hundred and seventy five feet (eighty four metres) high and claims to be the tallest folly in the world. Normally it is open and those who are fit enough can climb to the bottom of two viewing platforms (three hundred and sixty nine steps up). Regrettably, when we were there Covid regulations meant it was closed to the public. How many times have I written that?

We loved Sowerby Bridge. It is truly a 'canal' town, with its previous prosperity being built around the junction of the Rochdale Canal and Calder and Hebble navigation. I have detailed, in an earlier chapter, the chequered past of the link between these two waterways. Goods were off loaded, warehoused and reloaded here at Sowerby. It may have been the result of the much vaunted competition between the canal companies and carriers, but, whatever the reason, the consequence was a thriving town that, despite being nestled in the heart of the Calder valley, was on a vital link to the industrial powerhouses of Manchester and Leeds. Today there is a new connection between the two waterways, via the two Sowerby locks, a short road tunnel and, finally, the deepest lock in the UK - Tuel Lane, which we will tackle on the next leg of our odyssey.

CHAPTER 39: THE ROCHDALE - A TALE OF TWO CANALS

Every boater has a story to tell about the Rochdale Canal - and most of them are not positive. I wanted to start the chapter by coming to the waterway's defence. The Rochdale is, at the same time, one of the most beautiful and dramatic waterways I have ever had the pleasure of cruising AND one of the most difficult and unattractive. There is no conflict between these two observations. The stretch from Sowerby, via Hebden Bridge and up to the summit is glorious. The views at the highest wide lock on the UK waterways are staggering. The height that gives you those lovely views, however, brings with it a cost. The canal is fed by limited water supplies and this has an impact - particularly from the summit west - which I will expand on later. The approach down into Manchester has other challenges and, at this point, I'll just say that the CRT were invaluable as both 'water suppliers' and escorts on our descent. I explained, in a previous chapter, how we had met another boater who had just turned around, 'beaten' by the Rochdale and I can certainly understand this. I would also add that, after our experience, I would never want to travel east from Manchester along the canal. On our descent into this metropolis, we met a couple moored just above Slattocks Top Lock - facing east. They looked drained and told us, emphatically, that they would never tackle that route again. "It was hell" the female boater said. Halfway down the descent into Manchester we also met a family heading east who were so pleased to see us coming in the other direction. We were 'bringing' water with us and that at least gave them a couple of pounds they could safely traverse before having to work the locks two or three ahead to prepare their route. But more on all this later. Would I repeat the Rochdale? Overall, I think the rewards outweigh the challenges and I would tackle it again - but ideally with another boat, crewed by the 'right' fellow boaters.

Anyway, I digress. On Wednesday 7th July, our oven was repaired and we had no reason to put off the ascent up the Rochdale. We had to wait until one o'clock for Tuel Lane Lock (3-4) to open. The hour came and we crept out of Sowerby Basin and swung sharp right on our way to the first Sowerby lock. Another boat was coming down through Tuel Lane and, as a consequence, the already full Sowerby double locks were overflowing with the huge surge of water that comes from the deepest lock on the network emptying (many locks on the Rochdale do not have bywashes and excess water simply breaches the top of the gates into the lock - which looks dramatic and makes the locks harder to use). Tuel Lane is over nineteen feet and eight inches (six metres) deep. It was built, along with the road tunnel under the A58, in 1996 and combined two previous locks (hence its number) as the link to the Calder and Hebble was reinstated. It holds an incredible one hundred and thirty thousand gallons (five hundred and ninety thousand litres) of water. When you go through, needless to say, with the help of a CRT volunteer, you get a little certificate which reads: '*I braved the deepest lock in Britain*'. I will never forget the cavernous void that met us as we turned left out of the road tunnel. I pulled over to the towering wall and threaded a line behind a vertical pipe, built into the side of the lock, to ensure that we were not pushed around as it filled. The lock keeper was very cautious and let the water in gently - despite what looked like at least six inlets for the ground paddles - and we glided up seamlessly (albeit very noisily!)

We stopped early that day as England were playing Denmark in the Euros semi final. Our mooring, by the aqueduct at Luddenden (near bridge 6), was right behind a pub and throughout the very nervy match (which England won 2-1), the shouts from the bar framed the action we were seeing on screen.

The next morning we set off for Hebden Bridge. We quickly noticed that whilst the locks were longer than the Calder and Hebble, their mechanisms were all very stiff and Pip was finding them hard to open. We struggled on, however, and approached Hebden via the Falling Royd Bridge (14). This caught me completely by surprise. I would describe It as a very short tunnel, rather than a bridge and, in Nicholson, the canal looks like it bends sharply to the left at the centre of the crossing. In reality it swung sharply to the right and, as a result, unsighted for a short time, I managed to steer us hard into the tunnel wall. At the entrance to the 'bridge' there is a sign warning of the kink - but it was covered in undergrowth and I did not spot it. The TV aerial pole took a battering and I had to shorten it later that day to stop it being a constant reminder of my incompetence. We also made a small hole in the corner of the

Cratch Cover - which was much more of an annoyance. Just after Falling Royd we saw evidence of a sinkhole which the CRT were in the process of repairing and had been flagged in warnings a few days ago. They had already managed to seal the breach that had led to significant water loss.

That afternoon we explored Hebden, which is lovely and was the setting for much of the filming of *Happy Valley* - which is set around the Calder. We returned to the boat for a pump out. This particular pump out was going to be a challenge. The self service point was on a wharf near Hebden Bridge (16A) but we knew the hose was too short for us to reach the waste outlet if we continued to face up the canal. So I had to wind (in a small inlet by a boatyard) and then back up about a hundred yards to the wharf - before reversing the process so we were once more pointing towards Manchester. I was really pleased with the way the manoeuvre went - especially as the gongoozlers were out in force that day. That night we moored between locks 9 and 10, still in Hebden. I was slightly nervous as the day before we had word of water shortages at Lock 9 and I had fears we would be woken up in the middle of the night at a forty five degree angle and with no water left in the pound.

Thankfully, our sleep was undisturbed and the next morning we set off for the metropolis of Todmorden. Pip took the helm all day and I worked the locks. The highlight of this section was our meeting at Callis Bridge Lock (21) with David Johns of *Cruising The Cut* fame (see Chapter 2 for my reference to his great Vlogs that really helped us when we were boat hunting). He generously posted our meeting in his next video and our followers rose by about three hundred overnight! The day we met him, he was meeting up with Robbie Cummings (famous for Channel 4's *Canal Boat Diaries*) and was driving his van and, unusually, was not on the cut.

Excitement over, we pressed on towards Todmorden. At Lobb Mill Lock (16), we saw a generator and water pump bringing water from a nearby river to top up the canal - a step the CRT had taken following the breach at Hebden. At Todmorden, we stopped before we reached the visitor moorings, which sit just after Shop Lock (18), as they looked very busy. Our spot was opposite some private moorings and alongside the Asda car park (glamorous!) This decision did give us a comic moment the next day. Two days later was Pip's birthday so we needed to stock up with provisions ahead of the celebration. We ordered a Sainsbury's 'home shop' and gave the Asda car park as the delivery address. The driver thought that was hilarious and we all felt very furtive as we filled our bags with the other shoppers looking on in confusion.

Todmorden is really sweet. There were the usual signs of post industrial poverty here and there but overall the town was busy and the market on Saturday morning was teeming with people. Pip's birthday was a strange one. We had a late morning and I prepared a favourite lunch of ours: bruschetta topped with seared fresh figs, basil leaves, Burrata cheese and runny honey. This is a *Pizza East* recipe (thank you) and if you have not tried it - you must. We ate far too many and then headed into town to walk them off. It was Sunday so the town was quiet. Todmorden sits in the lovely Upper Calder Valley and is banked on both sides by higher ground. Both the Pennine and Calderdale Ways run through here and it is popular with both walkers and mountain bikers alike. We found the beautiful Centre Vale Park - where a cricket match was in full flow. We sat for an hour or so and just soaked up this very English (and Yorkshire) scene. That evening I cooked Lamb Shanks (amazing) and we overindulged before watching England lose to Italy in the Euros Final but it wasn't this that cast a shadow over our celebrations.

There was a much more serious reason why we were reflective that evening. We had been in contact with our good friend, Julie, in Penzance, who had been looking after our beloved dog, Bimble, since we set off on our cruise. He was very old and hated the boat and whilst, ideally, he would have shared the odyssey with us, we did not want him to be unhappy and distressed in his latter years. Reluctantly, therefore, we agreed that he should stay with Julie (who had recently lost her own dog, Ozzy, to illness). We were looking forward to being reunited with Bimble when we finished our trip. Regrettably, whilst we were away he developed pancreatitis and was soon in acute pain and discomfort. His condition was so bad that the vets had recommended we let him go. His 'appointment' was the next day and we will be eternally grateful to Julie for making that final journey with him on our behalf. My eyes are filling with tears even now as I write this account. He was a beautiful dog, a great companion and we will miss him forever. The day he passed it rained all day and we stayed on our mooring - having no inclination to do anything. With heavy hearts we spent the time reminiscing about our precious Bimble, which was some comfort to us both.

It was now Tuesday the 13th of July and we left our mooring to start the climb to the summit and cross the border into Lancashire. I am currently reading Tom Rolt's account of his first cruise on his narrowboat *Cressy* in 1939 (in his book *Narrow Boat - see Chapter 17*). In it, he describes many waterways that were coming to the end of their industrial value and, as such, were being neglected by the companies that owned them (many of these companies being railway operators). Without regular traffic, it does not take long for a canal to silt up, for undergrowth to take over and for lock mechanisms to get very stiff. Because the Rochdale is 'underused', we were experiencing a slightly less severe manifestation of this neglect. Whilst the canal was not silting on this side of the Pennines, the lock gates were still becoming really difficult to operate. This section was at least still traversed by hire boats out of Sowerby and Hebden - but even so the condition of the lock gates was not great.

Our journey started with a 'normal' lock and a water refill, followed by our second guillotine at Library Lock (19). Just beyond this we encountered the 'Great Wall of Tod' - an enormous Victorian structure supporting the Railway embankment, that is estimated to contain over four million bricks. Around a sweeping left hand bend we were faced with Wadsworth Mill Lock (20) - the next of the thirteen that sat in the two mile section that carried the canal out of the valley and towards the summit. Water was gushing over the top of the lock gates on the next eight or nine locks - which seemed to make a mockery of the 'water' issues this canal is supposed to have. Little did we know what lay ahead on the descent.

We had read in Nicholson that Copperas House Bridge was very low, so I had taken down the chimney and the TV aerial in case of issues. In reality, there was plenty of clearance and our biggest challenge turned out to be Gauxholme Highest Lock (24). Pip and I together could not move the top gate after filling the lock. Luckily for us, the owner of the nearby cottage was doing some stone work in his garden and he brought his not inconsiderable muscles to help. Finally, we got it to move and we were on our way. The next day we read we had been the last boat through that lock and that the CRT had closed it entirely for essential repairs. The canal remained closed for several weeks and we heaved a huge sigh of relief that we had managed to get through. That night we moored in one of the most attractive spots on the entire network - just after Winterbutlee Lock (30). We were surrounded by stone walls, steep grassy banks with clumps of verdant trees - all under a sky of bright blue patches punctuating moody dark clouds. We settled in for the night - contemplating the remaining six locks that would take us to the summit.

The next morning we tackled three more locks before passing the 'blink and you will miss it' entrance to the impressive Summit Railway Tunnel. Built between 1838 and 1841 by the Manchester and Leeds Railway Company, at just over one and a half miles it was the longest railway tunnel in the world when it was constructed and is still used today. Two more locks were completed (Warland Lower and Upper (34 and 35)) and we were approaching the highest point on the Rochdale Canal. The summit lies between Longlees Lock (36) (six hundred feet above sea level) and West Summit Lock (the first 'down' lock on the canal that claims to be the highest broad lock on the network). The surrounding moorland was stunning. Set against a lovely blue sky dotted with the odd 'cotton wool' clouds, we were certainly seeing the summit at its best. It turns out we were also seeing it at its worst. We moored on the landing pins for West Summit Lock and immediately realised that the pound below it was almost empty. We made our first call to the CRT.

By coincidence a CRT volunteer was walking the towpath and I stopped him to ask what he recommended. He explained the problem was being caused as the North West CRT (who looked after the Lancashire side of the Rochdale Canal) had already 'taken' a large part of their annual allocation of water from the reservoir that sits just to the east of the canal above the summit. I pointed out the irony that the Yorkshire side is 'awash' with water all the way down to Todmorden. I also explained that there will be no boats coming along behind us for some time now that Lock 24 was out of action. He understood but still said we needed to wait until the next morning before we could move and that he would get another volunteer to attend and help us down. That afternoon we chilled and watched the water in the pound below slowly rise. We walked down the towpath past the next five pounds and after the first three, the water level appeared to be better - but we still had to reach it.

It was whilst we were moored on 'top of the canal world' that Pip and I had our first proper contact with the production company that makes the '*Escape To The Country*' television programme. We knew that in a few months we would be house hunting and thought it would be fun to see if the programme makers were interested in our story and would help us search. They were and they did. The first step, after a few emails and calls, was a long 'Zoom' call - which amounted to an interview - assessing our suitability for the programme. This went well and we were told we were suitable for filming. The 'interviewer' asked us to make a few short films that they could use in the introduction to the broadcast and also said they wanted to come and film us on The Frog. We were excited by the opportunity and it was going to be another adventure but we never really expected to find our new home in this way. Little did we know!

The next morning the pound below us was still very low but on the bridge we spotted our saviour - Gerry from the CRT. He was a really friendly guy who explained he was here to 'help us down'. He opened the paddles into Lock 37 and when it was full opened the bottom paddles to pass water into the pound below the lock. Whilst this process was underway he expanded on the water issues. As I have already recorded, at one time the Rochdale Canal was closed to all traffic (it only reopened in the 1990s - see my previous note about the building of Tuel Lane Lock). In the interim, whilst the canal was closed, its owners (probably British Waterways) sold off the reservoir to a local water company. When the canal reopened, the water company and the CRT agreed an allocation each year - which is now, clearly, insufficient. He also added that what makes matters worse is that the Yorkshire descent takes most of the allocation as their section has active hire companies - meaning that part of the canal is much busier (most hire boats only cruised as far as the summit before turning and heading back to Sowerby). 'We hardly see any boats on this section'! We were not sure how that comment made us feel: intrepid yes, but also anxious that the journey ahead was going to be interesting.

It was slow going as we moved the water with us through pound after pound - with only just enough to give us the draft we needed to keep moving. Gerry told me to stay in the middle of the channel and to 'hover' at each lock entrance to ensure I did not ground by trying to go into the landing pins. This continued until we reached Sladen

Lock (44). He explained that the next section is fed by Hollingworth Lake, which is still CRT water and, as such, could be fed into the canal at whatever rate they wished (water levels permitting). We said goodbye to our CRT 'hero' at Littleborough and, after a quick coffee, pressed on alone until we found a lovely mooring at Smithy Bridge, just before Little Clegg Swing Bridge (54A).

As with our approach to Liverpool, we had taken advice from fellow boaters and had looked online to establish how we should approach Manchester (that is to say, where we should moor). By stopping at Smithy Bridge we had set up a seven mile and fifteen lock cruise the next day to reach *The Rose of Lancaster* pub by the River Irk aqueduct. Not only were there good rings for mooring here, but it was also recommended as the last 'safe' stopping point before the New Islington Marina in the centre of Manchester. We also went online to arrange two things: to ask for a CRT volunteer to escort us from Failsworth down into Manchester and to try and find another boater who was on the same schedule as us. Luckily we managed to achieve both.

Pip was at the helm as we started out the next morning. Fifteen locks and three swing bridges awaited us and we needed to share the leg/arm work. This section would include passing through the town of Rochdale itself. We noticed a couple of things: the canal became dirtier with a lot more litter floating on its surface and there was a growing number of gongoozlers who fell into two categories: on the one hand there were the 'great to see a boat passing through here - we don't see very many' and on the other there were those who were clearly enjoying some other form of stimulant (and earlier in the day than most of us do.) A group who fell into the latter category were congregated at Moss Lower Lock (50). The initial sight of them was a bit intimidating so I ensured Pip was at the helm and that I was working the lock. In reality I need not have worried. Two of the group were so excited at seeing us that they insisted on 'helping' to raise the paddles and open the gates. I am not sure their help could ever be described as such but it was a reminder to me not to 'judge books by covers'.

We cruised under the very low Edinburgh Way Tunnel, which carries the A627(M) over the canal and our Vlog shows the chimney about an inch below the roof. I had obviously had no prior warning of how low this was or I would have almost certainly taken it down.

The Rochdale Canal renovation took place after the M62 was built - directly over the then disused waterway. The renovators knew that putting a new bridge under the motorway was impossible, so, instead, a short section was diverted into an existing water culvert that already ran under the 'new' road. The diversion meant that Lock 53 was also relocated and in Nicholson you can see a distinct 'kink' where this happened. The culvert is very narrow, partly because the towpath has also been taken through the opening on a pontoon and we passed with care.

Progress was hard but steady until we reached the top of the Laneside (Slattocks) flight (54-59). This is where we met the ashen-faced couple heading in the other direction who said they felt like they had come 'through hell'. They also told us that water levels below lock 62 were very low. At this point, we did not have a CRT volunteer with us - so we took matters into our own hands. The pound above lock 54 is almost a mile long so we stopped above lock 55 and opened all the paddles on the lock above us letting the water feed down via the bywashes and into the lower pounds. After about thirty minutes we closed these paddles and set off - only to repeat the process at lock 61, thus ensuring that the pounds approaching the Rose of Lancaster had enough water for us to complete our passage. Our efforts meant that water levels were low but manageable and, after a tiring day, we reached our mooring just after four. After stopping, we walked down to say hello to Ian and Sarah who would be coming down with us the next day. They were long-standing liveaboards who had arrived at Todmorden about a month before us. Unfortunately, their journey was interrupted as Ian had suffered a heart attack. This had happened only five weeks prior and I was amazed that they were now about to tackle one of the most demanding sections of the UK waterways - respect! That night we ate at '*The Rose*'. Pip and I agreed that it felt a bit like a 'last meal'. We were nervous about how things would go the next day and wanted to ensure, if nothing else, that we would be well-nourished.

It's Saturday 17th July 2021 - and my diary opens with the words: *Happy Birthday Beautiful Sophie X* (my youngest daughter's twenty ninth birthday). When I wrote those words we would have already been moored in the 'safety' of The New Islington Marina but that haven was a long way off when we awoke at six am. Our first task was to take anything moveable off the top of The frog. We were told to do this in order to remove temptation from anyone who may approach us on our descent. We were meeting Mike from the CRT at Failsworth Lock at eight and we quickly realised that we had not allowed enough time to reach him by then. We had to manage a lock and a very slow vertical swing bridge as well as covering three miles of canal before we got to the rendezvous and we finally arrived at about eight thirty. Luckily Mike was still there. Not long after we met up we realised why he was needed. The quality of the canal deteriorated quickly and drastically. In one short pound we counted twelve shopping trolleys and, in many more, water levels were so low we could not progress until Mike had let water through. The weed and rubbish in the water was thick and I had to access the weed hatch three times to clear the prop of a variety of materials - including, on one occasion, a coat. Buddleia was in full bloom - which would have been lovely had it not been growing out of the middle of the lock gates, making opening them very tricky. In one pound the canal had been filled on both sides with concrete/stone - leaving a very narrow channel that was navigable but full of weeds. I can only guess that this was done during the period the canal was closed and proved impossible or too expensive to fully remove at the time of the restoration. Either way I was glad that the passage was marked with signs warning of the underwater hazards.

At one point we reached an almost completely empty pound. We were already in the lock so we took a further thirty minutes to empty the lock and then refill it before emptying it again. I had never been in a lock when the paddles at the stern were opened and the sensation was very strange. Ian and I were using reverse gear to keep our bows from hitting the front gates - which are not designed for boats to 'slide' up them (unlike the gates that sat behind us).

As we approached Manchester City Centre the quality of the buildings improved but Mike also warned us to keep walking when we were on the towpath. In reality we were engaged by only a couple of locals, both the 'worse for wear' but friendly despite (or maybe because of) their condition. Finally, Lock 81 completed, we approached The New Islington Marina. Its entrance was impeded by a badly moored boat that jutted out into the channel but I managed to make the sharp turn and we said our goodbyes to Ian and Sarah. We learned later that they had continued to the end of the Rochdale and moored on the Bridgwater - completing the infamous Rochdale Nine through the heart of the city en route. What a day of cruising they had!

Meanwhile, back at the marina, our booking had been taken by phone the previous day by the marina boss - who was now absent. John, the poor guy on duty, did not know anything about our reservation but thankfully believed we had booked (I am guessing this had happened before). He allowed us to moor on the waterpoint and we tied up with some relief. We had made it. In a couple of days we would complete the final two locks on the Rochdale and say goodbye to this interesting waterway. In the meantime, we enjoyed the modern setting of the marina, with its collection of small shops (including an amazing bakery), bars and attractive residential buildings. A huge sense of achievement washed over us and, despite the noise of the local bars, my Apple watch still registered nine hours sleep that night.

CHAPTER 40: THE ASHTON CANAL

We stayed two days at New Islington and took the opportunity, whilst there, to walk down to the Piccadilly Basin and Dulcie Junction, where the Ashton Canal, our next waterway, branches off from the Rochdale. I had winded The Frog over the weekend and we woke very early on Monday 19th July to start our cruise up the Ashton. The early start was deliberate. Much of the Ashton also passes through the outskirts of Manchester and the CRT advises all boaters to get through as early as possible, avoid school holidays, only moor at recommended spots and to keep your doors locked. We did not need to be told twice. The final two locks of The Rochdale went smoothly and we soon passed under the graffiti-strewn Leech Street Bridge (89) to enter Piccadilly basin and turn sharp left at Dulcie Junction to join the new to us waterway. We immediately passed through the beautiful residential development of Piccadilly Village and onto the first of the three Ancoats Locks. These are single width and we reflected that we had last seen a single lock leaving Middlewich on the Trent and Mersey - which seemed a long time ago. The sun was shining on a beautiful day and it was hard to imagine that the CRT were right with their doom-laden warnings.

Before I detail our passage through the Ancoats locks, a few facts about the Ashton Canal. It was opened in 1792 and was built to link Manchester to the textile mills of Ashton-Under-Lyne. It is only six miles long but has eighteen locks. Its terminus is at Portland Basin where Dukinfield Junction sees the confluence of the Ashton, the Huddersfield and the Lower Peak Forest canals. Its route passes close to the Etihad Stadium (Manchester City's home ground) and the National Cycling headquarters.

Pip took the helm after seven locks and I walked the towpath. The locks, whilst single, were anything but easy. The mechanisms, like those on the Rochdale, felt neglected and were hard to move and in some locks only one paddle was operational. The gates also had an annoying habit of swinging open on their own. As we were ascending, this caused us problems when we tried to close the bottom gates to fill the lock. On more than one occasion we had to ask passers-by to hold them shut until the water pressure did this for us.

Navigational notes in Nicholson warned us that Bridge 21 (Lumb Lane) was very low so we had taken down our chimney and TV aerial before we set off. This was lucky as there was no warning whatsoever about Bridges 5 and 7 (Beswick Street and New Viaduct Street). Take a look at Vlog 29 and you will see the footage of us passing underneath these bridges with no more than a couple of inches clearance. What was worse, both crossings were positioned in such a way that I could not measure the air draught before we tackled them. As Pip says in the Vlog: *'We just held our breath and went really slowly'.* When we reached Lumb Lane I was able to check the draught and, ironically, soon realised we had much more clearance than the bridges at 5 and 7. Future cruisers of the Ashton beware.

Less than two more miles and we emerged into the lovely Portland Basin. Directly ahead was the west entrance to the Huddersfield Canal (we passed the east entrance at Cooper Bridge on the Calder and Hebble), to our left stood the impressive Social and Industrial History Museum, whilst to our right, under a low, stone tow-bridge, we could see the start of the Lower Peak Forest Canal - our next waterway of choice. We had completed the Ashton in less than a morning and now we needed lunch and some diesel.

CHAPTER 41: THE PEAK FOREST CANALS

We had already researched and knew that there was a small boatyard just after the junction. As we approached, I saw two moored boats on either side of the narrow entrance to the yard and turning in was tricky without clipping either of them. I made it but winced as I clocked that I had entered a water cul-de-sac and realised that, after filling with diesel, I would be faced with reversing back out to the canal. The challenges of reversing The Frog are well-documented but, luckily, there was no wind and whilst it took a long time, I was finally back on the main channel - even managing to avoid an underwater obstruction on the bank opposite the boatyard.

The Lower Peak Forest Canal is only eight miles long, stretching from Dukinfield in the north to Marple in the south - where it joins both the Upper Peak Forest and the Macclesfield canals at the top of a lovely lock flight. The Peak Forest canals are really scenic. Their unique setting makes them lovely to cruise and fabulous countryside, glorious views and interesting features can be found all along their route. As such, they were a welcome contrast after the demands of the Rochdale and the Ashton. I still rank the Upper Peak Forest as one of my favourite waterways and even though it is an 'out and back' experience, the route definitely bears repeating.

That afternoon we cruised just another three miles and found a lovely quiet mooring south of Captain Clarkes Bridge (7), on the outskirts of Hyde. I am looking at my Nicholson Guide as I write and am surprised just how urban this mooring was. As I rewatch Vlog 30 I am struck by how pastoral this section felt, with trees dipping low into the water on the offside and more trees hiding all traces of buildings by the towpath. The bridges are all quaint and many are partly covered in undergrowth, adding to the feeling that we were moored out in the countryside. We were glad to stop, as whilst my diary says we had only covered nine and a half miles, the route had included twenty locks and all of this after a very early start.

The next day we intended to rest but after we went for a walk in the nearby nature reserve, we received a call from the Escape to The

Country (ETTC) team. They wanted to come and film us in two days time and we needed to commit to being in a certain place. We consulted Nicholson and agreed a rendezvous at the top of the Marple Flight. All agreed, I spent the afternoon of one of the hottest days of the year rubbing down and varnishing various parts of The Frog. We wanted her to look her best for the television.

The locks were not far away, so the next morning we cruised down to the opening of the Rose Hill Tunnel and moored - just south of Romiley. En-route we passed through the short Woodley and Hyde Bank tunnels and under the wonderfully named Top of Th' Hill bridge (which, from underneath, looks like two bridges stuck together). That afternoon we walked the three mile round trip all the way up the flight, looking for a suitable mooring spot to do the filming the next day. Our afternoon was spent cleaning and getting finally prepared. On our walk we noticed that the locks were manned by volunteers but the water levels were quite low. We agreed that we would set off early the next day to be the first boat up and ensure we got moored ahead of the film crew arriving in case of any delays.

We woke early to nothing more than the sound of crows and the sheep grazing in the field opposite our mooring. As planned, we set off early and I took the helm, steering us through the narrow one hundred yards of the opened up Rose Hill Tunnel. Just after this striking feature we cruised past an even more impressive one: the Grade I listed Marple Aqueduct. This crossing, over the River Goyt, sits alongside an even bigger railway viaduct doing the same thing. It is one hundred and five yards long and, standing at almost one hundred feet, is the highest aqueduct on the English waterways and the second highest in the UK after the Pontcysyllte. It took four years to build and cost the lives of seven men before it finally opened in 1800.

As we approached the bottom lock we saw another narrowboat, with people on the aft deck, moored near the lock pins. I pulled in and ran ahead to ask if they were planning to go up the flight (it would be boating etiquette to ask permission to go ahead if they were). As it turned out they had not even had breakfast and were more than happy that we went first.

The Marple Flight is made up of sixteen locks and rises a total of two hundred and fourteen feet. Whilst the canal was opened in 1796, the locks, linking to the Macclesfield and Upper Peak Forest Canals, were not added until 1804. In the intervening years, a tramway was built to transport goods up the hill. Most of the finance for the flight was provided by Richard Arkwright Junior, son of the well known industrial revolution pioneer. In 1799 he was a very successful financier and investor and one of only ten known millionaires in the UK.

The deepest lock has a rise of sixteen feet and we were pleased to be met by three CRT volunteers a little way into the climb. After the first lock, Pip and I swapped roles and she took the helm. In the pound above lock 5 she regretted this decision as low water levels forced her aground. The CRT volunteers let down some extra water and she was soon on her way again. The climb took us three and three quarter hours and we were very pleased to see the beam of Lock 16 swing open to let us out of the final chamber. As we emerged, we could see the start of the Macclesfield canal under a bridge to our right but we followed the channel to the left and onto the Upper Peak Forest Canal. We pulled in to moor and waited for the film crew to arrive.

It was a hot day and we spent a big part of the afternoon being filmed and re-filmed from lots of angles - having pretend/repeat conversations as we did so. We were captured doing the dishes (about seven times - ensuring we washed the items in the same order each time), walking the towpath and knitting (Pip - not me). Lucy and Sam, the ETTC crew who carried out this initial shoot, also wanted to film us pulling in to moor. This involved me untying The Frog and reversing back down the canal (we searched the bank ahead of us for another mooring spot but could not find one) and then pretending that I was approaching the mooring for the first time. It took three takes before they were happy - not really appreciating how tricky this was to do in a boat that hated reversing. All of this for a few seconds of footage that made the final programme! Whilst they were with us, I noticed a boat trying to moor into a very tight spot between two boats just behind us. I instinctively stopped everything to do with the filming and ran over to take a line and help pull them in (they almost had to come in sideways - such was the tightness of the mooring spot). Whilst there, I also saw that a moored boat was close to having one of its mooring pins pulled out of the ground (the result of passing traffic). I came back and grabbed my mallet to drive the pins back into the bank. Lucy asked if my actions were normal and I explained that most boaters would give priority to helping fellow boaters. No doubt, the shoe will be on the other foot one day. She was impressed and it gave her a good insight into the 'community' on the cut - a theme that was relevant to the relocation we were about to undertake.

Filming finished and excitement over, we settled in for the night and the next morning resumed our course along the Upper Peak Forest Canal. This waterway was completed in eighteen hundred and links Marple to Whaley Bridge and, via a short arm, the iconic Bugsworth Basin. It is only about six miles long but makes up for its lack of miles with fabulous views. A large part of its length has been cut into the westerly edge of the Goyt valley and this positioned us much higher than the surrounding countryside. The canal swings around a long sweeping bend at New Mills and a sweet smell fills the air. Right next to the waterway stands the Swizzles sweet factory - which was relocated here in 1940 when the company left London to avoid the Blitz. It produces, amongst other things, Parma Violets, Love Hearts and Drumsticks all still firm favourites of many with a sweet tooth. The smell really was lovely and I slowed down as we cruised past just to savour it.

Our only obstacles on this waterway were lift and swing bridges and we soon completed the trip to the junction that led to Bugsworth (the village is called Buxworth - the locals having changed its name for fairly obvious reasons). The canal folk were clearly less concerned and, to this day, the basin still carries the original name. The whole site is a scheduled historic monument and is a must visit if you are a boater. It is clearly a canal terminus but it once would have had a six mile tramway link to the huge limestone quarries at Dove Holes. Limestone was brought down the hill to Bugsworth. Some was processed in the large number of kilns on the site before being loaded onto barges to be taken away to buyers across the UK. The rest was shipped out to kilns elsewhere. Forge Mill Bleach Works, at Whitehough, also used the tramway to bring bleached cloth to the basin for onward transport and further processing. It is clear that, in its heyday, the basin would have been a hive of activity and one contemporary observer even described it as a *'hell hole'*! Today it is a blissfully quiet hideaway and the only business in evidence is between visiting boaters and the many trade boats that add colour and interest.

To slate their understandable thirst, the many workers on site would have wandered over to The Navigation Inn. Nestling at the end of the road that enters the far end of the basin, it is now almost as famous as its former owner, Pat Phoenix, who played Elsie Tanner - an original and long-lived character in Coronation Street. We visited the pub and had a very strange dinner (sausages and fish fingers) before joining in a pub quiz.

In the afternoon we walked to Whaley Bridge - rather than cruising and winding The Frog in the basin. The most interesting feature here was what I will call a 'transfer shed'. Inside there is an inlet of the canal and, on either side, a road and a railway line. This meant that, protected from the elements, goods and raw materials could be easily transferred from one mode of transport to another. At the edge of the basin, a large pipe was drawing water from the River Goyt and topping up the canal. Essential work taking place on Todbrook Reservoir meant this additional, temporary water source was needed.

On Saturday 24th we headed back towards Marple. We stopped for lunch on a bend just before Hill Top Footbridge (20), where the view to our right was stunning. It was so good in fact that we decided to stay all afternoon - allowing me to do a few tasks and complete the Rochdale Vlog ready for publication. We said goodbye to the Upper Peak Forest the next morning and, at Marple, we turned left to join the Macclesfield Canal.

CHAPTER 42: THE MACCLESFIELD CANAL

The Macclesfield canal was commissioned in the early nineteenth century from a design by Thomas Telford. Following the completion of the Trent and Mersey there was a growing demand for a further link between the Midlands and Manchester and the obvious route was through the manufacturing town of Macclesfield. The course is just over twenty seven miles long and runs from Hardings Wood Junction with the Trent and Mersey - all the way to Marple - where we were about to join it. The canal is a classic Telford waterway and in many places follows a dead straight route - employing cuttings and embankments to do so (similar to the Shropshire Union). This made it commercially attractive once finished and it continued with traffic until about 1954. It also had only thirteen locks along its route - twelve in the flight at Bosley and a stop lock near Hardings Wood. Having cruised it, it is no surprise to us that leisure boating started here as early as the end of the first world war - it really is a lovely waterway.

On the very edge of Marple we passed by the enormous Goyt Mill. It was built in 1905 and is a great example of an Edwardian factory - producing cloth using raw material brought in on the canal and sending its finished product out in the same way. Thankfully it was not demolished when production stopped and today it is full of small workshops.

We cruised for only another two miles and moored between Bridge 10 and 11 at High Lane. I walked the two miles or so back to Marple to buy some DIY materials to complete a few jobs onboard. Tasks completed, we set off the next morning intent on reaching Bollington by lunch time. This was important, as that afternoon we were walking to Hollins Hall Hotel to have 'high tea' - a birthday present for Pip from her son, Ian and his wife, Brittany. En-route we stopped for water at Higher Poynton and as we filled up, we noticed a nearby boatyard called Vernon's Wharf. Any boater who has cruised widely will know this name as it is painted on the cabins of some of the loveliest craft on the network.

We reached our destination and moored between the impressive Clarence Mill and the Bollington aqueduct (bridges 26A and 27). We explored the village - which took about five minutes - and headed off for our afternoon feast. Many sandwiches and cakes later, we staggered back to the boat and collapsed in front of *Only Connect* and *University Challenge* (sad - but we love both programmes). That night I was surprised to receive a direct message from the CRT saying that they had viewed our Rochdale Vlog and would take a good look at the issues we raised about the condition of the canal. I am still not sure that anything was actually done about it but it was nice to think we had done a little bit to raise the profile of the waterway.

We travelled only three miles the next morning and moored on a floating pontoon near Bridge 37 in the middle of Macclesfield. We explored the town and Pip had a pre-filming haircut. The following Monday we were heading south, by hire car, for the filming of ETTC and needed a few things. Unfortunately we could not find any independent shops to explore. The centre also felt a little run down and the very heavy rain did not help change our view of the town. Instead we completed a big food shop and sat on the pontoon for the afternoon - bemoaning the weather and working on the next Vlog.

Our journey the following morning started with Buxton Road Bridge (37). The pre-fabricated concrete feel of this bridge was in sharp contrast to the majestic brick splendour of the old Hovis Mill that sat just beyond it. Very few Britons have not heard of Hovis Bread and its flour was milled here from 1898 to 1904, when the success of the business meant the building was too small and production moved to Trafford Park in Manchester. The Mill produced the flour, using a special technique that retained more flavour. The magic white powder was then shipped out to different bakers all over the country who then made bread that could be branded as 'Hovis'.

The three bridges from 39-41 are lovely. The Hydrangeas were in full bloom on the canal side and the grey/pink stone of the bridge architecture set them off beautifully. We were soon passing under Foden Bank bridge (43) - with its distinctive 'crossover' design carrying the towpath from one side of the canal to the other - and over the quaint Gurnetts Aqueduct. We knew the weather was closing in so we pulled in to moor just south of Crow Holt Bridge

(52). The mooring was onto Armco, but the towpath had clearly not been trimmed for some time and I had to get out our grass shears (for the first time, I think) to cut a path through to the bow and stern of the Frog. Ten minutes later the heavens opened and we took video footage of the biblical rainfall that followed (see Vlog 32). There were very few occasions when we timed our mooring right but that was certainly one of them. When the deluge finally stopped, we emerged from The Frog and walked the half mile to check out the Bosley lock flight. We needed to pump out and we had been examining the peculiar diagram in our Nicholson guide that showed the approach to the sanitary station that sat at the top of the flight. It was useful to see it 'in the flesh' as I was able to work out that the pump out hose would reach all the way over our roof to the outlet on our port side. This meant, the next morning, I would be able to cruise straight into the diagonal cutting without having to wind. After pumping out, I would simply need to reverse, using the tight banks of the cutting to keep The Frog pointing in the right direction and then swing the bow to starboard to point at the locks.

The next morning, the manouvre went without incident and we were soon descending the one hundred and eighteen feet of the flight. I was on the tiller for the first seven locks and we benefited from how busy this section was (many locks were set in our favour as other boats were ascending as we went down). We completed the flight with no volunteer lock keeper help and after turning the sharp left just before Lock 12, we set our course for Congleton. Not long after we started following a VERY slow boat and decided, rather than following it any further, to moor at Buglawton (near Foden Bridge 67) - a couple of miles from the middle of Congleton itself. We walked into the bustling town centre and Pip bought a dress for filming the following week (understandably, we only had very practical clothes on The Frog).

The next two days we stayed in our mooring - largely because we were not booked into the marina at Scholar Green for another two days and it is only five miles away. On Sunday 1st August we set off on this final stretch. Our route through Congleton itself was interesting. After Flyover Bridge (74) the canal passed under three other crossings that came thick and fast. The channel narrowed acutely as the addition of bridge supports for the relatively modern A527 must have meant moving the bank a few feet on either side. The narrowing felt even more acute as directly behind this modern bridge was the old Park Lane Bridge (75) and the unnumbered railway crossing. Luckily there was nothing coming the other way and we were pleased when we emerged unscathed out the other side.

Five miles on we pulled safely into *Heritage Narrow Boats* Marina at Scholar Green - where The Frog would spend the next week while we set off to Somerset and our ETTC filming.

Escape to the Country

We loved the filming experience and we took the opportunity to meet up with my three children in Bristol for a lovely Persian meal. It was great to see them after so long! We were put up in a hotel in Midsomer Norton with the film crew and, from there, we visited Clevedon, Bishop Sutton, Congresbury, Uphill (near Weston Super Mare) and Ilminster. As well as viewing four houses, the team knew we were bell ringers and arranged a surprise visit to Bath Abbey to film us ringing the bells. Pip and I had only been ringing a few years (not long in Bell ringing terms) and we had not been able to visit any towers throughout our cruise because of Covid. So to say we were terrified, after a year of not ringing, was an understatement. The bells in the Abbey (which is effectively a Cathedral) are huge. The Treble (smallest bell) weighs a quarter of a ton, whilst the largest (the Tenor) comes in at one and a half tons! We rang bells three and four - so somewhere in between. To get to the ringing chamber we had to climb up a very narrow spiral staircase to the level of the nave roof and then walk a narrow balustrade along its edge. Because we were still in the grip of Covid, protocols meant we had to go outside every fifteen minutes, so we spent a lot of time out on the roof - enjoying the views of this beautiful city. Luckily, the Tower Master was kind enough to let us just ring 'rounds' (one bell following the other) and there were no disasters. It was a wonderful experience that we would not have had if we had not applied to 'Escape'. In summary, we had a fabulous week and, to cap it all, we found the lovely house that I am now sitting in. All followers of our Vlogs will know we are now based in Uphill and we have Bryony May Williams (presenting her first ever show) and the rest of the crew to thank for that. The programme was Episode 26 of Series 22 - in case you want to see it.

Adventure over, we drove back to Congleton and took a taxi to Scholar Green to be reunited with The Frog. It felt a bit strange. We had already made an offer on our new home and having had such an intimate relationship with The Frog, we felt slightly disloyal - albeit excited that our longer term future was taking shape.

It's Monday 9th of August and we left Heritage Marina and set off for the Trent and Mersey and the Harecastle Tunnel. The junction was only a couple of miles away and the only obstacle to overcome was the final lock on the Macclesfield Canal - Hall Green Stop Lock - which has a drop of only one foot. It is situated over a mile from the junction and this is explained by the history of the merging of the two canals. The owners of the Trent and Mersey agreed with the link to the new Macclesfield Canal at Hardings Wood but were worried about losing water to it. They applied for an Act of Parliament in 1827 and were granted permission to build the first mile and a half of the new canal themselves. They insisted that the water level in the rest of the Macclesfield be set one foot higher than their short section ensuring they always gained water from, rather than lost water to, the new cutting. The lock is flanked by two beautiful stone cottages, one whitewashed, giving another picture postcard image (one of many on our travels).

Shortly after the lock, the canal crosses the Trent and Mersey on the Poole Aqueduct and turns a sharp left to run parallel with it before turning another sharp left at the junction itself. Finally, we passed under Bridge 98 and having said our goodbyes to the Macclesfield, we rejoined the Trent and Mersey and headed for Harecastle.

CHAPTER 43: AN UNWANTED DETOUR

The Harecastle Tunnel is nearly one and three quarter miles long and is the second longest on the UK waterways (after Standedge). It is notorious for being very low in the middle. At its mouth, a hanging wooden template gives an indication of how high the roof is at its lowest point. Unfortunately for us, there had been lots of rain recently and on the day we approached the tunnel the water levels were higher than normal. A CRT volunteer, standing at the tunnel entrance, was not happy for us to proceed. Whilst we knew our roof boxes JUST fitted under the template, it still meant I would have to stay dead centre through the length of the tunnel to avoid a box being dragged off the roof. This was not something I had a strong track record of doing and the thought of losing the boxes mid tunnel was horrendous. It was not a risk I, or the CRT, were happy for us to take.

This was very disappointing. We would not now be able to 'tick the Harecastle box' on our odyssey wish list and, in many ways worse, to get to where we wanted to be we would now have to cruise back to Middlewich and down the Shropshire Union. Whilst we had not covered this part of the Trent and Mersey before, there were thirty locks between us and Middlewich. Additionally, we had already cruised both the Middlewich Branch and the very long Shropshire Union before. To add insult to injury, there is no room to wind in the basin at the tunnel mouth and we had no option but to reverse the quarter of a mile back to the junction where there was room to turn. Knowing how difficult this would be on The Frog, we decided to take a line each and tow her back whilst walking the towpath - a physically demanding but low risk option. We must have made a very strange sight to anyone passing by.

I remember the feeling I had that day. I knew that Pip was particularly upset with the decision not to go through the tunnel and I suspected she secretly thought that my 'tunnel phobia' was influencing the decision not to proceed. All that day she walked the towpath and managed the eleven locks we completed until heavy rain forced us to moor at Rode Heath - between bridges 140 and 141. We had only covered 5 miles from Heritage marina and the weather and our mood made it a sombre evening. Looking back now at Vlog 33, I reflect that this section of the Trent and Mersey is really quite lovely. Yes it is 'lock heavy' and quite hard work as a result, but the locks were in good order and the canal architecture en route was really attractive. It is a shame we were not really in the right frame of mind to appreciate it - well not on day one anyway.

The next evening we aimed to moor on familiar territory - just after the very short Wardle Canal in Middlewich. This meant cruising nine miles and completing twenty locks. The day started frustratingly; Thurlwood Lock (53) had a queue of four boats ahead of us waiting to descend. After this initial wait we then found ourselves following a group of lady boaters who, despite having fifteen years of boating experience (they told me this), did everything very slowly and hit every lock entrance as if it were compulsory to do so. I know Derek once described narrowboating as a 'contact sport' but this was taking it to the limit. We managed to get ahead of them at one of the many double locks (two locks side by side rather than a wide lock) and were pleased to make steadier progress. In my diary I take the time to explain why I referred to the other boaters as 'ladies': *'(I am) not being sexist - (it's) just the best way to remember them'*. Their lack of ability clearly did not have anything to do with their gender. Some of the best helms people I have met on the network have been women. I refer particularly to: the boat moving heroine in Crick who winded The Frog when I had no clue how to deal with the very windy conditions; Kathie aboard NB *Coo-ee-Too* whom we met on the second day of our odyssey, who had completed a helmsman course and was fearlessly skilful and, of course, the lovely Katherine on NB *Double 0* - who has the cut running through her veins.

Anyway, where were we? Oh yes - en route to Middlewich. The rest of the locks were completed without incident. We knew we were approaching Middlewich when we passed the huge British Salt Ltd works and, not long after, we were leaving Kings Lock (71) and preparing to swing hard left onto the Wardle Canal. I remember this manouvre well. I knew how low the bridge was and that it was really important to avoid cutting the corner (this would have risked scraping the roof and cabin had I done so). As a result I let The Frog drift slightly wide and then swung in a very sharp arc to get around the turn. There was a boat moored on the right of the Trent and Mersey with two people sitting on the well deck watching the proceedings. I revved hard to create the tight turn I needed. As I pulled the throttle back I heard a distinct 'tut' from one of the onlookers and I guessed I must have disturbed their tranquil G&T. After a hard day of cruising a canal I did not want to cruise I was not in the mood for any sanctimonious, inconsiderately moored, boating critics (who should have known better). I swung around, gave them a big smile and forced out a not too sarcastic: 'Hello'. The 'tutting' male smiled broadly back at me and gave me a wave - clearly not willing to say anything to my face.

We pulled under the towpath bridge and stopped in front of Wardle Lock - which was full of water and being entered from above by another boat. Pip went to help with their descent and I jumped off and put the centre line through a ring. I am so glad I did. Boaters who have passed through here will know it's very narrow and when the paddles were opened to empty Wardle lock (which was only a few feet away from me) it was all I could do to stop The Frog flying backwards and re-joining the Trent and Mersey! Had I not put the rope through a ring I would never have been able to hold her using my own strength. I even ran the rope back through the ring again to give me better traction and at one point I was convinced the line was going to snap.

After we entered the lock the hire boat that had just descended met another hire boat coming onto the Wardle under the towpath bridge. This made the tricky turn even more difficult and both boats were still trying to pass each other when we left the lock. We moored in almost the same spot we had on our previous visit but on this occasion we noticed a plaque that we had missed before. The cottage overlooking Wardle Lock was once the home of a lady called Maureen Shaw. She was so kind and helpful to passing boaters that many had renamed Wardle as 'Maureen's Lock'. The plaque describes her as a 'Boat Woman' and its erection is testament to how fondly she is remembered.

I won't go into detail about a waterway we have already cruised and will simply say the next day we covered thirteen miles - which is the full length of the Middlewich Branch and back to Nantwich - mooring by Nantwich Junction Bridge (92). En-route we had to wait an hour to go through the first lock but our day was brightened by seeing NB *New Dawn*. This was the home of the couple from Sunderland that we had helped find a mooring spot in Kintbury (see Chapter 11). They had not forgotten our help that day and we chatted animatedly as the boats passed each other - cramming in as many updates as we could before distance meant we could no longer hear each other.

A quiet night in Nantwich ended with a beautiful dawn on the glorious 12th of August. The clouds of the previous day had disappeared and we set off before breakfast under an azure blue sky, lit by a sun still sitting quite low on the horizon. We stopped immediately for water and I only tell this story because I remember meeting another boater who moored up just after us. He told me that the last time he was here a passing walker had defecated in the shower - just before he went to use it. He went into great detail, telling me that he: "...*did it in the grate and the wife and I christened him Richard The Grate*". This pun is made funnier if you have seen a Ronnie Barker sketch or know Cockney Rhyming slang. A 'Richard' (as in Richard the Third) can mean a bird (a real bird or, more derogatively, a woman) or a turd. In the sketch, Ronnie Barker, dressed as a vicar, preaches to a congregation of Cockneys and relates a parable in which he uses the former meaning in such a way that it becomes hilarious when you apply the latter. He describes an errant drunk who, walking home, "*..saw a small brown Richard the Third lying on the ground*". He, thankful that he had not trodden on it, picked it up and placed it on a wall! Ronnie Barker had his audience in stitches. I was less amused and, with a completely straight face, thanked him for sharing and tried to put all thoughts of the conversation out of my head before I sat down for breakfast.

We were soon on the move and, as before, we made good progress on the wide and straight 'Shroppie' - which is good because we planned to moor that night at Market Drayton (a distance of 12 miles and twenty two locks later.) We swapped roles until we reached the bottom of the Audlem Flight when Pip was walking and I was at the Helm. The bottom lock was full and was manned by two CRT volunteers who were helping a trade boat with a 'butty' attached (a butty is a second craft, with no independent means of propulsion, that is attached to a powered vessel). He was struggling to get out of the lock above and was taking a very long time to do so. The CRT volunteers, unusually, suggested that they would empty the bottom lock to allow me to progress - on the basis that we would have filled it again before the trade boat reached us. I entered the lock and the volunteers opened the paddles to fill it. Meanwhile, Pip walked along the towpath towards the next lock and, en-route, was berated (with very aggressive language) by the helmsman on the trade boat. He accused her of 'stealing his lock'. Pip explained, in vain, that the volunteer had suggested the manouvre and that he was not going to be delayed as a result. He wasn't listening and continued his tirade. Pip radioed me. By this point I was 'up' and ready to leave the lock (proof that our decision to go ahead was the right one). However, I could not leave as the trade boat had come up really close to the gates and was blocking the exit (clearly in a fit of pique). The CRT volunteers asked him to move back and he finally did. As I left the lock I shouted at him in no uncertain terms that if he had an issue with what happened, he should have taken it up with the CRT volunteers and not my wife, I may even have called him a tosser. The only valid concern he could have is with wasted water but the Shroppie is not short of water. He could not point to any delay because the only hold-up was caused by his intransigence in sitting outside the lock.

I stayed at the helm until Lock 12. Pip took some great footage of me entering this lock. If ever evidence of the abundant water supply on the Shroppie were needed then the bywash entering the very narrow approach to Lock 12 provided it. Watch Vlog 34 and you will see me hit the strategically placed wooden barrier to the left of the lock gate. The barrier is obviously there as an acknowledgement that every boat will be pushed sideways when the bywash is running fast and it does its job of guiding me into the lock. The only alternative to hitting it would have been to approach the lock at very high speed - which would have been very tricky in such a narrow channel.

Pip took the helm after a couple of locks and was further irritated by somebody telling her not to 'ride the gate'. I was walking further on so did not hear the conversation. Firstly, Pip maintains that her bow was nowhere near the gate on this occasion - but even if it was, the upper gates on single width locks usually have a metal 'rising' plate or are finished with a flush surface to avoid any issues if the bow touches the front gate. I have even been advised by some experienced boaters to actually place the bow on the front gate to avoid being buffeted around in rising locks. Indeed, many solo boaters, who have to get off of their boats when using a lock, will sometimes leave it in forward gear so that it stays away from the troublesome rear gates and slides up those at the front. Either way, this comment added to Pip's irritation. They say things always come in threes and, sure enough, at a lock further up the flight Pip was shouted at by another boater for not leaving the landing pins of the lock quickly enough for him to moor easily. In reality, as boater etiquette demands, Pip had left the lock she had just exited full of water and with its gates open - so the errant boater could just cruise straight in without needing to moor. I am not sure what was in the air that day but it seemed everyone was in a very tetchy mood and we were glad to reach our mooring in Market Drayton without any further incidents.

The route the next morning started with two familiar obstacles: Tyrley Locks and Woodseaves Cutting. The former, as I have already recounted, have wicked bywashes, and, true to form, I planted our bow into the outer wall at Lock 4 when the current swung the stern forcibly to the left. I was already steering to the right to allow for the current, but stupidly forgot to switch direction as the centre of the boat passed the stream - schoolboy error! The latter, you may recall, is a mile long, very narrow cutting with few passing places. What made us particularly nervous today were the recent CRT reports of a boat that had grounded on a large log, following a landslide. We proceeded with care - with Pip walking ahead, looking out for obstructions (until the overgrown and muddy towpath made it impossible to keep walking). Despite meeting one boat coming the other way, thankfully near a passing point, we got through unscathed.

The rest of our cruise to Gnosall passed without incident. We flew through Norbury Junction and the nearby CRT yard and were soon approaching the lovely canalside village. It was somewhere we did not have time to explore on our 'up' journey, so we decided to stop here for a couple of days. It also had a bus link to Stafford - where we had arranged to meet Marlene and Wolfgang for lunch (thinking we would be coming down the Trent and Mersey). We moored near the Navigation Inn, having cruised thirteen and a half miles and completed five tricky locks before two thirty.

The next morning we caught the bus to Stafford town Centre for our lunch appointment. We will never forget the journey, as the driver was a lunatic! The only other occasion I had felt that unsafe on a bus was when we had negotiated the Amalfi Coast on a coach driven by an Italian who clearly thought he was in a Ferrari. The road to Stafford was much less precarious, but we were still both holding onto the seat in front for dear life.

Having survived the drive to Stafford, we were walking through the pedestrianised shopping area and were amazed when a lady ran up and said how much she loved our Vlogs! We were often recognised when cruising (the Frog is very distinctive and a lot of our followers are also boaters) but this was the first (and last) time Pip and I had been recognised some miles from a canal.

Lunch, in a town centre hotel, was lovely. We gave Wolgang a present of a copy of Bradshaw's *Canals and Navigable Rivers: of England and Wales*. With his passion for all waterways in the UK, we knew he would love the level of detail in this publication. There then followed an embarrassing moment which we still chuckle over. Almost immediately he had said thank you for the book, Wolfgang handed us a collection of printed and bound photographs - chronicling one of their recent cruises. I assumed it was also a present and put it into my bag. Pip was more aware however, and told me to get it back out so that we could peruse it, before GIVING IT BACK. Ouch!

Sunday 15th of August saw us set a new canal cruising personal best. We left Gnosall with no particular goal but hoped that we could finish the Shroppie and get back onto the new to us water of the southern section of the Staffordfshire and Worcestershire Canal. I have already documented how easy the Shroppie is to cruise (well, for the most part) and we covered sixteen and a half miles, tackled three locks and pumped out - all before four o'clock. Our mooring that night was just above the picturesque Wightwich (pronounced 'wittick') Lock. At last our detour was over and we were back on the route we would have taken had the Harecastle Tunnel been more accommodating.

CHAPTER 44: AUTHERLEY TO STOURPORT

The Staffordshire and Worcestershire Canal (S&W) is a lovely canal and I have already laid out a brief history in the opening of Chapter 30, when we cruised from Haywood to Autherley in April. The lower section of the canal is different, but equally scenic. In places it bends around tight sandstone banks - which rise high above the tranquil waters. Many of the bywashes are really special with the water entering a stone basin and dropping down through an aperture, protected by what looks like an upturned metal hanging basket. I haven't described them very romantically but they really were lovely and you can see for yourself in Vlog 35. We had also forgotten just how low the bridges are on the S&W, passing within a few inches of the arches on more than one occasion. A lot of the lovely locks are entered or, more accurately, exited (as we were descending) under attractive brick bridges with very narrow, low archways - reminiscent of those on the Trent and Mersey near Fradley. This is best illustrated at Dimmingsdale Lock (the locks are not numbered on this canal). In Vlog 35 Pip records me leaving this lock from the lock bridge and I do the same from the helm - clearly showing the very low archway as I pass under where she is standing.

Not far from Autherley, the Birmingham Main Line Canal can be seen leaving Aldersley Junction under another low, narrow bridge. From here a flight of twenty one locks climbs all the way into Wolverhampton and the canal makes its way into the heart of Birmingham itself - just one of many routes into the Birmingham Canal Network (BCN). On a previous boating holiday we cruised through the middle of the city and, having been pelted with stones from more than one overhead bridge, we made a conscious decision to leave the BCN off of our Odyssey list of 'must dos'. By contrast, considering how close we were to some major conurbations, the S&W canal felt like a well kept secret, hidden away, as it was, behind lush, mature evergreens, through which the milky sun cast alternate shadows and then bright reflections of the cloudy sky.

Early the next morning we walked from our Wightwick mooring to Wightwick Hall, a gem of a National Trust property not far from the canal. It is well worth a visit - if only to view the amazing Arts and Crafts interior, which includes original William Morris wallpapers. At eleven thirty we upped pins and continued our journey south, heading for the fascinating Bratch Locks. If you look at the Nicholson Guide, it is easy to miss the little 'bubble' diagram off to one side that 'expands' the one lock shown on the main waterway into the three locks that actually sit here. I would hazard to say that they are unique on the waterway. They were designed by Brindley and opened in 1772 and were originally built as a staircase. I am not sure why they were redesigned, but they were and are now three distinct locks with VERY small pounds in between (literally a few feet long). The total drop for all three locks is just over thirty feet. The paddles between them (of which there are two sets for each 'transition) are colour coded and, thankfully, manned by CRT volunteers who know the order in which they should be opened. The rhyme goes like this: *'Blue before red is what the man said. Red before blue - that won't do!'* I was reminded of the rhyme that ensures you consume alcohol in the right order: *'Cider then beer makes you feel queer but beer then cider makes a good rider'*. The problem is the rhyme could just as easily be: *'Cider on beer makes you feel queer but beer on cider makes a good rider'.* The same could be said for the Bratch Lock paddles. What if I remembered it as: *'Blue after red is what the man said. Red after Blue - that won't do*! Either way, Pip captured some great footage of the vortex that is created as the paddles are opened to allow the water to pass from the small pounds into the next lock. I did not fancy my chances of survival if I had fallen into it, unless the paddles were closed very quickly to stop me being dragged down to the sluice. Again, I was very pleased that the CRT were in control. As well as these intriguing design features, the whole complex is really attractive with a lock cottage and a very quaint toll house sitting at the exit of the top lock where the towpath crosses the canal.

Bratch locks completed, we then waited for three other boats to go through Botterham Staircase - two locks with a drop of twenty feet and three inches. We caught some lovely images of the entrance to the bywash and, as we descended in the second chamber, the view behind the helmsman was really dramatic. At Marsh Lock we met a Vlog follower who recognised the boat and Pip. His wife was also from Burnham on Sea - where Pip and I used to live. One nice chat later we were on our way again, completing two more locks before mooring on the bend between bridges 39 and 38 (just before the aqueduct at Hinksford). It had been a long day with fourteen interesting locks completed over our six and a half mile cruise.

The following morning we were looking forward to exploring this interesting canal further and planned to get to Kidderminster - a cruise of twelve miles and ten locks. This section has lots of the sandstone walls I mentioned above. Brindley designed the canal to follow river valleys, where he could, but in many places the sandstone had to be cut away to complete the navigation. The result was a lovely backdrop to our cruise - albeit some of the blind bends were challenging. We made good progress and did not meet a lock queue until we reached Debdale Bridge - a distance of about ten miles. En-route we passed Stourport Junction (also known as Stewponey), and noted the start of the Stourbridge Canal that links to the town itself, Halesowen and the BCN via the Dudley Tunnel. Stewponey lock has a quaint toll house on its approach and the short Dunsley Tunnel sits just around a sharp right hand bend. It reminded us of the Cowley Tunnel on the Shroppie - being unlined and having clearly been hewn out of solid rock. Our course took us through the well known Canal town of Kinver - where our cratch cover was tailor-made for us - and on to the Whittington Lock. I remember this lock really well - it is flanked by a lovely yellow cottage and whilst we were descending a friendly face appeared through the open french windows. The owner clearly loved where she lived and passing the time of day with boaters using the lock.

At Cookley, another tunnel (sixty five yards) has been blasted through solid sandstone and carries the canal under the main road through the village. Unlike Dunsley, the Cookley crossing has subsequently been lined with brickwork - presumably to add more stability and protect passing boaters from rock falls. At Debdale we did have to wait and I remember holding The Frog on the centre line, just around a bend out of sight of the lock. It was then I received an excited radio message from Pip: Ed Balls and his family were cruising through the lock in the other direction and Pip, after a chat, had cheekily asked for a photo. Ed and his well known wife, the labour politician Yvette Cooper, kindly posed at the tiller of their hire boat.

The lock at Wolverley Court caused a long delay. For some reason the water level here was very low and a CRT barge had grounded out trying to get into the lock (they were coming the other way to us). It took ages for them to work themselves free from a sandbank near the lock gates. Pip was at the helm but I took it back to take us through the lock as I expected a potential problem as we left. When the gates were fully open I put on high revs and cleared the initial hazard. As soon as I was free of the lock walls I accelerated even harder and, whilst I felt a twisting sensation as we crossed over it, we managed to get past the sandbank. We moored at Kidderminster, just after Limekiln Bridge (17) - near a large Tescos. A few days before, we had been passed by a very familiar boat but with faces on board we did not recognise. Mark and Katherine were taking a short break from cruising and had lent *Double 0* to Katherine's brother, Matthew, and his wife. When we emerged from the supermarket in Kidderminster we bumped into them again.

We departed Kidderminster the next morning and had to wait for a while at the nearby Lock, but I really did not mind. The backdrop of St Mary's Church, reflecting on the still mirrored water surface early in the morning, was really lovely and I relaxed at the helm just enjoying the view. Kidderminster is most well known for its carpet industry and this canal played an important role in its development. On this stretch, Pip was walking the towpath and captured some great images as we passed Weavers Wharf and the Museum - with its iconic tall brick chimney. We soon passed out into the countryside again and the canal's approach to Stourport was beautiful. We were blessed with sweet low bridges, sandstone walls and lush vegetation all along its winding course. The town itself has long been a busy inland port and at the terminus of the S&W we entered a lock that gives access to several basins that sit above the mighty River Severn. Once through the lock we followed signs for narrowboats - effectively passing through a large marina. When we reached the two sets of staircase locks that give access to the river, there was a queue of three boats waiting. I noticed a sign pointing to another 'wide' lock so I turned around and headed into a different section of the basin. Unfortunately, this lock was both enormous and locked - so I had no choice but to wind again and head back to the smaller staircase. The queue here took up the whole jetty so we breasted alongside another boat until the one at the front of the queue descended and gave us room. We took the opportunity to reattach the anchor and don our life jackets and after about an hour, we were joined by Double O. Matthew, Pip and I filled our time watching the alternating pattern of one boat leaving the river and ascending the four locks up to the basin, followed by another going the other way. Another hour passed and eventually it was our turn.

The two sets of staircase locks are manned by volunteers so we felt in safe hands. The only challenge was crossing the narrow basin that lay between the two sets of locks. It looked like it should have been easy, but I had to turn the bow to the left quickly enough to then turn back to the right to straighten up. This was made harder by the lock wall behind me and it took a few forward and backwards manoeuvres before we were properly lined up. The last two locks completed, we passed under a stone bridge and out onto the wide majesty of the River Severn.

CHAPTER 45: THE RIVER SEVERN - STOURPORT TO TEWKESBURY

The river was such a contrast from the windy, sandstone lined S&W. It felt like a long time since we had left the River Calder and we had forgotten the strength and breadth of such a big channel. In a bizarre way, it almost felt good to be back on a river - not my natural reaction to these intimidating and unpredictable waterways.

Our mooring plan that night was Worcester, about 12 miles away. This was quite a trek but our timetable was being driven by a planned meeting with family who were holidaying at Bredon, on the River Avon. We were due to meet up the next day, after about thirty miles of cruising! On the canals this would have been impossible, on Rivers it was definitely doable - especially as we were cruising downstream on the Severn. Pip and I took turns at the helm - not because it was challenging but simply to break the monotony that you rarely get on a canal (where there always seemed to be something to negotiate/avoid). The Frog loves calm, deep rivers and we made quick progress towards our night mooring. The river locks were typical - huge but electronically operated by permanent lock keepers - so all we had to do was not miss the short channel that took us safely to the controlled descent and not over the accompanying weir. Before long the Malvern Hills were looming in the distance and we knew we were approaching the home of Elgar.

About two miles out of Worcester we passed the entrance to the 'blink and you'll miss it' Droitwich Barge Canal - which cuts through that town before joining the Worcester and Birmingham Canal and, ultimately, the BCN through the legendary thirty locks at Tardebigge. Our final approach to Worcester was accompanied by the dulcet tones of Cornelius Lysaght, erstwhile BBC Racing Correspondent, who was coming over the Public Address system at Worcester Race Course. We moored right next to the course on good mooring rings (needed on a strong flowing river), where we spotted a short footpath that took us right up next to the race track. This provided fabulous entertainment. If you have never seen a horse race up close then I recommend it. The power, speed and athleticism of the horses is only matched by the bravery of the jockeys. A real spectacle. We fired up Pip's betting account (normally used once a year for the Grand National) and made our picks for each race. After placing our bets, and between drinks, we strolled back up to the course to watch us lose every penny. As a final ignominy, in one three horse race, our nag came in last - sixty four lengths behind the winner! It was great fun though.

The next morning will live long in my memory. Despite being an overcast day, the architecture of the ornate Victorian railway bridge, crossing high above the river, was wonderful. It was only topped by Worcester Road Bridge, where, at one point, the majestic Cathedral was beautifully framed by the centre arch. If you want to see it for yourself, watch Vlog 36 where Pip captured the image from the bow.

Shortly after passing through Diglis Lock, we started to see more evidence that this river is still very much a working thoroughfare and has some very big vessels moving up and down it. Conversely, the wildlife was abundant. This included a heron that did its typical 'cat and mouse' act with us - zig-zagging across our path, landing, letting us go ahead before catching us up again and then repeating the process three or four times. It was lovely to witness; they are such majestic birds.

We made great progress that morning and were soon approaching the junction at Tewkesbury where the River Avon joins the Severn. We needed to make a sharp left turn to enter a controlled section of water that was protected by a lock giving access to the slightly higher waters of the Avon (the main stream of which, called Mill Avon, tumbled over a weir and joined the Severn about a mile further down). It would have been very difficult to turn onto the Avon in full flow, so it was clear why the navigation had been configured in this way. The only challenge we had was a navigation warning that there was an underwater spit on the inside bend of the sharp left turn. This meant I had to keep to the right, whilst not allowing the flow of the Severn to push us past the exit as we turned side on to the stream. With the help of some extra throttle at the right time, the manouvre went smoothly and we were soon cruising gently up the channel towards the landing pins for Avon Lock. Goodbye River Severn: it may have been a short, fast moving relationship but some of your highlights will live long in my memory!

CHAPTER 46: RIVER AVON - TEWKESBURY TO STRATFORD-UPON-AVON

In the UK there are several River Avons - probably the most well known of which enters the sea near Bristol after passing through the deep gorge that Brunel conquered with his magnificent Clifton Suspension Bridge. The river we were on is often referred to as the Warwickshire (or Shakespeare's) Avon, to distinguish it from the others. It rises in Naseby in Northamptonshire and runs eighty five miles until it joins the Severn at Tewkesbury. We were going to cruise almost all of its navigable length, finally leaving it at Stratford-Upon-Avon.

Access to the River Avon was not included in our CRT licence. The Lock Keeper asked us for evidence that we had paid the sixty pounds for our fourteen day permit before allowing us to go on our way. In the lock we saw a pole that is the same height as the only navigable arch on the nearby King John's Bridge. This measure helped me to be confident that we would fit under the bridge - before actually having to tackle it. In reality, we had lots of clearance and the only slight challenge was the lack of visibility of any oncoming craft. I sounded my horn as a precaution but we were soon clear and pulling in for an expensive pump out and lunch. To be clear, the pump out was expensive, not the lunch.

As I have explained before, mooring on Rivers is much more of a challenge than canals and Pip had wisely phoned ahead to secure a private mooring at a site called Rectory Meadows near Bredon. As we approached, we saw about ten mooring points - but they all had small jetties and were clearly meant for short, river cruisers. Thankfully four or five of these were unoccupied, so we pulled in along the end of these and tied ourselves off on the poles that rose from the water at their end. I was happy that the boat was secure but getting on and off was interesting - the jetties were quite a bit higher than our well deck and we had to hang on for dear life as we lowered ourselves down onto The Frog. We did not complain however - we were in Bredon (where Robbie and Sue and family were on holiday), we were in time for our rendezvous and the owners of the moorings were charging us just ten pounds for the night (they were also very friendly and welcoming). Incidentally, that day we had created a new record by cruising a distance of just over twenty miles!

It's now Friday 20th August and my diary opens with: *Happy Birthday Charlie* (my eldest daughter). Robbie, Pip's brother, and Sue, our sister-in-law, were really great help to us when we had been forced to moor on the Thames at Cavendish and we had not seen them since their farewell wave from the bridge at Pangbourne (in the rain.). It was great to meet up for dinner at their rental property in Bredon. In conversation, Robbie mentioned that they had looked into hiring a day boat for a cruise on the Avon but found that they were prohibitively expensive. We suggested that they join us on The Frog and I looked at Nicholson and worked out that we could cruise through Strensham Lock, wind and return to our mooring in a couple of hours. The next afternoon, loaded with our guests (including one great nephew and three great nieces - two of which were loving our walkie talkies), we slipped our moorings and headed for Strensham Lock. The lock was interesting. The landing pins were on the left hand side, almost at a right angle to the lock. The lock was not in our favour (and was un-manned) so I had to tie us up and jump onto a narrow concrete walkway to reach it in order to prepare it. When it was ready, I jumped back on board and turned sharply left to enter, trying to miss the wall in the process. The gang enjoyed their six mile circular cruise and Robbie and James (our nephew) both took the helm for a while.

Safely back, we said our goodbyes at Rectory Meadow and Pip and I set off immediately to continue our journey upstream towards Eckington. Having completed Strensham lock for the third time that day we cruised for just another two miles and were pleased to see a mooring spot right next to the iconic Eckington Bridge. There has been a crossing at this point since 1440 but the current bridge dates from 1720. In Vlog 37 I quote from a poem:

'Nor the red tear nor the reflected tower abides;

But yet these elegant grooves remain;

Worn in the sandstone parapet hour by hour;

By labouring bargesmen, where they shifted ropes'

From: **Upon Eckington Bridge, River Avon (by Arthur Quiller-Couch)**

The bridge is built from different sized sandstone blocks, which are easily eroded, and under the arches the 'elegant grooves' are still very visible, along with evidence of weathering on many of the other blocks. Later that evening we were joined by two intrepid wild swimmers entering the river next to our mooring. We have seen quite a number of these brave souls on the Avon.

We awoke to heavy rain. That day we were meeting our lovely niece, Laura, in Pershore and had no choice but to set off and tackle the six miles and two locks that lay in between us and our destination. After about a mile we reached the Swan's Neck, a 'hairpin' bend that really tested the sweet spot on the tiller, and shortly after that we reached Nafford Lock. When we arrived the lock was in our favour and a widebeam, coming in the other direction, was approaching the higher lock gates. Unfortunately, the cut is quite narrow here and, after rising, we could not leave the lock until the widebeam reversed back out of the approach. The crew, who helped with the lock, did not know what order to do things in, and the helmsman was really struggling to manouvre the boat - so I guessed that this was probably their first time out. Quite an undertaking to take a wide beam onto the Avon on your first trip. As I write, I reflect how many people may have looked at some of my handling and drawn the same - inaccurate - conclusion.

Despite the rain, Pip and I appreciated just how lovely the river was on this stretch. We were cruising by lush grasslands as we swept around the wide arc that took the waterway past the village of Great Comberton. One more arc in the other direction and we saw Pershore New and Pershore Great Bridges in the distance. Here the river turns gently to the right. As we approached the New Bridge, the five arches of the Great Bridge, just beyond it, were perfectly reflected in the still water between the two crossings. The rain had stopped and it made a beautiful image. There has been a crossing here since 1413. The original bridge was built by monks, responding to the untimely death of their Abbot, who had fallen into the river whilst using the stepping stones that had previously been the only way of getting over the river. A later bridge was damaged and almost destroyed in the English Civil war and the bridge that we can now see was only closed to road traffic in 1926 - presumably when the 'New Bridge' was opened.

We tied up on a free mooring set at the bottom of the lovely lawned gardens behind The Angel Hotel. That afternoon a lucky couple were holding their wedding reception on the lawns - which was duly adorned with a decorated marquee. It was nice to be a 'fly on the river' observer of the festivities - which continued well into the evening. We did not mind the noise as we were also over-imbibing and playing board games with Laura.

Groggy but happy, we woke the next day to a clear blue sky and set off past the many willows on the nearby park, whose branches kissed the water surface, to cruise the remaining ten miles to Evesham. What a gorgeous stretch of water. The river courses through several wide meanders in beautiful countryside and has some interesting locks. The first of these was at Wyre Piddle. Unusually, this lock was in the shape of a diamond. I have explained elsewhere why this design was used on canals (normally at confluences with rivers to bring extra water into the canal network) - but I was at a loss to understand why this one was the shape it was. A little research told me that the explanation was quite prosaic. The rise was originally a turf lock and when the masonry was added, it simply followed the line of the eroded banks. I cannot vouch for the accuracy of this explanation but I do know that the shape made tying up a real challenge. At Fladbury lock, you can see how narrow the earth bank is that separates the short lock cutting from the main river flow. The river level would not have to rise much to reunite the two channels. My diary says that the lock only had gate paddles and Pip and Laura had to open them gently at first to avoid swamping our welldeck. Chadbury lock was memorable because the really impressive weir was set off to the left of the river and was clearly visible across from the lock landing pins.

After this final lock, the river course turned from south east to almost directly south and we entered the outskirts of Evesham. Just before the river sweeps around the town to head north again, we passed the Hampton Ferry. This small pedestrian vessel crosses the river from Evesham to Hampton and is pulled along a cable. There has been a ferry here since the thirteenth century, when monks created one to access their new vineyards at Clark's Hill. A navigation note, in Nicholson, reminds boaters to sound their horn three times as they approach the crossing so that the ferryman can drop the wire to the river bed and allow you to pass. Excitement over, we entered the town and moored at the first visitor moorings we found - near the slipway opposite Abbey Park (the next day we moved down to a nicer spot before the iconic Workman Bridge in the centre of Evesham).

Evesham is an attractive town. The word 'homme' is Old English for 'land on a river bend'. Eof was a swineherd who worked for the Bishop of Worcester and originally the town was named Eof's Homme (or land on the river bend belonging to Eof). Over the years it became Eveshomme and, finally, the more modern form we use today. The town is dominated by the river that helped to name it. Pip and I had stayed here before and had discovered the best Thai restaurant we have ever visited (*Thai Emerald on the High St*) and that evening we didn't hesitate to take Trish (Laura's mum and Pip's sister) and Laura back there.

On Monday 23rd, Pip and I, alone again, were delighted to get a message from an old school friend, Kate, who was walking through the park and had spotted our distinctive boat (having followed our Vlogs she knew what it looked like). We agreed dinner plans for the following evening and it was really good to catch up with her and her husband Dave - whom I met at University (to explain: I went to school with Kate and she, Dave and I all went to Lancaster University - Kate and Dave graduated and I dropped out - but that is another story). We also met up with an old friend of Pip's daughter, Rachael. Rachel (the friend) met Rachael at University and had kept in touch ever since. She was accompanied by her lovely three week old son, Tommy.

On Wednesday we had arranged to meet friends of Val and Ade (the owners of NB *Jack 'N Janner* - whom we met in Warwick - see Chapter 18). Roy and Sonia had expressed an interest in buying The Frog and their visit would be a first viewing. Needless to say, they loved her and things were looking good for a sale ahead of our farewell to the water later in the year - but more on that later. I still remember how I felt when we showed them around. It was hard to imagine somebody else owning The Frog. We knew, from Val and Ade, that Roy was a very talented joiner who has refitted yachts in the past. We agreed that if The Frog had to go to anyone, then it should be to someone whom we knew would not only look after her but may even make her nicer (if that was possible).

The moorings we were on were time limited, so even though we were meeting family here the next day, we pushed off and immediately passed under the glorious Workman Bridge. This crossing was built in 1856 and replaced a mediaeval version on the same spot. It is named after Henry Workman - a long time mayor of the town. We passed through Evesham Lock with its long weir and then cruised out into the countryside for about two miles - mooring at a remote location just after Simon de Montford Bridge. The next day we cruised back into Evesham and noticed the interesting lock keeper's cottage. It looks like a cross between a swiss chalet and an indonesian coastal shack - being 'toblerone' in shape and built up on stilts to protect it from flooding (other chocolate bars are available). In Vlog 38 you can see an image of the deluge in 2007 when water came more than halfway up the inside of the lodge - causing major damage (thankfully now repaired by the Avon Navigation Trust - who manage the river here). Incidentally, the lock marks the end of the Lower Avon Navigation and the start of, yes you guessed it, the Upper.

Before we left Evesham, we spent a nice couple of days with Pip's son, Ian and his wife Brittany along with three of our grandchildren (Billy, Lyra and Seren). Sleeping arrangements were interesting. We let Ian and Brittany have our bed and they slept with Seren - who was about nineteen months old at the time. Pip and I 'slept' (I use the term loosely) on the 'noisy every time you moved' leather dinette - whilst Billy and Lyra shared the bed settee at our feet. The next day we cruised back out to near the mooring we had used the night before, just to give the family the chance to go through Evesham lock and enjoy The Frog for one last time. When back in town, we said our goodbyes and turned our eyes south to look out for the familiar shape of *Double 0* and our good friends Mark and Katherine - with whom we were being reunited after what felt like a long break.

The 'Leeds and Liverpool Conquerors' were back together and we set off the next day intent on reaching Bidford on Avon, on our way to Stratford. Our first lock was at Offenham - also named George Billington Lock after its sponsor. The generous Mr Billington was terminally ill at the time of his donation and, remarkably, the lock was built in only six weeks - just in time for him to see it completed (he died a week later - just before his thirty seventh birthday). Confusingly, at the site is a memorial to Eric Pritchard, 'Navigator and Craftsman' who was heavily involved in building the locks between Evesham and Stratford.

We noticed that the river was slowly becoming narrower and shallower as we moved further up stream. This was never more evident than at Marlcliff Lock - where the weir looks like it should have salmon jumping up the many exposed stones. It was here that a passing boater told us all the moorings in Bidford were full. When we reached the beautiful river side village, however, we found a lovely mooring opposite The Frog public house (yes - The Frog) and resolved to have a photograph (and a drink) later. Pip and I walked up through the village and got a spooky sense of deja vu. Our memories slowly cleared and we recalled visiting the village and staying in a bed and breakfast - which we even managed to find - but for the life of us we could not remember why or when we were there!

On Sunday 29th August (happy birthday to Pip's son, Ian) we made the final leap to Stratford. To leave Bidford we passed under the only navigable arch of the six that make up the sublime, early fifteenth century, Grade I listed stone bridge. I clearly remember the church bells were ringing as we did so - which only added to our wonderful sense of pastoral bliss. The river really was changing quite rapidly - with stronger currents, shallower water and some precarious rock outcrops just below the surface. The shallow water also had other consequences: we picked up what looked like a sari around the prop and I had to use the bread knife to cut it off. Our troubles continued at Weir Brake Lock when Pip dropped the windlass into the chamber. Our sea magnets were rarely used but this was exactly what they were designed for. The magnet was attached to a long rope and after a few searching drops we heard the reassuring 'clunk' of the windlass locking on. We reflected that having completed in excess of eight hundred locks, it was amazing we had not dropped the windlass in before.

The approach to Stratford includes the Colin P Witter Lock. Being so close to the town, we were suddenly the subject of interest to a large number of gongoozlers. The rest of the short cruise, to a lovely mooring spot next to a public park, was lined with sightseers and we moored near the very quaint pedestrian chain ferry almost opposite the iconic Royal Shakespeare Theatre. The next morning we moved through the wide lock and into Bancroft Basin and the start of the Stratford Canal. There is much I could write about the town of Stratford but suffice to say, it is a glorious place and worth a visit. For us, Tuesday 31st was a red letter day: Roy and Sonia revisited us and we finally agreed on the sale of The Frog. We were racked with mixed feelings but were consoled by the fact she was going to a very good home. From that point on it felt like we were saying a long 'goodbye' and we were determined to savour every moment we had left with our precious Frog.

CHAPTER 47: THE STRATFORD-UPON-AVON CANAL

It was Wednesday 1st September and we decided we would treat ourselves to breakfast out in a lovely cafe called Mor (if it's still there, try it). Fully fed, we started our ascent of the Stratford Canal. This waterway was conceived as a means of shifting coal from Dudley to London and Oxford - without having to use the BCN. An act of parliament was passed in 1793 and work began. The canal linked with the Worcester and Birmingham canal at Kings Norton and travelled south to Kingswood, where a short cutting, just below the impressive Lapworth flight, connects it to the Grand Union (and hence London and Oxford). The northern section was opened in 1802. Cutting then ceased until a businessman, William James of Stratford, saw the benefit of creating another link between the Midlands and the River Severn via his hometown. He even went as far as buying the upper reaches of the River Avon (the stretch we had just cruised) to ensure his plan could be realised. A new Act of Parliament was passed in 1815 that authorised a link to the River Avon at Stratford. This southern section was completed but the River Avon proved to be too treacherous and prone to flooding to be a reliable navigation. After spending even more money on improving its locks, poor Mr Jame's was declared bankrupt. In 1947 the northern section became subject to a vigorous campaign by the newly formed Inland Waterways Association (IWA). Attempts to close the canal were challenged and the IWA even forced Great Western Railway to raise a bridge at Tunnel Lane to allow boats to pass underneath. This was the first step in securing the future of the waterway and after the National Trust took ownership of the southern section, it was renovated by the Stratford Canal Society and ownership was finally passed across to British Waterways (now CRT) in 1988. We owe a huge debt of gratitude to all those visionaries who fought hard, on our behalf, to save these beautiful and historically important waterways.

We would only cruise the southern section to Kingswood, about thirteen miles and complete the first six of the twenty six Lapworth Locks. Those of you with good memories will remember that Pip and I walked up the rest of the flight at the end of October 2020 - just as Boris announced a new lockdown for November. It was the day we decided to turn around and head for winter moorings and it will live long in our memory as we never did get to take The Frog all the way up this lovely flight.

To leave the basin I first had to reverse out of our mooring and swing our bow around. This went ok, with Katherine guiding me, but I neglected to check the lock to my right. A boater had ascended and had to sit whilst I completed what turned out to be a fifteen point manoeuvre! I was not popular. To make up for his wait, we pulled over and let the frowning helmsman go ahead and start the five locks that would take us out of the town. Our next challenge was the very low bridge (69) that crosses the exit to the basin. We made it under but the lovely Sunflowers sitting on our roof were gently brushing its concrete underside. After the five locks in Stratford, we stopped for water and lunch and Pip took the helm for the first few of the eleven locks to Wilmcote and our mooring near Featherbed Lane Bridge (59). In the afternoon we both agreed that water levels felt very low and The Frog was less responsive as a result. This made negotiating the VERY narrow bridges more interesting than it would otherwise have been. In Vlog 39 we highlight Canada Bridge (60) - which is a really good example of what I mean. The canal is crossed by lots of these very attractive wrought iron bridges. At first sight they appear to be solid but closer examination reveals that the span is actually split in the middle. This gap allowed the passage of the rope that was attached to draft horses pulling barges along the waterway. Canada Bridge also had great chunks taken out of its brickwork, serving as a warning to all boaters of what can happen if you don't treat these bridges with respect. Passing underneath them was akin to entering a lock and it was vital you were lined up properly as you approached. Before we had tea that night, Pip made the short walk into Wilmcote and photographed the nearby Mary Arden's House. Mary was Shakespeare's mother.

The next day the dark cloud cover created a real autumnal feel but at least it wasn't raining. We planned to get to Wootton Wawen and fill with diesel by lunchtime. En-route, just after Drapers Bridge (57), we crossed Edstone (or Bearley) Aqueduct, whose four hundred and seventy five feet carried the canal over a road, a river and a railway line. It was the first aqueduct we had crossed where the towpath is set at the same level as the bottom of the canal. This must give a very interesting eye line for any walkers who are crossing the aqueduct at the same time as a narrowboat. The same was true of the crossing at Wootton Wawen - which sits just before the canal widens into a basin next to a boatyard - and the source of our diesel. Before filling up, however, we moored canalside and walked to the nearby Yew Tree Farm Shopping Village. This was really pretty and had a fabulous range of shops with lots of artisan offerings. We bought a new bread knife (having used our current one on the prop a few times too often) and had a fabulous hog roast sausage roll for lunch. We also spotted a garden patio set which we both really liked (and as I look out of our patio doors today I can see it sitting in the corner of our garden).

Lunch over, we reversed into the basin to fill with diesel before cruising another four miles through the Preston Bagot and Bucket locks and approaching Lowsonford. At Preston Bagot we saw the first of the 'barrel-roofed' lock cottages that can be found in a few places along the canal. The shape of the roofs is easily explained: it is the same as the humped-back bridges that cross the canal - the engineers having used the same 'forms' to build both.

At Lowsonford Lock (31) a moored boater, seeing Double 0 approaching, spilled his glass of wine in his hurry to pull out right in front of Mark and beat him to the lock. Mark is very easy going and thought the whole thing very funny - especially when the interloper rammed into the lock gate. We eventually got through the lock and found great moorings opposite the Fleur-de-Lys pub. It looked amazing and we immediately agreed that we would cross the lock gates and pay it a visit. Three drinks later, Pip fell off of her seat and we decided it was time to go back to The Frog! (To be fair to her, her seat was on a grassy slope.)

The next day we completed the last two miles and eight locks to reach the basin at Kingswood junction. I swung The Frog around so we could pump out and then reversed before swinging our bow to the left and slipping into the short link that would take us back to familiar territory. We had enjoyed the Stratford Canal but we were also glad to be back on the wide and forgiving Grand Union.

CHAPTER 48: GRAND TO BE BACK

We cruised another mile that afternoon and moored at Turner's Green (near the same spot we had moored in the previous October). We had arranged to meet Val and Ade and we all popped to the Tom O' The Wood pub for a drink and a catch up. They had not met M&K before and, as experienced boaters, they had a lot to talk about.

The next morning we said our goodbyes and, with M&K, headed for our third transit of the Hatton Flight. The twenty one locks are hard work so we girded our loins once more with bacon baps at the cafe by the top lock. Carbs and fat topped up, we headed off with Mark and I at the helm. The gongoozlers were out in force and we were showboating a bit by moving from lock to lock in tandem. As we descended we swapped roles and Pip and Katherine took the helm. The weather was great, we made good progress and were soon negotiating the sharp left hand bend at the mouth of the Saltisford Arm. We hoped to moor at the Cape of Good Hope again, but there was no space and we had no option but to complete two more locks before pulling in to moor, on our own pins, between bridges 49A and B. M&K came around for celebratory drinks following our third conquest of the infamous flight.

Double 0 was having solar panels fitted, so, the next morning, we said a temporary goodbye to our good friends and headed off. In two days we were meeting up with our lovely neighbours from Cornwall, at Calcutt locks - so we needed to press on. After a water stop at the student accommodation in Leamington (which we knew well) we headed out into the countryside and the Radford, Fosse and Bascote locks. It had been a while since we had been alone tackling these big Grand Union locks and they were hard work. When we approached Bascote we saw a hire boat pulled into the towpath. On board were an elderly couple on the first day of their holiday. They had completed the Radford and Fosse locks but didn't fancy tackling the Bascote flight alone. We were happy to pair up and help them through - particularly as the top two locks are a staircase - a real challenge for 'new to lock' boaters.

When we left the lock we noticed the water level seemed low and, sure enough, when pulling over to pass another boat, we ran aground. Barge poles and reverse gear were enough to get us moving again but we didn't fancy tackling low water levels any longer. I noticed some moored boats and an empty length of armco and took the opportunity to pull in for the night. We had covered about eight and a half miles and ten locks and the clock had ticked past five - so we were happy to stop (near Long Itchington - between bridges 27 and 26A).

Our next challenge was the ten locks of the Stockton Flight. The holiday makers we met the day before joined us as we approached the first lock. The man was about to get off and help with the locks but his wife was not happy to take the boat on her own. She was also too fragile to help with the locks - so I 'volunteered' to do them on my own - with Pip at the helm of The Frog. Seven tiring locks later we were joined by a CRT volunteer. He was slightly less understanding and, rather sarcastically, asked the holiday makers if they had lost their windlass. Abashed, the man got off and helped with the last three locks. This turned out to be a good thing. His wife was really very capable at handling the boat and her confidence grew with every lock. We cruised three more miles and stopped by bridge 19 - ready for our rendezvous the next day.

Kat and Sadie, our fabulous friends from Cornwall, arrived mid morning. They parked at the nearby Napton Reservoirs and Pip and I walked up to meet them. We met here because we wanted to take them onto the Oxford Canal and complete most of the Napton Flight - which is so picturesque and one of Pip's favourite sections. Our cruise started with the three Calcutt locks and we were immediately facing a problem. A hire boat was ascending the flight and was sitting in the top lock. Being new to boating, they had managed to leave all of the paddles open on lock 3 and, as a result, the pound above was almost empty. We had to sort this out before we could go anywhere. Kat, Sadie and I walked up the flight and opened all the paddles of the top two locks. In this way we brought water from the large pound above the top lock all the way down through the flight. It took about twenty minutes to get back to workable water levels. Amazingly, there was a narrowboat and a wide beam moored in the bottom pound - both seemed to be occupied and both seemed to be oblivious to the fact that their boats were temporarily sitting on a bed of mud. Luckily for them, the canal bed was flat - and even more fortunate, they did not get stuck to the bottom of the canal as the water levels rose.

We cruised the last mile of the Grand Union and turned sharp right at Wigrams Turn onto the Oxford Canal, heading for Napton. Sadie took a turn at the helm and was very good - this was quite a busy section of canal but she was not fazed at all. We went through the bottom lock of the Napton Flight and moored in the same place we were moored when I had the embarrassing visit from the RCR mechanic who explained about the tiller sweet spot! I am still blushing slightly when I think about how I explained the steering problems to him and blamed The Frog. There was another reason for mooring here - The Folly Inn was about a hundred yards away. Before visiting the pub we walked across Folly Bridge and into the village itself. En-route we noticed a Cider Tap bar and resolved to pay it a visit on the way back. We were glad we did. The hot weather and the walk to the village had given us a thirst and Kat and Sadie are both cider fans. If you are in the area and you like Cider, pay it a visit.

Back to our mooring, and after salad prep we took a very short walk to The Folly. We sat outside in the lawned garden and were only dragged away by the pressing need to light the barbecue. We spent a lovely evening sitting on the towpath, drinking and eating overcooked food. It was so good to be reminded why we loved having Kat and Sadie as our neighbours. Kat described it as a 'millionaire's day' - on the basis that even if she had a million pounds to spend she would still have chosen to do what we did. What a lovely expression.

The next day Kat was running out of superlatives. It was gloriously sunny and we were taking the girls up six locks to the winding hole at the Old Engine House Arm. Kat joined me at the helm so she could experience what she described as the 'surfing' feeling as the locks filled with water. At the winding hole, a boat had thoughtlessly moored right opposite - making the turn tighter than it needed to be. We got around with no collisions and after a quick coffee we began the descent - this time Kat and I worked the locks and Pip and Sadie were at the helm. Halfway down we got some great shots of a herd of wallowing water buffalo in a field right next to the canal, and concluded that some enterprising farmer must be branching out into Mozzarella production.

We reached Folly Bridge and filled with water just as M&K appeared - with their new solar panels. They wind and follow us to a mooring spot near Bridge 109 where we said our goodbyes and walked the girls, cross country, back to their car. It was so good to see them again and, as I write, we are about a week away from another visit. Can't wait!

That night we joined M&K in a walk back towards Napton and a visit to The Kings Head pub on Southam Road. Our travels now sound like one long 'beerfest' and I guess to a certain extent they were. Our view was this: summer and our odyssey were both drawing to a close. One day soon we would be saying goodbye to The Frog, M&K and our life afloat and we really did want to make the most of what little time we had left. Don't forget, Covid had stopped us doing this for many months at the start of our trip - we were just making up for lost time!

In the morning we agreed that we would take a leisurely cruise to Braunston and moor on the Oxford, before we reached the junction at Bridges 94 and 93. We made great progress and arrived before midday - mooring near bridge 96. Despite being on the towpath side, the bank here was tricky and whilst we managed to get The Frog in reasonably close, Double 0 was moored about two feet out and a gangplank was needed to get on and off. We walked into Braunston and visited the shops - which we now know so well - before grabbing lunch at The Gongoozler's Rest Cafe (I have fond memories of a huge bacon and mushroom roll).

Remarkably, we did not visit a pub that night and were feeling very fresh the next morning as we set off to climb the Braunston Flight and tackle the tunnel once more. I remember that the bottom lock was really busy with a waiting boat on the landing pins. At this point, the canal is lined with hire boats belonging to Union Carriers and we had no option but to breast up with one of the empty, moored boats so that we could safely wait for the lock to become free. Ironically, the business of the locks helped us once we started our assent. Boats coming down were leaving the locks in our favour and we were soon pulling out of the Top Lock and heading for the tunnel once more. Mark was leading as we entered, which helped a little with visibility. Half way through we met a boat coming the other way and had to trust the engineers had got their dimensions right and we could just squeeze through. I breathed in and waited for the chimney to crunch as I moved over to the right hand wall but thankfully all I heard were the faceless pleasantries of the passing helmsman (who was wearing a head torch). We cruised out into the muted daylight under the trees that line the canal here and made our way to very familiar territory to moor near Bridge 10 (exactly the same spot where we had spent a week in the previous November).

The next day we knew we were saying goodbye to M&K. They were turning left at Norton Junction and heading up the Leicester Line - whilst we needed to cruise down the Grand Union to meet friends at Milton Keynes. So, that evening we went for a farewell drink at the New Inn - the pub that sits right next to Watling Bridge and the Top Lock of the Buckby Flight. It was bitter sweet - knowing we were parting the next day - but we made the most of it. After a few drinks I remember we decided to go online and register the name 'Raducanuridge.com', mistakenly thinking that this would be the new name for Henman Hill (or Murray Mount - depending upon your persuasion), at Wimbledon. Then, if anyone wanted to use it in future they would have to pay us some form of royalties. I am sure it doesn't actually work that way but our rash purchase only cost about four pounds and was made after a few drinks (and Emma had just won the US Open).

We woke up in a sombre mood. M&K were not moving off straight away so they walked the towpath and, very kindly, helped us with the seven locks of The Buckby Flight. The last lock sits right next to an old 'home' of The Frog - Whilton Marina. The previous owner to us bought her here and Pip and I had stupid thoughts about her 'recognising' her surroundings and, somehow, feeling at home! With each day we were becoming more and more emotional and our attachment to The Frog only grew stronger knowing our days together were numbered. M&K came on board for a final cup of coffee and we said our goodbyes. This would be the last time they were on The Frog but it would not be the last time we cruised together. Long after we had settled in Somerset we took two trips with them on Double 0. One on the Regents Canal to Paddington Basin and another from Bath to the Bristol floating harbour along the River Avon (the Avon that empties into the sea at Avonmouth and not the one that joins the Severn at Tewkesbury). We will be firm friends for life and we will never forget our shared time afloat. Thank you Mark and Katherine for your kindness,friendship, boating advice and great humour!

CHAPTER 49: THE FINAL CHAPTER

We moved off from Whilton and stopped soon after at Bridge 18 to visit the fabulous Heart of The Shires Shopping Village - a short walk away. We stocked up with a few things we needed and a few more we didn't and then cruised another three miles to moor at Weedon Bec - on one of the highest embankments I have ever seen.

This village has an interesting history. That afternoon we explored the local church and stumbled upon a special war graves celebration. An organisation had taken the time to highlight all the graves and memorials, around and in the church, that belonged to commonwealth combatants who had fallen in action. It was very moving and we loved the short stories about each of these brave individuals that were attached to each of the graves. It made us feel like they, and their sacrifice, had not been forgotten.

Weedon Bec has an even greater military connection and the next morning we walked to the Royal Ordnance Depot. Now a museum with a smattering of antique and other shops, this large collection of buildings was built in 1804 and until 1965 was one of the military's largest store houses. All manner of things were kept here - including armaments. The site was chosen as it was about the furthest you could get from the coast (and any invading force) and it was right next to the Grand Union Canal. The buildings are arranged into two rows facing each other across a channel, still filled with water, with bridges connecting the two. This channel once continued right out through the entrance of the site and under what is now a housing estate, to join the Grand union. Next to the canal there is a railway line. Once upon a time, the tracks were on a swing bridge that could open to allow boats to leave the Depot and join the canal - right opposite our mooring spot. There is an obvious logic to carrying gunpowder and armaments by canal - the same logic that made Josiah Wedgwood invest in this 'new' technology all those years ago: canals provide a smooth passage and a reduced risk of anything getting broken (or, in this case, exploding)! The Depot's magazine was made up of a series of buildings with very thick walls - each capable of holding one thousand tonnes of gunpowder. The canal was so important to UK military and commercial logistics that, during World War Two, coal dust was sprinkled on the water surface to make it harder for German bombers to find their target.

The lack of locks on this stretch of the Grand Union meant that we made great progress in our afternoon cruise - covering seven and a half miles and reaching Gayton Junction. We knew this patch very well of course - being the site of our very first cruise out of Gayton Marina (tucked just up the Northampton Arm). Our heart strings were pulled once more as we thought back to those early days of boat 'love at first sight' and just how close we were now to giving up our wonderful friend! We walked up to the marina - partly to get water and partly just to be nosey and reminisce some more.

The next morning we walked into the lovely village of Blisworth to collect a parcel and then returned to prepare for another passage through the infamous (in our lives) Blisworth Tunnel. You may remember that, not only was this our first tunnel experience with The Frog, but it was also where our headlight failed and we went through using only Pip's iPhone to guide us. On this occasion I made sure we were properly equipped before we set off. On the subject of lights, not far from the tunnel we passed under Bridge 50, better known as Candle Bridge. This moniker is explained by the fact that there was once a shack that sold candles to boatmen as they approached the long, dark tunnel - many years before such luxuries as headlights.

As we approached our nemesis, we found ourselves behind another boat. At first I was pleased that their lights would give me some orientation in the darkness of the third longest passage on the UK waterways. After a few hundred yards, however, I changed my mind. The ventilation at the centre of the Tunnel is limited to the vertical shafts that were originally used in its construction. They do not provide much fresh air and the diesel fumes of the boat ahead were soon making me feel queasy. I was relieved to see the tunnel exit looming large and to breathe the fresh air it brought with it. In my diary, I was surprisingly positive about the tunnel writing: *'The Blisworth is actually an OK tunnel. It is long (3075 yds) but it is straight and has a long renovated section in the middle - giving a feeling of even greater space. You can pass two boats here (sic) as we proved again today'.* Oh yes - I had forgotten that we passed a boat coming the other way.

Blisworth, Stoke Bruerne and Gayton are classic canal villages. Blisworth came to prominence in the late eighteenth century - before the tunnel was built. Between 1796 and 1805, whilst the tunnel was being constructed, its inland port became an important terminus of the horse drawn tramway that carried goods over Blisworth Hill between the village and Stoke Bruerne. In this way, cargoes could continue their journey along the Grand Union - being unloaded, trammed over the hill and then reloaded onto another boat on the other side.

We stopped in Stoke Bruerne at the water point right outside of the low slung Boat Inn before tackling the seven locks of the eponymous flight. I started at the helm but the mechanisms were really stiff and after two locks we swapped to give Pip a 'rest' at the helm. We cruised a further six miles to Cosgrove and after passing under the beautiful Soloman's Bridge (65) we pulled in to moor. The bridge was built in 1800 and is ornately decorated in a gothic style. There are possible links to the architect John Soanes (he designed the Bank of England) but there is no documentary evidence to support this. Whatever the case, being made of such ornately decorated stone, the bridge is almost unique on the Grand Union and, as far as I can establish, no-one is really sure why.

Our journey continued two days later, having 'lost' a day to heavy rain. The canal takes a huge left turn as it reaches Milton Keynes and, in my diary, I described it as a 'ring road' - cutting through only the eastern edge of the conurbation. In reality, whilst I am not entirely clear on my history, I do know that Milton Keynes (now a city of over a quarter of a million people) was only conceived as a 'new town' in the 1960s - long after the canal had found its route south. So there must have been some other commercial or engineering reason why the canal twists in the way it does here.

The day began with Cosgrove Lock (21) which sits next to the now truncated Buckingham Arm. The canal straightened and we crossed the short Great Ouse Aqueduct. It was hard to believe that once upon a time the waterway descended and ascended through nine locks to cross this narrow valley. In 1807 the original brick aqueduct collapsed and its longer replacement was built using the iron trunk method (similar to Pontcysyllte), being completed in 1811.

Our progress was slower than hoped as the whole route seemed to be lined with moored boats. Not far from Cosgrove, we caught up with a very large hotel boat - which, understandably, was cruising very slowly to allow its guests to enjoy the sights and to fit through the bridges, which were not much wider than the boat itself. The helmsman spotted us and kindly pulled hard to one side to let us pass.

At Wolverton, near Bridge 71, the canal is adorned with a fantastic train mural painted on a long brick wall. It was originally painted in 1986 by local artist Bill Billings and represents this section of the canal - naming towns along its route. It had been renovated recently and looked stunning as we passed it - taking several minutes to do so (some great footage can be seen in Vlog 41).

Just after Bridge 82 we spotted signs which highlighted a really exciting development. The Inland waterways Association is building a NEW canal - linking the Grand Union to the Great Ouse (and, as a result, the Fens). The idea for such a waterway was first muted in 1810, long before the building of the M1 and the A421 - two major roads that the canal will now have to underpass. The business case for the development is clearly no longer one based on industrial factors. That said, leisure boating is now big business and the new waterway will also create footpaths and cycleways through existing nature reserves and water parks. As I write, I am not sure of any proposed completion dates but the fact that the project is underway is already making history.

The canal along this section is really beautiful. In places, it felt like we were out in the countryside and in others we passed through some of the many parks that Milton Keynes boasts and autumn was starting to add golden hues. We moored after Bridge 89.

Whilst we were meeting our friends in Milton Keynes, we needed to top up with food and we had a couple of days to fill before they arrived. So the next morning we continued our cruise south towards Leighton Buzzard. The landscape here is very flat and there is only one more lock as we continue to cut through the outskirts of the city. At Fenny Stratford, Lock 22 looks and feels like a stop lock - but it's in the middle of the Grand Union - a long way from any other canal. A little research solved the mystery: it seems the canal was being built in sections and two of these met at the lock. Unfortunately, a miscalculation meant that the two meeting tracts had different water levels and an expensive lock had to be built to correct the error. Legend has it that the engineer was so upset by his mistake that he threw himself into the new lock and drowned (I can't vouch for this.) It also has a swing bridge across it - adding another task for passing boaters.

We completed nine miles and five more locks en-route to Leighton Buzzard. The highlight of which were the Soulbury Three Locks (26-24) - which took the canal up twenty feet alongside the pub named after the climb. We talked to a boater who was stranded near the water point having had serious engine trouble. He had just left the pub having given the new staff there a lesson in operating the locks. I asked him why they would need this and he explained that the pub sits between two of the locks and its entrance is level with the top of the canal. If the paddles are left open in the wrong combination the pub has been known to flood. Knowing how to correct the problem quickly could avert an expensive disaster in the future. We finished our cruise to Leighton Buzzard and moored on the visitor moorings right beside Tescos - perfect for the big shop we would need to do the next day before our visitors arrived.

We stayed a couple of days and explored the attractive town. It was Saturday 18th and we needed to head back to Milton Keynes to meet an old friend of Pips for lunch and wait for our special guests. It was only when we went to leave that we read the mooring sign properly; we had moored in a two hour mooring space - designed for boaters visiting the supermarket - for two days. Oops! We consoled ourselves that there had always been additional mooring space in front of us and, consequently, we could be pretty sure we had not caused anyone a massive inconvenience.

I took The Frog under Bridge 114 and turned in the winding hole just beyond before heading north again for one last time. We had researched the best place to moor on the way down and so we stopped about a quarter of a mile below the Fenny Stratford Lock. This spot, near Bridge 97, had a fourteen day mooring limit - so we could stay for the three days we needed to, and it was quite close to a bridge, giving access to the nearby conurbation of Fenny

Stratford. The next morning Andy Cassels, a friend of Pip's from her teenage years, paid us a visit and we lunched at a local pub. It was good to catch up with Andy and over lunch we spotted an advertisement for Bletchley Park. We had no idea it was nearby and as we had a day to kill we resolved to walk the three miles round trip to pay it a visit.

If you have never been to Bletchley I can heartily recommend it. Not only is it an oasis of beauty in the middle of a sprawling conurbation, but it oozes atmosphere. Its importance in shortening the second world war and saving thousands (if not millions) of lives is well documented and I will not repeat it here but nothing compares with standing in the footsteps of Alan Turing and the other quiet heroes of Bletchley. We loved it so much we visited again the next day with our newly arrived guests.

Tuesday 21st September we hired a car and drove to Heathrow to collect Julie, Pip's best friend from Canada and her new partner Dave, whom we had yet to meet. Julie was also a navy wife and Pip often talks of the camaraderie and the very strong bonds that developed between the spouses when their husbands were at sea. Pip had not seen Julie for over twenty years until they were fortuitously reconnected on Facebook. Julie wasted no time in coming to see us in Cornwall in February 2019 and we were looking forward to seeing her again. Whenever they meet up, it's just like they had seen each other the day before - a sign of true and everlasting friendship.

We drove back to The Frog before heading out to Bletchley again. After the visit, Dave and Julie were starting to flag (jet lag kicking in) but they were determined to try and get onto a UK 'cycle' as soon as possible. To keep them busy and alert we decided to head off and we used Fenny Stratford as a gentle introduction to the world of locks. We didn't go far but both Julie and Dave had a turn on the tiller (Julie is a very accomplished sailor and is used to holding a tiller - normally in much more challenging circumstances). We moored near Little Woolstone - between bridges 83 and 82. I remember the evening well. We were right next to one of the many parks that grace the canal here. It was early autumn and the leaves on the poplars that lined the path were just turning. The sunset was getting earlier and was beautiful after a lovely sunny day. I set up a towpath barbecue and Julie and Dave managed to stay up until nine o'clock before sleep finally claimed them.

Refreshed, we set off the next morning intent on making it to Stoke Bruerne. This was over twelve miles away but we knew there was only one lock (at Cosgrove) so it was absolutely doable. As it turned out, we arrived at the bottom of the flight early in the afternoon and moored just before the services. On our approach we noticed a large outlet pumping water into the canal. It was connected to the River Tove, below, and was being used to top up the canal. With time to kill, we walked up the flight to the village and explored the National Waterways Museum and had a cuppa at the Navigation Inn (the one below the top lock). Whilst there, we noticed that there was a quiz that evening and decided to walk back up for a meal and the quiz. My diary reads: *'Lovely evening - food questionable - but we won the quiz (£20)!'*

Reality kicked in the next morning, however, as we faced the flight and, for the FOURTH time, Blisworth tunnel! There were volunteers on the flight and, with the help of the newly trained Julie and Dave, we made the top lock very quickly. As we approached Blisworth, Julie came to the stern - wanting to experience the tunnel from the helmsman's perspective (it's much darker back there). The crossing went without incident and Pip captured some great footage of us passing another boat coming the other way (see Vlog 42). After lunch, at Blisworth, we cruised another seven miles in glorious sunshine and moored near Bugbrooke Wharf - close to Bridge 36.

The next day we set off intending to reach Braunston. The sun was still shining and we made good progress and the six miles to the Buckby flight passed with Dave and I swapping time at the helm. We approached the flight and saw a boat climbing two locks ahead of us. They were a couple on their own and all the locks were set against both of us. This meant we were effectively using three locks of water to move two boats through each lock. I spoke to the other boaters who, finding the going tough, were happy to wait for us to catch up. I then walked ahead and, having checked that no other boats were coming the other way, prepared the locks to speed up our ascent. Near lock 9 stands a little cottage selling the iconic Buckby Cans (adorned with the classic Castle and Rose decorations) - amongst other things. We already had a bucket, so Pip bought a bird house that looked like it could have been made of driftwood. Today it takes pride of place under the laurel tree in the corner of our garden.

We turned hard left at Norton and after our final passage through Braunston tunnel, we moored near the Admiral Nelson pub (between locks 2 and 3). That night we celebrated two milestones: first, it was our sixteenth wedding anniversary and, second, we had exchanged contracts on our house purchase. Anyone who has gone through the house buying process in this country will know just how significant (and relieving) this moment was. We went to the pub!

The next morning was surreal. We needed to get to Daventry to do some boring stuff so we took a taxi (Pip and I having almost been killed when we walked the same route about a year before). In my diary, I described the taxi driver as a 'nutter'. He was a conspiracy theorist who claimed, emphatically, that COVID was a 'creation of government' in order to control and coerce the populus. Under questioning, he couldn't really explain why the disease was a global phenomena or why killing the elderly and vulnerable would help the powers that be in their quest for world domination! Pip brought the conversation to a polite close and we resolved to get a different taxi company on our return trip.

Back on board, that night we reached a nice mooring between bridges 107 and 108, near Wigrams Turn and I decided to stop early and not risk being unable to moor at Napton. The locks there would be a nice start to our Sunday morning. The next day started with mist but with the normal autumnal promise of later warmth, when the waning power of the sun would finally manage to burn through the dampness. By the time we reached Wigrams, the sun was winning its battle and the temperature quickly rose about five degrees. We had a phone call from the proposed new owners of The Frog. For reasons I will not go into here, they needed to move her into moorings, in Newbury, by the 1st of November. This meant our proposed handover at Gayton was not going to be possible and we were asked if we could cruise as far down the Oxford as possible to shorten their trip down the Thames and onto the K&A. We agreed, of course, and I clearly remember helping with the locks up the Napton Flight whilst simultaneously making various phone calls to marinas to unbook and rebook us in for a handover. We finally settled on Cropredy Marina for our final destination. The fact that our odyssey was coming to an end suddenly felt very real.

The flight was really tough. We were following two boats up and, as these are single locks, this meant a lot of waiting around. We finally reached the top lock at Marston Doles after 3 o'clock. My mind went back to the challenge a hire boater had had when we descended these same locks all those months ago (you may recall that he drifted hard to the left and ended up pinned against the wall of a house on the far side of the canal). The wind was up, and blowing in a direction that would have made this fate even more likely for us. The trouble with this lock is that the canal turns right as soon as you leave it. What you want to do is start the turn whilst you are still partially in the lock, but it is so narrow (and the lock exit extends in a straight line for a few feet beyond the gate), making it impossible to swing the stern around until you are fully out. I decided to improvise and I gave Dave the bow line and asked him to walk along the towpath as I emerged from the lock - pulling The Frog towards him as he went. This not only stopped the bow drifting towards the wall in the wind, but also meant that as soon as the stern was clear of the lock we swung sharply towards the towpath and away from the wall. It went well and having picked up Dave, we cruised on to stop just after Priors Hardwick Bridge (123) and have pasties for tea.   That night we went online and bought a new car (a Citroen EC4). It was a bit of a risk as we had obviously not seen it but we also knew we would need transport when we reached Cropredy and said our goodbyes to The Frog.

The wind strengthened overnight and the next morning was a real challenge. This part of the Oxford is where you see the greatest evidence that it is a contour canal. We twisted our way down towards Fenny Compton, with the wind getting stronger and stronger. We were pleased to finally pull into the marina and fill with diesel. After paying we stood on the wharf and talked about where we would moor that night. The very kind marina owner overheard and said she would not cruise any further in these conditions and offered us a mooring at the end of their service wharf for the night. This was a godsend. To be able to moor on rings when the wind was blowing so strongly was really reassuring but I still attached the centre line to stop us bouncing around in what was quickly becoming a gale. With time to kill, Dave and Julie taught us the card game *Golf* and we showed them how to play *Newmarket* in return. Life in the fast lane.

The wind died down overnight and we set off the next day before breakfast. Pip and I had a video call to complete the car purchase at 9.30 am and we wanted to be clear of the wharf and to have put a few miles in before we took the call. We passed under Tunnel Bridge (137) and entered the famous 'tunnel that isn't a tunnel' (see Chapter 17 for detail). As we were so early, we did not meet another boat in the very narrow cutting and were soon approaching Claydon Top Lock (17) where we stopped for our call and to have breakfast. The Claydon flight reminded us that from Marston Doles we had effectively been on a plateau and the canal was now starting its descent all the way to Oxford via Banbury. Video evidence shows how tough the mechanisms were on the descent through Claydon. Julie, who is no shrinking violet, really struggled to raise the paddles. Dave and I were helping but it still took a while to empty the locks. Pip was on the helm for what would be her last time steering The Frog. She did not realise it at the time or I know she would have found the whole thing very upsetting (as it would be for us both a few days later).

Whilst we were booked into Cropredy Marina, which sits about a mile and a half from the bottom of the Claydon Flight, we still had some time to kill. Today we did pull into the marina - but only to pump out. As I turned The frog into the large basin and we emerged from the protection of the entrance, the wind hit us with a vengeance. I had not anticipated this or I would have steered hard left and taken a loop around to enter the pump out station. My mind flew right back to Ventnor Marina and my hilarious efforts to enter their station in high wind. I just about managed to avoid hitting the boats that were moored on my right side, but when I tried to pull out and swing around to enter the narrow bay, The Frog was not playing ball at all. I eventually ran out of marina and as I slowed down to avoid hitting the far bank, the wind pushed me even further to the right and I ended up being pinned across the bow of three moored boats. I was resting on their respective bow fenders so, apart from my pride, nothing was damaged. If you have read this far into the book you will already know that my pride was vanquished a long time and many cock-ups ago. After some clumsy manoeuvring, I finally got into the pump out bay. When I walked over to the office to pay, the lady behind the counter, unprompted, said: *'It's good to see The Frog back again'*. It turned out she had seen her under previous ownership and remembered her striking portholes and unusual name. We talked about our plans, how sad I was feeling about the looming goodbye and how I would see her again in a few days when we came back for our final mooring.

We left the marina, stopped for bacon sandwiches at Cropredy village and continued through heavy rain to get closer to Banbury. Wet through, I finally gave in just after we had passed through Hardwick Lock (28). We moored on our own pins next to the railway bridge that crosses the canal just below the lock chamber. We had covered eight and a half miles and completed twelve locks and I for one was ready for a rest. As we settled in for the night, I soon regretted my mooring decision. The trains here were regular and very noisy and I was woken up several times throughout the night. Pip always wears ear plugs - something to do with my heavy breathing (snoring) - and she did not hear a thing.

The next morning we completed the last mile into the heart of Banbury, finding a mooring spot about a hundred yards from Tooley's Boatyard (see Chapter 17 for more background on this iconic location). We walked to the station and caught a train to Oxford. One of the bonuses of our change of plan was the opportunity to show Dave and Julie the fabulous 'city of dreaming spires', where Pip and I had moored the previous year. We had a great day and if you want to see more, take a look at Vlog 42. One highlight for Julie was visiting the Botanic Gardens and sitting on Will and Lyra's bench (fans of Philip Pullman's *'His Dark Materials'* will understand this reference).

CHAPTER 50: SAD GOODBYES

Having labelled the previous section of this book The Final Chapter, I guess I lied. This final, final chapter is worthy of its own title. Not only were we saying goodbye to Julie and Dave but we were also taking our final cruise on our lovely Frog.

It's Thursday 30th September 2021. It's a landmark day. We left our mooring in Banbury and headed south through the lift bridge (164) that forms a pedestrian link to the shopping arcade. The rest of the crew got off to operate the mechanism of Banbury Lock and I pressed on alone to the winding hole about half a mile down the canal. For the very last time I turned The Frog around. True to form, as the winding hole was on the right, her tendency to pull left as I reversed meant it was an eight, rather than three point, manouvre. I would not have had it any other way and I smiled wistfully as I patted the tiller in an act of final submission: *'You win old girl - you always did'!*

I cruised back into the town to pick up the rest of the team and we went back through Banbury Lock. Pip and I knew there were only four more to complete and we counted them down with a very heavy heart. It was raining, which fitted our mood. This melancholy was only lifted slightly as we entered Hardwick Lock (28) and Pip received a text from our solicitor telling us we had completed the purchase of The Beach House. We now owned our new home and, whilst we were happy about this news, it was as if the future was pressing, uninvited, into our present. We wanted to focus on The Frog and not think about the days ahead. This was her time and we quickly brought our minds back to the task in hand.

Bourton Lock (27) and Slat Mill Lock (26) passed in a blur of emotion. In the last Vlog I can even be seen stroking the stern of The Frog as I contemplated our final few moments afloat. Before we knew it, we were entering Cropredy Lock - the nine hundred and eighty seventh and, more importantly, LAST lock we would ever negotiate on our blue goddess! Pip captured the moment on video. If you look closely you will see me swallowing hard and the tears that welled up in my eyes as I pull back the throttle to slow her down for one final time. I can hardly see the keyboard now as the same strong emotions come flooding back.

Our last half mile passes too quickly and I am soon turning back into Cropredy Marina - this time more prepared for the high winds. Luckily, our mooring was off to the left and I dropped Dave off so he could run down and stand on the end of our pontoon so I knew exactly where to aim. The marina was choppy, but as I was heading into the wind, whilst progress was slow, there were no mess ups as I manoeuvred The Frog into her mooring for the very last time. I was relieved - not because I did not want the further embarrassment of yet another poor piece of boat handling - but rather I did not want our final active moments together to be sullied in any way. She is a dignified lady and it was only fitting that my last act at her helm was smooth and professional. She deserved nothing less!

That night we went to the fabulous Brasenose Arms, in the nearby village, for a 'last supper'. Both Julie and I misread the menu and whilst we thought we were ordering a burger with a portobello mushroom - we were actually ordering a burger that WAS a portobello mushroom. Both avid meat eaters we did not let it spoil the evening (although we both suffered extreme food envy looking at Dave and Pip's choices).

Fully refreshed, we hired a car the next day and drove, via Port Sunlight, to Birkenhead in the North West. We had an AirB&B booked for our much delayed (thank you Covid) Genesis concert in the M&S Arena in Liverpool. Julie is a huge fan and Pip and I have always liked their music. Whilst in Liverpool we did the usual tourist things - some a repeat of our visit in June - but some new (like a visit to Paul McCartney and John Lennon's childhood homes). We took Julie and Dave to the Cavern Club and this time we sat in the smaller but more intimate vaults. There was a live band and the place was packed - despite it being two o'clock on a Sunday afternoon.

All good things must come to an end, and, after a brilliant concert, we packed up and drove south to Heathrow to say our goodbyes to Julie and Dave. We hoped they had had a great time - we certainly loved seeing them and it was particularly hard for Pip to be wrenched away again from her best friend. We were very quiet on the drive back to Cropredy - not just because of recent farewells but also because of what we knew lay ahead.

We filled the next couple of days with two trips to Somerset - filling our hire car with the staggering number of personal possessions we had managed to squeeze into The Frog. But finally we could not put it off any longer. It was Thursday 7th October 2021 and we had been packing, and cleaning for the last two and a half days. The Frog was empty of everything that suggested she was still ours. There was only one more thing to do - say goodbye. Pip and I recorded our final moments on board just before Roy and Sonia arrived for the handover. I have just rewatched the final few minutes of Vlog 42 and, once again, I have tears in my eyes. The strong feelings we both had at saying goodbye are written all over our faces. I kept kissing Pip's head as a diversion every time I was about to lose it!

We signed off then with *'What a year we have had'* and shared some statistics. For those who like that sort of thing: we cruised 1386 miles, completed 987 locks, went through 36 (bloody) tunnels and 121 moveable bridges. Oh - and we recorded it all in 42 Vlogs.

But our YEAR ON THE FROG was about so much more than just numbers. We learned a huge amount about ourselves and our relationship - which grew even stronger. We spent so much quality time discovering the gems that are the UK waterways. We saw places we would never have seen in a car and spent nights in places that you could not even reach by car. We met many like-minded people and a few we were glad we would never see again. We made life-long friends and for that we will be forever grateful. And finally we fell in love - with a fifty seven foot, gorgeous mix of wood, granite and metal. She was not just a boat - she was our home and an extension of us for so long that leaving her was one of the hardest things we have ever had to do.

Goodbye dearest Frog! May your future be full of many locks and may they all be in your favour. We will always miss you!

THE END

APPENDIX

Our Vlogs can be found at: *YouTube.com/c/vlogfromthefrog*

Our Blogs can be found at: **myblogfromthefrog.wordpress.com.**

Happy viewing.

Printed in Great Britain
by Amazon